HESS AND THE PENGUINS

THE HOLOCAUST, ANTARCTICA AND THE STRANGE CASE OF RUDOLF HESS

Adventures Unlimited Press

Other Books by Joseph P. Farrell:

HESS AND THE PENGUINS

THE HOLOCAUST, ANTARCTICA AND THE STRANGE CASE OF RUDOLF HESS

BY
JOSEPH P. FARRELL

Hess and the Penguins

by Joseph P. Farrell

ISBN: 978-1-939149-85-5

Published by:
Adventures Unlimited Press
One Adventure Place
Kempton, Illinois 60946 USA

auphq@frontiernet.net

www.adventuresunlimitedpress.com

Cover by Terry Lamb

10 9 8 7 6 5 4 3

HESS AND THE PENGUINS

THE HOLOCAUST, ANTARCTICA AND THE STRANGE CASE OF RUDOLF HESS

Table of Contents

Table of Contents

Table of Contents

Table of Contents

Table of Contents

Table of Contents

ACKNOWLEDGEMENTS AND DEDICATIONS

And to all my extended family and friends:
Scott D. deHart, and sons: Wesley, Alex, and Bennett:
Thank You is inadequate;
And to Calvin deHart,
in gratitude for helping "proofread" the manuscript and being a
second, trustworthy pair of eyes, and for putting up with my
"I want it yesterday" schedule!

To Catherine Austin Fitts,
Who, with me, wonders what really is going on "down there";

To "Al" in Norway, who told me during an interview that I should
finally write "the Hess book";

To all my website members and subscribers for your support and
prayers;

To "Maria" in Spain, and so many others,
for boundless support beyond my ability to repay;

And to the late George Ann Hughes, for so many good times and
conversatons;

To Matt S. for sharing your good heart and conversation;

To Mr. S.E.J. for helping me authenticate the Nordau Quotation
many years ago in the Library of Congress;

And Above All to T.S.F., who told me to write:
You are, and will always be, sorely and deeply missed.

You are each and all a true

FOREWARNED IS FOREARMED

"Readers may form their own conclusions on these facts and deductions, but without such a challenge, acceptance of the official version continues, and with it misrepresentation of this critical moment when history failed to turn in the way that Hess and Hitler and so many in the highest circles of British life wished. It is high time the official story is confronted, for consideration of the path Churchill did not take in 1941 casts a more brilliant light on the morality of the path he did take, the history we know. Hence the sub-title of this book: The Real Turning Point of the Second World War."
Peter Padfield[1]

T HIS IS THE PLACE WHERE REGULAR READERS OF MY BOOKS have come to expect a rather lengthy Preface, laying out in abstract form the basic contents and argument of the book which follows it. Prefaces and Introductions are the places where normally I or other authors attempt to clarify the main details and argument of the book, according to the old adage, "tell them what you're going to say (Preface), say it (main book), and tell them what you said (Conclusion)."

But with the Hess affair—or as I have called it in this book, the Hess Mess—one is confronted with something else entirely, something that does not easily lend itself to the usual oversimplifications; it is, as I have designated it, a first-class gold-plated *mess*. Like the two Kennedy assassinations or the assassination of Dr. King, or the still-debatable Watergate affair ("What was *that* really about?"), or the Waco tragedy or the Oklahoma City Bombing or 9/11, it is a pivotal event of the twentieth century, and perhaps even *the* pivotal event. But unlike the rest of them, it is not "neat" or "tidy." A multi-layered conspiracy it most certainly is; a neat and tidy one, like the others, it most definitely is *not*. Yet, like the Kennedy assassination or 9/11, there are aspects of the Hess Mess that are classified to this day, and that should tell us something of its real significance.

---

[1] Peter Padfield, *Night Flight to Dungavel: Rudolf Hess, Winston Churchill, and the Real Turning Point of WWII* (Lebanon, New Hampshire: Fore Edge [University Press of New England], 2013), p. 21.

Preface

What I have is a *speculation*, a *proposal*—to be sure, not one that is based solely on contextual argument, but one based on careful parsing of details unearthed—but unnoticed (perhaps!)—by some other researchers. Why the "perhaps" in the previous sentence? Because like everything else in the Hess Mess, the details, when we shall encounter them, are capable of more than one interpretation. My interpretation of those details, as we shall discover, makes eminent *sense* simply on a logical basis of their implications. Thus, they become other components of the Hess Mess, and perhaps the principal ones.

In any case, the Hess Mess *is* a mess, and thus, rather than try to tidy-up the mess in the usual Preface or Prologue, I want the reader of this book to experience the same mystifications that I and others have experienced when researching it, in all their complexity and fulsome messiness, for there is a huge, nagging, gnawing Question at the heart of it all, that *no* one, to this day, knows the answer to. I certainly do not have an answer either. All I have is a speculation, a proposal. That said, I want the readers of this book to experience the *confusing* clutter of the Hess Mess in all of its apparent junkyard disorder, and hence I have attempted to present the affair as a *Gestalt,* which can only be appreciated as a series of layered, compounding mystifications, all networked and interlaced with each other, so that when my "added layers" are added to the mess, they will at least fit the "pattern," for Sacrifices and Penguins are very much a part of the Hess Mess.

All of that said, I really wrote this book "for myself and in full freedom,"—to quote the words of C.P.E. Bach wildly out of context –as an exercise to set down all my thoughts on the record, once I had pondered those extra details in the context of the Hess Mess.

Joseph P. Farrell
From somewhere
2017, the year that, supposedly, all the Hess Mess files are to be
opened up

Part One:
The Hess Mess

"It soon becomes apparent that the whole Hess affair, from 1941 onwards, is riddled with so many contradictions and anomalies that it is obvious that the British authorities were desperate to conceal something. Judging by the fact that they are still desperate to conceal it, common sense dictates that they deem this secret to be unsuitable for public consumption, even after sixty years. But why? What could be so unacceptable to Britain, or the Allies, in the early twenty-first century? What does the Rudolf Hess story conceal that would in some way shock even today's cynical world?"

"How can the details of an abortive mission undertaken sixty years ago even begin to threaten today's Britain in any way?"
Lynn Picknett, Clive Prince, and Stephen Prior, *Double Standards: The Rudolf Hess Cover-up*, 2001, pp. xx, 17 respectively.

1
SPANDAU BALLET
(AND NO, WE DON'T MEAN THE 1980'S MUSIC GROUP)[1]

*"He certainly had lots of time to think in the nine months he was in
Landsberg. It was only after this, according to his intimate acquaintance,
'Putzi' Hanfstaengl, that the Führer cult began in earnest. Before then, he
was* Herr Hitler *to everyone. At Hess's instigation, this now changed, first to*
der Chef *and then to* Mein Führer. *Hitler seemed to enjoy the
transmutation.
"In prison, he had written* Mein Kampf *with the help of Hess."*
Dusty Sklar[2]

NOTHING ABOUT THE CASE OF RUDOLF HESS is normal, and
nothing about the "normal" or even the "revisionist"
explanations of the Hess case are reassuring or convincing.
Of all the high ranking Nazis imprisoned within the formidable
walls of Spandau Prison in Berlin after the war when the
Nuremburg War Crimes Tribunals had handed down their
sentences, Rudolf Hess stands out as a black hole of bizarrerie
almost unequaled in recent history. The Nazi Reich's Armaments
Minister, Albert Speer, and the two chiefs of the German
Kriegsmarine, Grand Admirals Erich Raeder and Karl Dönitz, all did
their "time" in the prison, as did former Reichsbank President and
Finance Minister Walther Funk, diplomat Konstantin von Neurath,
and Hitler Youth leader Baldur von Schirach. These were some of
the men that kept the gigantic war machine of the Third Reich
smoothly running and functioning as a military power right up to

---

[1] It should be noted, however, that the rock group, according to the Wikipedia
article on Spandau Prison, *did* get their name from the expression "Spandau
Ballet," which was the slang for the twitching and spasms of the nervous systems
of inmates executed by hanging in the prison during its years as a military and civil
prison under the German Empire and Weimar Republic. I use it here in an entirely
different sense, to denote (1) the theatrical dancing of the Four Allied Powers—
France, Great Britain, the USA, and Soviet Union—in their handling of the prison's
sole remaining inmate until his death, Rudolf Hess, (2) their explanations of the
case, and (3) the equally bewildering mass of research and speculation that the
case has engendered since the death of Spandau's most infamous inmate in
August, 1987.
[2] Dusty Sklar, *The Nazis and the Occult* (New York: Dorset Press, 1977), p. 54.

the end of the war, and in Dönitz's case, had nearly brought Britain to its knees in the unrelenting U-boat warfare. Indeed, of all the "designated successors" to Hitler, it was Dönitz that finally succeeded Hitler as the legal head of state and government after the latter's problematical "suicide" in the Berlin *Führerbunker*. But these men, crucial as they were to the smooth functioning of the German military juggernaut, were released, some of them—Grand Admiral Erich Raeder and Walther Funk—having been sentenced to life in prison like Hess himself. Funk and Raeder were released early for health and humanitarian reasons, a point already raising a serious question about Hess, for clearly in the last decade or so of his incarceration, he had begun to suffer health problems as well. Why was he not also released on similar humanitarian grounds? Speer and von Schirach served their full twenty years sentences and were released on the same day: September 30, 1966, while Grand Admiral Dönitz, sentenced to a mere ten years, was released on the same day, ten years earlier.

Only Hess remained after the release of Speer and von Schirach, and he lived another twenty-one years past their release, finally dying on August 17, 1987, at 93 years of age.

Hess in SS General's Uniform

*Prisoner Number Seven: an elderly Hess (or "Spandau Hess"?)
at Spandau Prison.[3]*

Buck-toothed, somewhat goofy-looking Rudolf Hess—with his perilous overbite, his dull fanatical eyes, his eccentric obsessions with the occult, and his bizarre and (many would say) insane behavior, not only during the Nuremburg tribunals but long before, during his infamous flight to Scotland in May of 1941 to negotiate peace with the British—only Hess was required to serve his full life

---

[3] See Abdallah Melaouhi, *Rudolf Hess: His Betrayal and Murder* (Washington, D.C.: The Barnes Review 2013), p. 28. This picture is often seen on the internet without attribution, but as far as I have been able to determine, it appears to be from Melaouhi's book, and to date from the period that Hess was Melaouhi's patient.

sentence in Spandau, the only remaining prisoner after the departure of von Neurath, Speer, von Schirach, Funk, Raeder, and Dönitz. It's an absurd picture: the Allied powers—France, Great Britain, the USA, and the Soviet Union—all contributed to the maintenance and upkeep of the entire Spandau Prison, changing their military guards at regular monthly intervals, just to guard this one man.[4]

Even if one was *not* tempted to believe the absurd tales spun by neo-Nazis of secret Antarctic Nazi bases constructed and maintained by the German Navy, or even if one was *not* tempted to maintain that there may be some kernel of truth lurking within them, it would still seem far more likely that the Allied Powers and the Soviet Union would have contrived reasons *not* to release Speer, Raeder, and Dönitz. After all, these were pragmatic, sane, and in Raeder's and Dönitz's cases, professional military men, and as such, they all knew secrets. Yet, with the exception of Raeder, they were not sentenced to life; and in spite of whatever secrets they knew, they were all released. Similarly Walther Funk—President of the Reichsbank, German finance minister, and sponsor of the 1942 I.G. Farben-Reichsbank study on how to create a European federation (a study looking all too conveniently like the current structure of the European Union)[5] and who could also, most assuredly, tell secrets—was also released.

But the allegedly insane occult-obsessed lunatic that remained—Hess—the Allies and Soviets for some reason held under tight guard. *This* man—reviled and ridiculed in private by some in the Nazi hierarchy even before his infamous May 1941 flight to Scotland to negotiate peace with the British, even while Nazi domestic propaganda continued to laud and extol him, and universally rejected as insane by both the Nazi and British hierarchies *after* his "crazy stunt"—*this* man had to be guarded at all costs and his access to the outside world strictly and severely,

---

[4] The guard rotation shifted on a monthly basis, with French guards during the months of February, June, and October; British guards in January, May, and September; American guards in April, August, and December, and Soviet guards in March, July, and November.

[5] See my *The Third Way: The Nazi international, European Union, and Corporate Fascism* (Kempton, Illinois: Adventures Unlimited Press, 2015), pp. 167-218.

and some would say, cruelly, controlled. This man alone of the Spandau Seven, had to remain imprisoned—in solitary confinement—for the rest of his 93 years.

Indeed, there is only one other story that is as badly obfuscated and whose official narrative is so blatantly silly as the story of Rudolf Hess, Prisoner Number Seven, and that official narrative silliness concerns the assassination of President John F. Kennedy.

That, perhaps, ought to tell us something.

The question was, and *is, what* does it tell us?

In the case of the Kennedy assassination, the problem is that several plausible theories can be put forward as to who was involved in the conspiracy, and why.[6] In the case of Hess, however, theories abound to be sure, but without the benefit of anything near the supporting evidentiary weight that approaches that adduced for the JFK conspiracies. On the contrary, the Hess case is a wild roller coaster ride through a hall of mirrors enclosed in a fog of obfuscation of claim and counterclaim and a badly conflicted and contradictory narrative, a narrative also overlaid with wild postwar neo-Nazi assertions of Antarctic survival and UFOs, and the usual academic attempts at debunking them.

A. *The Harvey's Barn Methodology:*
The Hess Mess as an Epistemological and Historiographical Puzzle

My mother had an expression that, through my use of it in interviews over the years, has come to be known to at least a few people. That expression is "going around Harvey's Barn," by which she meant that a seemingly simple question could elicit from my father and/or me a long peroration of prelude, tangential perambulations and explanation prior to giving an actual "answer" to it. In point of fact, those long prologues and perambulations usually were, and usually are, a large part of the answer.

In the case of the "Hess Mess," however, the long prelude is necessary to highlight, not an *answer*, but rather the One Significant *Question* that hovers over the whole Hess affair, from

---

[6] See my *LBJ and the Conspiracy to Kill Kennedy: A Coalescence of Interests* (Kempton, Illinois: Adventures Unlimited Press, 2011), especially pp. 7-9.

his flight to Great Britain in 1941 and his sentencing at Nuremberg in 1946, to his long incarceration in Berlin's Spandau Prison and his final ignominious and suspicious end on August 17, 1987. That Question, which will remain unstated until the very end of Part One of this book, only gains its significance from a rehearsal and review of the salient and significant details of the "Hess Mess." Indeed, *all of the books on the Hess Mess are either an attempt to answer that One Question or a speculation on a plausible solution to it.* Such is also the case in *this* book: the lengthy review of other research and claims is a necessary component of the logic of the argument posed by that significant Question, and the speculative synthesis I offer here.

According to standard historical narratives, Hess was already beginning to fall from favor and influence in the Nazi "inner circle" by the time of his notorious flight to Scotland in 1941 and, according to those same standard narratives or popular perceptions, he thus knew no real secrets. In this respect, the Hess Mess stands as a kind of epistemological and historiographical Chinese puzzle-box, perhaps even a *challenge* to those disciplines: How much speculation should be entertained with respect to the Hess Mess? What types of evidence should be admitted and examined? What *about* those post-war stories of Nazi survival, of Antarctica, and their claims about Hess's involvement? Are they simply to be ignored (as most Hess investigators have done), or conversely, are they a possible crucial component of its resolution? Or have Hess Mess investigators perhaps not even considered the implications of their own evidence, doggedly researched and uncovered?

I knew, years ago, when I embarked on this strange series of books in "alternative research" and, more particularly, in the research of the hypothesis of post-war Nazi survival and secret research, that eventually I would have to deal with the "Hess Mess." For reasons that will become clear in the rest of the book, I could not do so without first introducing the concepts of (1) post-war Nazi survival, (2) the Antarctic component of that mythos, and (3) outlining, over the course of several books and interviews, why I regarded the Nazi-Antarctic-UFO mythology as untrue, and something masking, perhaps, a more prosaic, but also more sensational, secret.

Thus, the messiest aspect of the "Hess Mess" is that it *does* spin out of control, wildly and very quickly, into associations and relationships with mind control, Antarctica, Atlantis, into conspiracies of doubles and double-crosses, and into strange lore and myths, which Hess, no stranger to the occult, and as Hitler's Deputy in the Nazi Party, most certainly knew.

1. *The Questions that Lead to* **The** *Question*

One may gain an initial approximation of just how *large* and "messy" the Hess Mess is by considering the following questions, which are, to be sure, variations of that One as yet unstated Question:

Why was it necessary to maintain an entire prison, and the military guards and medical staffs of four world powers, just to keep watch over one individual who, by the end of his life, was a frail old man, and a threat to no one? *Why* was it necessary to bear such a financial cost? *Why* was it necessary to maintain such an absurd "Spandau Ballet"?

What secrets did he know that the Four Powers wanted to prevent others from knowing? Did they themselves even know what those secrets were, or did they only suspect? *Or:* were they trying to break him and learn those secrets?

Or: did Hess not know anything at all? Were the secrets located elsewhere? If so where? And if so, then why maintain what can only be characterized as a charade for more than forty years?

Worst of all: was the man they were guarding even really Rudolf Hess, one time "Deputy Führer" of Nazi Germany, at all? Was "Spandau Hess" really Hess? Or was "Spandau Hess" someone else, a double, substituted at some point in the drama? And was *that* the real reason for the "Spandau Ballet" of elaborate changings of the guard and maintaining an entire prison for just one man, and refusing to let him out, lest the substitution—the real secret—be discovered?

But if "Spandau Hess" *wasn't* Hess, then what happened to the real one? *Why* was the substitution made at all? And *when* was the substitution made? Of course, the question of *when* a substitution was made also is an indicator of *who* made the substitution.

While we're talking about *Doppelgängers*, what about the aircraft in which Hess made his flight? Was it the same plane that crashed in Scotland as took off from Augsburg, Germany? If not, when and why was the substitution made? Was *Reichsmarschall* Göring secretly involved, as some allege, in aiding Hess's secret flight through the then-state-of-the-art air defenses of Germany? If so, why did Göring also order the same air defenses to shoot Hess down? And what of Hess's crazy flight plan, and equally problematical explanations for it?

On the British side, why was the response of the Royal Air Force so lackluster, when Hess's plane was clearly being tracked by British radar? Was this because Hess was expected, and his flight was being aided by some on the British side, as some have alleged? And if so, what was the explanation for the "soft" response of the then-equally-state-of-the-art British air defenses? Was it because Hess had been *lured* to the United Kingdom as part of a British intelligence "psyop," a "sting" designed to embarrass the Nazi leadership? If so, then why was no major effort ever launched by Great Britain to capitalize on the propaganda value of his capture? Or did Churchill covertly use Hess for other political purposes, as some researchers maintain, and if so, what were they?

Equally, if Hess was *not* lured to Great Britain, then why the "soft response" of its air defenses? Was Hess *expected*, as yet others allege? And if so, *who* expected him, and why?

Why was Hess's flight made on the same day—May 10, 1941— that the *Luftwaffe's* bombing of London reached its most destructive pitch during the whole war? And why, after his flight, did the *Luftwaffe* suddenly drastically curtail its bombing of Britain, and why, conversely, did the Royal Air Force also apparently curtail its bombing of Germany?

We may add to this already strange list of questions the following:

Why did Hess undertake his flight to Great Britain in the first place? Was it, as some have persuasively argued, to offer a peace plan to Great Britain in view of Hitler's then-secret preparations and intentions to invade the Soviet Union a little over a month later? If so, did Hitler or other high-ranking Nazis such as Göring know about the peace plan effort? Were they involved with it?

8

If *that* is the case, did they hope that there really was a faction in Great Britain hoping for a negotiated peace with the Third Reich? Did Hess come as a plenipotentiary with a guarantee for his safe conduct under a flag of truce from high authorities in the United Kingdom representing King George VI himself, as Hess himself maintained in the early days of his captivity by the British?

And while we're at it:

What happened to Hess while he was in the custody of the British from 1941 to the German capitulation? Was he being drugged, as Hess himself claimed? If so, why?

And once the war was over, how does one explain Hess's bizarre behavior at the Nuremberg War Crimes Tribunals? What is the significance—if any - of the strange remarks that *Reichsmarschall* Hermann Göring made to Hess during the course of the trials? Is there any relationship between Hess's behavior and the *Reichsmarschall's* remarks?

Last but surely not least, what (if anything) is to be made of the claims advanced—long after the war had ended and Hess was dead—that Hess was somehow involved in Göring's Antarctica project? Are they to be simply dismissed as unsubstantiated rumor-mongering and story-telling by second-hand dead-man testimony of post-war veterans? Or are there any indicators that they might be true, and if so, what are they, and to what extent are they true?

As can be ascertained by the foregoing and by no means exhaustive list of questions, the Hess Mess is exactly that, a *colossal* mess with no easy resolution, a nagging and festering mystery that squats in the middle of the twentieth century for over forty years, unresolved to this day. The epistemological and historiographical problem of the Hess Mess is, quite simply, that each and every aspect of the story has more than one explanation, and many of the details of the story have been so badly obfuscated that extreme care must be exercised in reviewing them, and in reviewing what *others* have concluded *from* them, in order to highlight the importance and potential implications of that One Significant Question. The Hess Mess is, perhaps, the most significant unresolved historical question of the twentieth century.

In this case, it is best to begin at the end, with Hess's death, for even in death, Hess remains a mystery. Did he commit suicide? Or

9

was he "suicided," as his own son, Wolf Rüdiger Hess, and Hess's male nurse for the last half decade of his life, Abdallah Melaouhi, suspected?

B. "In my End is My Beginning..."
1. A Death in Spandau

The man we know as Rudolf Hess - one time Deputy *Führer* to Adolf Hitler himself as leader of the Nazi Party, and third in succession to become head of state and government after Hitler and *Reichsmarschall* Hermann Göring—was pronounced dead on August 17, 1987, around 4:10 PM at the British Military Hospital in Berlin. He had spent the last forty-one years of his life in Berlin's Spandau Prison, the last surviving major Nazi leader, and the only one who had been kept in captivity to serve out his full life sentence.

According to researcher and author Peter Padfield, Hess had been accompanied by the Black American sergeant Tony (Anthony) Jordan, whom Hess did not like because of his anti-black prejudice, into the garden at Spandau prison for Hess's daily walk. A small "garden house" had been placed in the courtyard for Hess, where he would typically spend his afternoons relaxing or reading. This occurred at approximately 1:30,[7] according to some accounts of Hess's prison warders.

Padfield notes that while strict regulations meant that Hess was to be watched at all times, the small summer house—which had a window facing the formidable walls of the prison, and a pair of sliding glass double doors, a small table and some electric reading lamps—was normally left unobserved by the prison warders to allow Hess some privacy, with the guards only checking on him at regular intervals a few minutes apart. As we shall also discover, Hess normally sat in such a way that his guards could see him through the small window.

Then at approximately 2:20, Sergeant "Ten"—the warders are numbered in the official reports of Hess's last day—made a routine

---

[7] Peter Padfield, *Night Flight to Dungavel: Rudolf Hess, Winston Churchill, and the Real Turning Point of WWII* (Lebanon, New Hampshire: University Press of New England, 2013), pp. 3-4.

check on Hess, noting that Hess had emerged from the prison in a tan raincoat and a straw sombrero, walking with his cane.[8] (Already there would appear to be a discrepancy, for was Hess accompanied to the garden house at 1:30, or 2:20 PM?)

Meanwhile, number "Thirteen," who as a switchboard operator had never seen Hess, or Prisoner Number Seven as he was officially known,[9] was alerted by his colleagues that Hess was in the prison yard. Finding a colleague to relieve him at the switchboard, number Thirteen walked into the yard hoping to catch a glimpse of the infamous inmate. There he saw Tony Jordan, sitting under a tree on a bench, located approximately fifteen feet from the cabin.

As he passed by the structure, he attempted to look inside the small window that faced the prison walls to catch a glimpse of the prison's sole remaining prisoner, but could not see him. At this juncture, he called out to guard number Nine in the prison wall watchtower, to inquire if *he* could see Hess. Nine responded in the negative, but reassured number Thirteen that Hess had indeed entered the garden house.

All of this had in turn been watched by "Lieutenant number Three" who had observed Thirteen's perambulation. "Lieutenant Three" also noted for the official record that Hess's normal practice was to sit and read in the garden house in such a manner that he could actually be seen by the guards on the prison wall through the small window facing it. On this occasion, however, Hess could not be seen.[10]

Then at approximately 2:35 PM, Jordan left his perch at the bench under the tree to check on Hess. In his subsequent statements, Jordan explained that he had looked through the window, and saw that Hess was lying on the floor with his back slumped against the very wall containing the small window, through which he was looking. At that point he quickly entered the garden house and saw that Hess's legs were stretched out, and that he had the electrical cord from one of the reading lamps around his neck, and tied to the window latch. According to Jordan, the cord

---

[8] Padfield, op. cit., p. 5.

[9] Spandau regulations officially prohibited any of the officers or warders from addressing any of their Nazi charges by name.

[10] Padfield, op. cit., p. 6.

was taut and was apparently supporting Hess's weight. Additionally, Hess's eyes were open and according to Jordan, he was still apparently alive. Jordan lifted Hess to relieve the tension on the electrical cord and removed it from his neck. After this he opened Hess's shirt, and then ran to seek assistance.[11]

According to guard number Nine on the prison wall, he saw Jordan exit the garden house and run to the prison, then turn around and run back to the garden house, and then, again, turn to run to the prison, this time entering it. At this point, the prison switchboard log records that Jordan had placed a call at 14:30, though as Padfield correctly observes, "it was surely later."[12]

At this point, Hess's male Tunisian nurse, Abdallah Melaouhi—whom we will encounter again when we consider *his* account of the events—and another medic, number Four, had been alerted, and had arrived. According to number Four, the time was 2:40 PM, for he had "looked at his watch." Collecting his first aid kit, he and Melaouhi ran to the garden house where he checked Hess's pulse, and tried to detect any breathing. Noting the red mark left around Hess's neck from the cord, and not detecting any life signs, he and Melaouhi began two-man CPR on Hess, ordering Jordan in the meantime to find and bring an oxygen tank.[13]

A few minutes later, he did so, returning with yet another medical orderly, "number Five," who brought the trauma kit, and inserted a breathing tube into Hess's neck. However, the connection on the tube did "not match that on the oxygen bottle"[14] and thus, Melaouhi had to breathe directly into the tube instead. The time was now, according to Padfield, around 3:00 PM.

2. But what Kind of Death?
a. The First Bit of Debris in the Hess Mess

At this juncture, accounts begin to diverge, and we encounter our first bit of "debris" in the "Hess Mess," for Hess's male nurse, the Tunisian Abdallah Melaouhi, refused to make any statement to

---

[11] Padfield, op. cit., p. 7.
[12] Ibid.
[13] Ibid., p. 8.
[14] Ibid., p. 9.

the British military police until he was well clear of the prison. Subsequently, as Padfield notes, in all versions of the story that Melaouhi told, the electrical cord—which in the official accounts Hess had removed and tied to the window latch to hang himself—was still plugged in to the wall socket. As Padfield notes, Melaouhi's statement about the electrical cord "was a feature of all his accounts. *If correct it virtually rules out the official account of the prisoner's death.*"[15]

Before continuing, it is worth pausing to consider two points:

1) Abdallah Melaouhi, while employed by the Spandau prison authorities, was *Hess's* nurse, and unlike the other figures involved in Hess's last day, was *not* subject to the military jurisdiction of any four of the Allied powers operating Spandau, but rather to the joint prison authority itself. It is thus intriguing to note that his version of events is ultimately the sole source for the idea that Hess's death was not a suicide, and that it occurred under highly suspicious circumstances;

2) Conversely, everyone *else* in the story *was* subject to specific national military jurisdiction, and hence could conceivably be ordered into silence on certain aspects of the occurrences that day, or simply ordered or be threatened to modify aspects of their testimony. And should such methods not prove persuasive enough, there's always the time-tested method of simply altering or falsifying documents, or removing them altogether, which, as we shall also discover, happens on more than one occasion in the Hess Mess.

Thus, at the outset of the Hess case, an investigator is placed into an ambiguous epistemological situation: who is he to believe, the official testimony based on more than one witness, but whose testimony can be coerced? Or the sole testimony of Hess's nurse, Melaouhi's testimony, the testimony of only *one* witness, who, nonetheless, has some claim as an *expert* witness?

Padfield continues his review of Melaouhi's account by noting that Melaouhi maintained that he saw two men whom he did not

---

[15] Padfield, op. cit., p. 9, emphasis added.

recognize, a large man and a relatively smaller one, both of whom wore American uniforms that were somewhat ill-fitting. Padfield interprets these men to be medical orderlies numbers Four and Five, although he notes that medic Five did not arrive until *after* Melaouhi was on the scene at the garden house.[16]

While Padfield is extraordinarily careful in his examination of the details of the case, one must pause to point out a problem with his analysis of this point: is it likely that Melaouhi—who by that time had been Hess's *fulltime* nurse for a number of years, and who had become thoroughly familiar with the operations of Spandau and who was therefore familiar with its regular personnel—would not have recognized two American medical orderlies? As Hess's nurse, he in fact had to know everyone with medical access to Hess. Rather, it would seem the converse is true: being familiar with Spandau's operations and personnel, it is more likely that Melaouhi would be particularly attuned to any break from routine, particularly where personnel were concerned. In my opinion his testimony in this respect takes on additional evidentiary weight.

Because the testimony of the American guards is consistent in the absence of any statement to the effect that there were strangers in the prison yard that day, Padfield rules out Melaouhi's story.[17] Additionally, Padfield observes that Tony Jordan's behavior prior, and subsequently, to his discovery of Hess, was radically different. Prior to the discovery, Jordan was calm, collected. The day's routine was unfolding as so many times before. *After* the discovery, however, Jordan was running back and forth "in complete panic... not knowing what to do."[18] Jordan had thus either to be "a consummate actor" or, contra Melaouhi's suspicions, "he had not killed Hess."[19]

The trouble is, Melaouhi's account is about a lot more than strangers in the prison yard that day, or simple "acting" on Jordan's part; here, the Hess Mess takes another strange epistemological twist.

---

[16] Padfield, op. cit., p. 10.
[17] Ibid, p. 11.
[18] Ibid.
[19] Ibid.

Before we address Melaouhi's account, however, it is worth noting the remainder of the official timeline as Padfield summarizes it:

At approximately 2:50 PM, as the medical orderlies, "Four" and "Five" (or, the "strangers in ill-fitting American uniforms," on Melaouhi's view) were arriving at the scene, the British Military Hospital was alerted by the code name "Operation Paradox," which was the operational plan in place for a medical emergency involving Spandau's infamous and sole inmate. Sometime circa 3:10, a military ambulance arrived from the hospital at the prison gate, with a British medical officer arriving in his own car at approximately the same time.[20] At this point Hess was removed from Spandau and ca. 3:50 PM his body arrived at the hospital, where it was taken to a very special suite built on its second floor, a suite built and dedicated entirely to Hess. At 4:10, Rudolf Hess was pronounced dead,[21] and with that, the curtain rang down on the last major Nazi leader.

Unfortunately, while the curtain came down on Hess, the curtain went up on a much bigger opera and the ones who kept the case alive to this day, Hess's last nurse, Abdallah Melaouhi, and Hess's own then-grown son, Wolf Rüdiger Hess.

b. Abdallah Melaouhi and Wolf Rüdiger Hess: The Problems with the "Suicide" Explanation Begin

It was 6:45 in the evening when American Colonel Darold Keane phoned Hess's son, Wolf Rüdiger, to inform him that his father had died. He could not give any further details. One day later, Colonel Keane telephoned Wolf Hess once again, and simply read to him the press release that had been prepared. This is the first official statement of the suicide explanation (and please note, the suicide explanation was already being promoted *prior* to the performance of the official autopsy by the British military authorities):

---

[20] Padfield, op. cit., p. 11.
[21] Ibid., p. 12.

Hess, as he was accustomed to do, went escorted by a prison warder to sit in a small cottage in the garden of the prison. On looking into the cottage a few minutes later, the warder found Hess with an electrical cord around his neck. Resuscitation measures were taken and Hess was transported to the British Military Hospital. After further attempts to revive Hess, he was pronounced dead at 16:10. Whether this suicide attempt was the actual cause of death is the subject of a continuing investigation.[22]

Wolf Hess, like Hess's nurse Melaouhi, found the claim of suicide to be incredible in the extreme, since his father, whom he had been to visit many times, was crippled and stooped over with arthritis, and was so weak he could not walk without the assistance of a cane and a warder; moreover his hands were so crippled and weak from arthritis that he found it unbelievable that his father could have (1) tied a knot in the electrical cord on the window latch (having to raise his arms to do it!), and then (2) loop the cord around his own neck.[23]

Hess's male nurse, Abdallah Melaouhi, was a young man from Tunisia who had completed medical studies in Hamburg to become a nurse when he was hired in the early 1980's about five years before Hess's death to replace the Dutch nurse who had tended Hess, and who was retiring. According to the Foreword to Melaouhi's book *Rudolf Hess: His Murder and Betrayal*, Melaouhi had been hired by the Allied authorities of Spandau—and, to be more accurate, the Russians, who did all the non-military hiring for the prison—because given the "language and culture barriers, Spandau officials felt safe, that with Melaouhi that there would be no fraternization problem with Hess."[24]

This surely cannot be correct, since each of the four Allied powers running Spandau for the sole inconvenience of Hess—France, Britain, the United States, and the Soviet Union—were well aware that Hess had been born in Alexandria, Egypt, in the small but vigorous German merchant community there, prior to World War One, and as such, Hess knew and spoke Arabic at least to the

---

[22] *The Daily Telegraph,* 19 August, 1987, cited in Padfield, *Night Flight to Dungavel,* pp. 12-13.
[23] Padfield, op. cit., p. 13.
[24] Abdallah Melaouhi, op. cit., p. 20.

extent that he was able to converse with Melaouhi in that language.[25] One is tempted, rather, to view Melaouhi's hiring as perhaps being an attempt by the Allies to get Hess to disclose to an Arabic speaker something he otherwise might not do to anyone else. While there is *absolutely no evidence* for this conjecture, in a case with so many twists and turns it is the possibility is worth mentioning.

This returns us once again to the epistemological problem. The problem, once again, is simply this: besides being the one "witness" at the scene that day who openly and consistently has *challenged* the official narrative at certain key junctures and details, and is thus one witness versus many, he is also an *expert* witness given his medical background, whereas most of the witnesses in the official narrative were soldiers and jailers, and not medical personnel. As noted earlier, it is Melaouhi who is the sole source for the doubts about Hess's death. "Every account of Hess's death insists he committed suicide, *except* for Abdallah Melaouhi's."[26]

Notably, Melaouhi first insisted that suicide could not be the explanation of Hess's death in sworn statements given under oath before German notaries and authorities. His statements thus "stand in direct contradiction to the official order given to Scotland Yard's chief, Howard Jones, by England's chief prosecution, Allen Green, to suspect all investigations into what *the Scotland Yard files labeled 'The Hess Murder Case.'*"[27] For Melaouhi himself, the case was clear, for he writes in his book, "the question was no longer whether or not Hess had been murdered, but rather who had committed the crime and why."[28] Indeed, as word of Melaouhi's testimony began to circulate in conjunction with Wolf Hess's own clearly expressed doubts, the media began to question the story, and sought Melaouhi out for numerous interviews.[29]

It is easy to see why, for Melaouhi's account is not only a direct, almost point-by-point refutation of the official suicide narrative, but it is also the testimony of the only medical technician at the

---

[25] Abdallah Melaouhi, op. cit., p. 20.
[26] Ibid., p. 21, emphasis added.
[27] Ibid., emphasis added.
[28] Ibid., p. 24.
[29] Ibid., pp. 25-26.

scene, who was not under *any* kind of military jurisdiction from any of the four Allied powers operating Spandau.

It's just after lunch August 17, 1987,

Melaouhi writes,

> and I'm sitting in the living room of my official residence in Wilhelmstrasse 23 in Berlin-Spandau, less than 100 feet from Spandau Allied Prison. I'm reading the newspaper when the phone rings around 2 p.m. The young senior guard of the day, the Frenchman Jean-Pierre Audouin, is on the phone and, panic-stricken, he beseeches me: *'Come quick! Dammit! Quick! Hess has been murdered, no, not murdered!'*[30]

Melaouhi sprang into action, putting on his shoes, but forgetting to tie them, and rushed to the prison, where, by his account, he was standing before the main gate approximately two minutes after receiving the call from Audouin.[31]

(1) The Delaying Tactics of the British and American Guards

Once at the gate, however, Melaouhi maintains that he rang the bell incessantly for some twenty minutes—becoming angrier and angrier in the process—"until the British guard, Bernard Miller, finally appeared. Peering through the small window of the iron prison door, he pretended not to see me and immediately closed the window again. I kept ringing the bell."[32]

Finally, some minutes later according to Melaouhi, "he looked through his window again and said: 'Mr. Melaouhi, it's all over, you can go home now.'"[33]

If one is keeping track of times, this would have been some time around 2:25-2:30.

Melaouhi, by his own admission, was by this point "really desperate to reach the prisoner whose care had been entrusted to

---

[30] Abdallah Melaouhi, op. cit., p. 29, emphasis added.
[31] Ibid., p. 30.
[32] Ibid.
[33] Ibid.

me," so he continued to try to persuade the British guard to open the gate and admit him to the prison, "using German, English, and French" for good measure.[34]

Then comes a significant statement, one that has gone largely unnoticed among researchers investigating the Hess Mess:

> Finally, he seemed to have had enough and, opening the door, he let me pass. I didn't get far because Miller had all the keys to the doors in the building complex and he wouldn't open the door leading to the wing where I would have been able to get to Hess in just a few minutes. An American soldier who was standing only six feet away behind the open door, pointed his rifle at me and shouted: "No, *nicht rein!*," "No, you can't enter!" Struggling and shouting, I pushed his rifle away from me. Then, suddenly, an American officer came on the scene *who knew me*. He ordered the soldier to let me pass.[35]

It is intriguing to note that Melaouhi's statement confirms that there *were* strange or unknown personnel in Spandau that day who —since Melaouhi, a steady fixture there and certainly one who would be well-known as Hess's personal charge nurse—was not recognized by them. In this, Melaouhi's subsequent assertion that he saw two *strangers* in ill-fitting American uniforms is at least consistent with the above statements.

Notwithstanding the American officer's intervention, however, Melaouhi records that the British guard, Miller, continued to refuse to open the door of the central wing of the prison, forcing Melaouhi "to take a detour of several hundred meters around the building" in order to reach Hess in his traditional afternoon retreat in the garden house.[36] Upon reflection on the delays he experienced with the British and American guards, Melaouhi wondered whether this was due to them not having received any clear orders or instructions on what do to on his arrival, or whether the delay had a more sinister purpose, namely, to ensure that Hess was well and truly dead, and

---

[34] Abdallah Melaouhi, op. cit., p, 30.
[35] Ibid., emphasis added.
[36] Ibid.

that any revival efforts "would not change things."[37] Indeed, the delay, according to Melaouhi, may have sealed Hess's fate:

> In my opinion—and I have inevitably seen many dead people during my career as an intensive care medic—Rudolf Hess was already dead for about 30 to 40 minutes when I got to the garden. It was exactly this time about 40 minutes, which I lost in the other delays I experienced trying to get to Hess on that fateful day.

Interestingly enough, this introduces yet another problem in the "Hess Mess," for in Padfield's reconstruction, Tony Jordan discovered Hess ca. 2:30 PM, and thus, any calls to medics and to Melaouhi, would have to have been made after that time, *if* Jordan's times are correct. Yet Melaouhi maintains he received a call earlier, at approximately 2 PM. It would appear that either the official narrative witnesses, or Melaouhi, are either confused about the times of events, or dissembling, or possibly a mixture of both

I, however, am inclined to believe Melaouhi for three specific reasons:

1) Melaouhi has little to gain by lying;
2) In reading Melaouhi's book, it is apparent that, as a medical professional, he strongly felt his first duty was to his patient's health and well-being, and that additionally he felt a great deal of compassion for Hess; and fnally,
2) Even on the supposition that he is confused about the timing of the phone call from Spandau urging him to come at once and the timing of his arrival there, the central core of his argument is *not* based on timing, but rather upon his professional judgment that Hess was simply physically unable to perform the tasks he would have had to perform in order to commit suicide in the manner described by the official story, as we shall see below. Even so, as a medical professional, he is trained to note times of events by habit, and hence it is unlikely that he was confused.

---

[37] Abdallah Melaouhi, op. cit., p. 118.

(2) The Scene of the Crime: Strange "Americans" in Ill-fitting Uniforms

Sometime ca. 2:30-2:40, Melaouhi arrived at the garden house, and here it is best to cite his own words more extensively:

> When I finally reached the small building out of breath after losing more precious time, I couldn't enter the house. When I finally managed to open the door, I immediately noticed *that a struggle had taken place.* I had cleaned and tidied up the small wooden house just the day before. Now the straw tiled mat covering the floor was completely untidy and the tall lamp had fallen over. *I clearly remember that the lamp's cable lying on the floor was still connected to the socket. The small round table and easy chair had also been overturned. Nothing in the room was in its usual place.*
>
> Rudolf Hess was lying lifeless on the floor, his arms and legs stretched out on the ground. *Two men dressed in American uniforms were standing alongside him—the men's uniforms were much too small, with the uniform of the larger man almost bursting at the seams.* Although I knew everyone who had access to "Prisoner No. 7," I had never seen these two men before. Not only that, but the black American guard whom Hess feared and deplored most, Tony Jordan, was also in the room—he seemed to be completely exhausted and extremely nervous, sweating heavily with his shirt almost soaking wet. He was also not wearing his tie, which was a highly unusual violation of the prison dress code.[38]

Later in his book, Melaouhi elaborates on this scene, speculating on what he thinks it represented:

> After arriving on the scene, my first impression was that a struggle had just taken place. This was where someone suffering from numerous infirmities and without much strength left in his body must have, in sheer panic, desperately yet unsuccessfully tried to defend himself. Looking at the people standing in the room, I then saw whom he had tried to defend himself against. The victim

---

[38] Abdallah Melaouhi, op. cit., pp. 30-31, emphasis added. Melaouhi's account subsequently in the book is almost an exact repeat, with the addition that the electrical cord that was still plugged in was "supposedly the cord that Hess had used to hang himself, according to the Allies."

was lying on his back with his hands and legs stretched out on the ground *almost in the middle of the small room* which measured about 70 square feet. Lifeless. Dead. The colored American guard, Tony Jordan, was standing near the feet of the dead body. He appeared overwrought and stressed, extremely nervous and sweating so heavily that his shirt was saturated with sweat and sweat was running down his face. He was also not wearing a tie, a clear violation of the Spandau prison military dress code. It was then that I first noticed the other two people who were standing next to Hess. I was now bent over my patient and I looked up from below at the two men in uniform. They both gave me icy stares and then, looking at Jordan several times with questioning glances, seemed to be asking, "What is *he* doing here?" There was one large and one small man, both of whom were wearing American uniforms.

But were they really Americans? *Guards wearing the uniforms of the four custodial Allied governments were **not** allowed to enter the inner area of the prison.* Soldiers were even categorically forbidden to approach the prisoner. They were not allowed to speak a word to him. *They were confined to their posts on the watchtowers and at other "sensitive" points of the prison... .*

But these two men were not Americans, at least not American soldiers—the uniforms that they wore were incomplete and they also didn't fit. The larger of the two men looked like a sausage pressed into a uniform that had been buttoned up with great effort and which now threatened to burst open at any moment. The smaller man's trousers were even too small for him. It looked as if they had just now hastily gotten these uniforms in order to conceal their illegal presence in the prison.

All of this crossed my mind as I was kneeling next to Hess to check his breath, pulse, and heartbeat. At the same time I reproachfully asked Jordan, "What have you done to him? He replied in a strange mixture of fear, anger, and even spiteful relief, "The pig is finished. You won't have to work anymore(sic) night shifts!" Mind you, he said "finished," not "the pig has killed himself."[39]

Melaouhi's account, if true, raises questions: who *were* the "strange men" in ill-fitting American uniforms? And what about the plugged in cord? As Melaouhi himself suggests, the latter raises three

---

[39] Abdallah Melaouhi, op. cit., pp. 120-121, emphasis added.

interesting questions of its own: was Hess strangled with it, and did the murderers reconnect it to the electrical socket? Or was it even the murder weapon at all?[40] Of course, according to the official narrative and witnesses, it was not connected but was wrapped around Hess's neck. In Melaouhi's testimony, it was never around Hess's neck, for in none of *his* statements does he ever mention seeing it there. For Melaouhi, suspicion fell upon Jordan because he was missing his tie.

In any case, Melaouhi records that he himself became panic-stricken, realizing that "something extraordinary must have happened here," and that "at least the Americans and the British must also be aware of what had happened here."[41] Fearing that the two strange men with the ill-fitting American uniforms "would not hesitate to allow another 'accident' to occur to cover up the first crime, this time to a small and unknown Tunisian male nurse,"[42] Melaouhi states that he decided to perform resuscitation, even though he knew Hess was already dead, largely in order to pretend that he did not suspect murder.[43] He ordered Jordan to get the first aid trauma kit and summon an ambulance, and in the meantime gave Hess mouth-to-mouth breathing. This being unsuccessful, he requested one of the two strange men to help him with heart massage. "This time," records Melaouhi, "the stranger demonstrated his strength and brutality by cracking several of the old man's ribs while he pressed down on Hess's chest."[44]

There is of course a self-contradiction here: how can Melaouhi maintain that there were signs of a struggle in the garden house, when Hess was so old and frail to begin with, and scarcely able to tie knots in anything, much less electrical cord?

Unless of course the struggle was between other parties, with Hess entirely uninvolved, and this is, indeed, the conclusion Melaouhi came to.

Melaouhi also notes that on August 17, 1987, the day of his alleged suicide, Hess did not appear to be suicidal or even

---

[40] Abdallah Melaouhi, op. cit., p. 119.
[41] Ibid., p. 31.
[42] Ibid.
[43] Ibid., p. 122.
[44] Ibid, p. 32.

depressed, and that Hess had even placed a requisition request with the prison authorities for certain items, and that he had made a similar request to Melaouhi to go shopping to replace a defective heating coil for his tea water.[45] Additionally, argues Melaouhi, there were other numerous opportunities to commit suicide with far greater success than in the garden house, where he was under closer supervision. The cell block itself, during the night, with plenty of electrical cords, was not under as close supervision.[46]

(3) Hess's Physical Inability to Perform the Tasks Required for His Suicide According to the Official Narrative

But garden house or cell-block, and notwithstanding possibly mis-remembered times, the real problem for Melaouhi was Hess himself:

> After a while I realized that Hess couldn't have hanged himself even if he had tried. In the last five years in which I had looked after him almost daily, I had gained a clear and precise impression of his physical condition and his physical capabilities, and it was impossible for Hess to have killed himself in the manner described by the Allies by placing a cable around his neck and tying it into a knot and then either hanging or strangling himself to death.
>
> Toward the end of his life, my patient was so weak that he needed a special chair with an electric lifting device to even get up. He had to be supported when he walked since he suffered from muscular atrophy in his left thigh causing a muscular debility and loss of the control of his knee joints.... *He was completely blind in one eye and only had 30% of his vision in the other one.* When he fell to the ground he could not get up by himself. He hands were crippled by an intense arthritis. He was even unable to pick up a spoon when he ate; I had to put it into his hand. He would therefore *have been unable to tie a knot in a cord or cable—he couldn't even tie his shoelaces. He also couldn't lift his arms above his shoulders so that he never would have been*

---

[45] Abdallah Melaouhi, op. cit., p. 116.
[46] Ibid., p. 117.

able to tie a cord to the handle of the window from which he allegedly hanged himself.[47]

The problem with the official narrative in other words, was that the Allies, having hired Melaouhi to begin with, were now confronted by first-hand medical testimony of Hess's own nurse that their narrative made no sense.

(4) Miscellanies: Champagne Parties, Tampered First Aid Kits, and a Familiar Pattern of the Destruction of Evidence

As noted above, Padfield observed that the tube from the first aid trauma kit did not fit with the oxygen tank, and that Melaouhi had to blow into the tube himself, and this appears to corroborate Melaouhi's statement about the first aid kit (and here, once again, note the timing difficulties when comparing Melaouhi's statements to the review of the official narrative provided by Padfield); having dispatched Jordan to retrieve the kit, Melaouhi states:

> I was desperately waiting for Jordan to return when he was suddenly standing next to me again. I immediately noticed that he had used his long absence—I estimated that he had been away for about 15 to 20 minutes—to change his clothes. The equipment that he brought had been clearly tampered with. That morning I had checked the first aid kit as usual and confirmed through an entry in my logbook that nothing was missing and that it was intact. Now the seal had been broken and the contents were in a state of disorder.[48] The battery for the intubation set was missing and the tube had been perforated. There was also *no oxygen in the oxygen bottle.* Yet when I had routinely checked the first aid kit and the oxygen device that very same morning, I am certain that both had been in complete working order. If any further proof was needed that things were not as they should have been, then this tampered first aid kit gave me an unmistakable sign that something had gone wrong here.[49]

---

[47] Abdallah Melaouhi, op. cit., pp. 126-127, emphasis added.
[48] Ed.: from prior use?
[49] Abdallah Melaouhi, op. cit., p. 123, emphasis added.

This is an important point of general agreement between the "official narrative" summarized by Padfield, and Melaouhi's account, and in my opinion, strengthens the nature of Melaouhi's allegations, for his behavior and observations are consonant with a medical professional's under such circumstances; he is noticing details that a non-medical professional would not.

Things took another bizarre turn for Melaouhi when, accompanying his patient—or his patient's body—to the British Military Hospital, he observed various British officials and "other officers" cheerfully drinking champagne and "apparently celebrating something," which he suspected was the death of Hess.[50] The British governor, Anthony Le Tissier, observed Melaouhi standing alone in the hospital lobby and asked him if he would like to see the body of his patient and so say "a last good-bye." Melaouhi naturally said yes, and was led to a basement room of the hospital where Hess's body was placed. Melaouhi, "very sad and shaken," observed Hess and "prayed for him in the custom of my faith because I believe that God is universal."[51]

The strange day was not, however, over for Melaouhi. Driven back to Spandau to identify a jacket which he had taken off while administering CPR to Hess, he was forced to wait four more hours before he was allowed to return to the garden house. There, the scene had already been altered, for "almost everything had been removed including all the traces of what had happened,"[52] and several strange men were milling about the area. Some of these approached him, handed him his jacket, and asked him to identify it. Having done so, Melaouhi was given his jacket and released. On the way out of Spandau, he inquired of the prison secretary who the strange people were, and was informed that they were "all officers from the U.S. Federal Bureau of Investigation."[53]

The very next day, the German tabloid newspaper, *Bild*, ran a story stating that bulldozers would soon appear at the prison to demolish the structure to make room for a new shopping center. The article stated that a plan had been approved three years previously

---

[50] Abdallah Melaouhi, op. cit., p. 124.
[51] Ibid., pp. 124-125.
[52] Ibid., p. 125,
[53] Ibid., p. 126.

26

that the old prison would be demolished beginning no less than 48 hours after Hess's death. What was the reason for the sudden need to destroy the scene of a possible crime? Answer: the Allies did not want the place to become a possible neo-Nazi shrine.[54]

There is, however, a deeper, darker, potential pattern here, for if Hess was murdered, then the rush to destroy the crime scene—in this case, a whole building—is paralleled by some other events in recent history where a similar "rush to destroy the scene" by destroying and removing whole buildings also occurred, events where there was also an unusual connection to Germany and extreme right wing Nazis: the destruction of the Alfred Murrah Federal Building in Oklahoma City after the Oklahoma City Bombing, and, of course, the removal of debris after the destruction of the World Trade Center complex after 9/11.[55]

(5) Melaouhi's Assessment of the Motivations: The "Gorbachev Hypothesis"

Like others involved with, or investigating, the Hess Mess, Melaouhi too is compelled to ask the all-important question: why? If Hess was murdered, why? And why do it so late in the game?

A clue, he argues, is provided by the fact that on the day of his death, there were no Soviet personnel present in the prison.[56] In touch with Wolf Hess soon after his father's death, Melaouhi informed him there was no doubt in his mind that his father had been murdered.[57] For Melaouhi, there is no doubt that is was a

---

[54] Abdallah Melaouhi, op. cit., pp. 141-142.

[55] In the case of the Oklahoma City Bombing, the connection is Timothy McVeigh's alleged sometime associate Andreas Strassmeir, a.k.a., "Andy the German," who, as I pointed out, appeared to have been some type of German intelligence agent. Strassmeir's father, Günther, was Chancellor Helmut Kohl's Minister without Portfolio entrusted with the reunification plan. (See my *The Nazi International: the Nazis' Postwar Plan to Control Finance, Conflict, Physics and Space* [Kempton, Illinois: Adventures Unlimited Press, 2008], pp. 209-216) The connection to 9/11 is via (1) Mohammad Atta, (2) Deutsche Bank, and (3) the "Nazi friendly" Swiss banker Francois Genoud. (See my *Hidden Finance, Rogue Networks, and Secret Sorcery: The Fascist International, 9/11 and Penetrated Operations* [Adventures Unlimited Press, 2016], pp. 11-33; 152-157; 167-174.)

[56] Abdallah Melaouhi, op. cit., p. 133.

[57] Andallah Melahoui, op. cit., p. 135.

crime of state, and that "the special interests that led to this crime *are apparently still valid*,"[58] though he does not speculate on what could still be so sensitive, so long after World War Two's end, that would require the political murder of a frail old man.

Melaouhi speculates that one possible reason was that the Allies discovered that Hess was successfully smuggling letters out of Spandau, and wanted to put a permanent end to the practice.[59] The problem with this view is that they would have had no idea of how many letters might already have escaped, and that might turn up with embarrassing revelations on Hess's death and any suspicions that its occurrence was not natural.

A much more serious hypothesis, however, and one that needs to be factored into any consideration of The Question, is the Gorbachev Hypothesis, and it was Melaouhi who was one of the first, but quite certainly not the only, individual who suspected it.

For years the western Allies had assured the Hess family, and the rest of the world, that they were indeed pressing for Hess's release on humanitarian grounds, and that it was the Soviets who continually played the "bad guy" and vetoed any such notion, conveniently enabling the western Allies to "blame Russia."

But then something happened, and that something was Mikhail Gorbachev, the new "liberal-minded" General Secretary of the Communist Party of the Soviet Union.[60] As we shall discover in more detail subsequently, through contacts in East Germany, Wolf Hess learned that Mr. Gorbachev was seriously considering a complete reversal of prior Soviet policy regarding Hess, and dropping its veto on his release for humanitarian reasons. It was even rumored that this would be announced when the Soviets took their next monthly turn at guarding Hess.

Melaouhi informed Hess of what he thought would surely be good news to the prisoner and his patient.

> But Hess failed to react at all. After about five minutes I asked him
> if he wasn't happy about the news. After taking a deep breath, he

---

[58] Ibid., p. 36.

[59] Ibid., p. 122.

[60] Of course, "liberal-minded" in this context is a highly relative term, given the previous occupants of that position in people like Stalin, Khrushchev, Brezhnev, Andropov, &c.

answered, "You fool!" Shocked, I asked him what he meant. He answered, slightly irritated, "Do you have to know everything?" I said no, but that I would still like to know this one thing, whereupon he said in a flat tone of voice, "If the Russians release me that would be my death. It would only be a happy day for me if the British published my documents internationally. Then I would be free." I didn't really understand what he meant until he explained to me, "I always wanted to have peace in this world, and I did everything I could to prevent war. Almost everything that people write about me is not true. That is why it would be good if these documents could finally be published, because then I would be a free man and I could finally see my family again. You must, however, not tell anyone about this as this would be more harmful than useful to me, and the Allies would twist every word I said as they pleased as they have always done before."

It wasn't until after his death that I understood what he meant, that the British—for reasons of state—would never allow him to be a free man.[61]

With this second-hand dead-man's testimony—always of very weak evidentiary value—we have the first intimation of yet another explanatory hypothesis in the Hess Mess: the "Peace Plan" hypothesis. According to this, Hess's flight was, as is now widely believed, a flight undertaken to negotiate a peace with Great Britain to end the war in the West. It is *this* hypothesis that lies at the central core of almost all investigation of the Hess Mess, and accordingly, we shall have much to do with it throughout the remainder of this book, for it, more than any other, highlights the unusual nature of the Hess Mess and the significance of The One Question.

We may, however, anticipate the problems that the Peace Plan Hypothesis poses to some extent by posing the related questions once again: is this hypothesis *really* sufficient, in and of itself, to explain why Hess was kept in prison for so long? And if the murder hypothesis be true, is it sufficient motivation to explain it? Why not murder him earlier? And if the murder hypothesis is *not* true, why would the Russians *not* release Hess *earlier*, and use whatever resulted from their about-face to embarrass the Western Allies and exploit its propaganda value? Or was there some secret the Soviets

---

were also attempting to preserve, of which the Peace Plan Hypothesis was only a component? Or were they willing to play "bad guy" in the service of some secret arrangement and agreement with the British? Did they change their position, knowing that Hess would be murdered by someone else to preserve that secret?

As Melaouhi puts it, "Outside of sheer cruelty, it would seem that there would have to be some quite powerful political reason why Hess needed to rot in jail."[62] But once again: What political reason would be relevant in 1987, fully forty-two years after the end of World War Two, and, if one considers the fact that some Hess files are only due to be classified in the year of the writing of this book—that is, in 2017—fully *seventy-two* years, almost three quarters of a century, after the end of the Second World War? What secret could possibly be relevant even up to the present time? Moreover, what possible secret could that be, that *Hess* might have been privy to, prior to his May 1941 flight?

C. The Autopsies

Such questions were instantly posed the moment the British announcement stated that the ninety-three year old Hess had committed suicide. But assuming for the sake of argument that Melaouhi's statements are totally unfounded—which this author does not believe them to be—is there any *other* evidence that Hess's death might not have been suicide? Indeed there is.

The British forensic pathologist and professor of forensic medicine, J.M. Cameron, a consultant for the British Army on forensic medicine, was ordered to Berlin on Hess's death to perform the autopsy. Cameron and his team discovered in Hess's clothes a note which they claimed was a suicide note, clearing indicating Hess's intentions of taking his own life. This note was read to Wolf Rüdiger Hess during a phone call.

Hess's son quickly concluded it was bogus because it used forms of expression and diction that his father had not used since the late 1960s and early 1970s, and, since it made direct and explicit reference to the Nuremberg Tribunal which had sentenced him to life, it was in any case forbidden under prison regulations. Wolf

---

[62] Abdallah Melaouhi, op. cit., p. 274.

Hess concluded, on this basis, that the note had probably been written in November 1969 during a period of severe illness for his father, and that it was confiscated by prison authorities on one of their many sweeps of Hess's cell years prior to its convenient appearance during his death in 1987. Under Spandau's regulations, Hess was forbidden, absolutely, speak or write about anything having to do with politics, with the Nazi era, or with the Nuremberg tribunals.[63] Wolf Hess, increasingly skeptical of the official report, decided to commission his own private autopsy.

In the meantime, Cameron's official autopsy found that Prisoner Number 7 had perished from asphyxiation that resulted from "compression of the neck" as a consequence of "suspension." In other words, strangulation by hanging.[64] Additionally, however, Cameron's autopsy also discovered other things, things which were left curiously "unexplained," which included a "circular bruised abrasion of the top of the back of the head," and deep bruises on the back of the head, and bruising on the right upper thyroid cartilage, and further additional bruising *behind* the voice box.[65]

Padfield, who does *not* believe Hess was murdered,[66] observes that while Cameron's autopsy was intended to dispel doubts and quell any political explanations or examinations of Hess's death, had exactly the opposite effect, because no explanation was forthcoming as to how the bruising occurred. It will be apparent to the reader however, that bruising might be consistent with Melaouhi's assertions that it appeared as if some sort of struggle had occurred in the garden house.

As for Wolf Hess's autopsy, with which we shall have more to do in a subsequent chapter, the German pathologists discovered "*two almost parallel* strangulation marks on the neck,"[67] a difficult feat for someone hanging himself to achieve, to say the least. However, in his final report, one of the German forensic

---

[63] Peter Padfield, op. cit., p. 14.

[64] Ibid., p. 15.

[65] Ibid., p. 13.

[66] Ibid., p. 350.

[67] Wolf-Rüdiger Hess, *Who Murdered my Father, Rudolf Hess? My Father's Mysterious Death in Spandau*, trans. from the German by Sonja Ruthard (Decator, Alabama: Reporter Press, 1989 [Printed in Argentina by Talleros Graficos, Genesis, calle Mrillo 2548, Buenos Aires]), p. 73.

pathologists hired by Hess to perform the autopsy, an eminent pathologist named Dr. Spann, went further in challenging Cameron's conclusions:

> During the second autopsy, findings were ascertained in the area of the skull and neck which lend themselves to explain the death by a central paralysis, caused by violence to the neck and accompanied by stoppage of the oxygen supply to the brain. Therefore, the findings ascertained by us agree with Professor Cameron's inasmuch as it is also his opinion that the cause of death was asphyxiation due to the compression of the neck. This presupposes that the decisive mechanism causing the death lay in a compression of the arterial vessels of the throat, accompanied by stoppage of the oxygen supply to the brain, and not in a compression of the respiratory tract.
>
> Dr. Cameron's further conclusion that *this compression was caused by the suspension is not necessarily compatible with our findings...*
>
> *In forensic science, the **course** which the ligature mark takes on the neck is considered a classic indicator for the differentiation between the forms of strangulation of hanging and throttling. A horizontally level course of the ligature mark around the neck is considered to be a characteristic sign of throttling. In the case of hanging, on the other hand, the ligature mark ascends in the direction of the fixed attachment point of the strangulation device...*
>
> If Professor Cameron, in his assessment of the cause of death, comes to the conclusion that this cause of death was asphyxiation caused by compression of the neck due to hanging, he neglects to consider the other method of strangulation, namely throttling. By definition, throttling entails strangulation by means of a device encircling the throat and the active constriction by another person, or very rarely by the victim himself, whereas in the case of hanging, the compression by the strangulation tool is achieved passively through the weight of the victim's own body. Making this distinction would have required an examination of the course of the ligature mark. The precise course of the mark *is not reported in Professor Cameron's autopsy report...*
>
> Here... *an almost horizontal course of the strangulation mark could be identified, this finding, as well as the fact that the mark on the throat obviously was **not** located above the larynx, is more indicative of a case of throttling rather than of hanging.* Under no circumstances can the findings be readily explained by a so-called

32

typical hanging. The burst blood vessels which we observed in the face, caused by blood congestion, are also not compatible with typical hanging.[68]

If one accepts Melaouhi's statements of Hess's frail health and strength, and considers them in relation to these remarks, it is clear that Prisoner Number 7 was in no condition to throttle himself. Add to this the bruising on Hess's head and around his neck, and one has clear signs of a struggle, and of murder. Even standing alone, Dr. Spann's report clearly implies murder, not suicide.

1. The Magical Year of 2017: Weeding the Files

The mysteries surrounding Hess's death are not likely to be solved even with the year 2017—this year and the year this book is being written—and the year that the remaining Hess files are to be declassified. Indeed, one may wonder about the wisdom of writing a book on Hess at all in the year that the files are supposedly going to be opened. But as Padfield rightly observes, the disclosure date in effect means nothing whatsoever, since *known* files, such as the inventory of items Hess brought with him on his notorious flight to Scotland, have already been "extensively 'weeded'"[69] leaving us with yet another epistemological conundrum, for the amount of files "that have been destroyed" or thus weeded is completely unknown, leaving one to argue from silence, or, at best, from what documentary evidence as *does* exist for the removal and "weeding" of certain files.[70]

Or to be as plain as possible about it: the 2017 disclosure date in effect means nothing, for while files might appear to challenge this or that detail in the Hess Mess, by the nature of the case, and based on the prior pattern evident in the Hess Mess, nothing is to prevent the removal of some files which might never appear on any index of files. In fact, it is even possible that files might be forged to challenge this or that aspect of the Hess Mess uncovered over the

---

[68] Wolf Rüdiger Hess, *Who Murdered my Father, Rudolf Hess?* pp. 89-90, all emphases added.

[69] Padfield, op. cit., p. 19.

[70] Padfield, op. cit., p. 20.

years by various researchers, and hence, the speculations will continue.

2. A Strange Remark in Melaouhi's Recovered Letter from Hess

As we shall see, those speculations *should* continue, for what *has* been uncovered in the Hess Mess by various researches is stunning enough. And it should continue for another reason, for some research has uncovered things whose implications have possibly gone unnoticed by the very researchers who uncovered them.

One of those "uncovered things" was a letter of Hess which Melaouhi himself had acquired, and which Hess had apparently written in Spandau and given to Melaouhi, with incredibly detailed and specific instructions on how to transmit it to people "on the outside." In this letter, at a certain point, Hess elaborates on a period of his imprisonment in England at Maindiff Court, a very *problematical* period as we shall discover in future chapters.

In this case, complaining of his treatment during this period, Hess also complained that he was being poisoned by his British captors, and then states, "I wasn't allowed to smoke."[71] For the health-and-homeopathy-obsessed Hess, Deputy Führer of the Nazi Party, which had itself during the years before the war embarked on an anti-smoking campaign worthy of modern America, this is stunning.

In fact, it's more than stunning.

Because Hess didn't smoke...

...and we're only *just* getting started.

---

[71] Abdallah Melaouhi, op. cit., p. 206.

2
THE SON SPEAKS ABOUT THE "SUICIDE"

"Then, in 1937—after ten years of marriage—they had their only child, Wolf Adolf Karl Rüdiger Hess 'Wolf' had been Hitler's codename in the early days of the Nazi Party, 'Adolf' is self-explanatory, and, of course, he was named 'Karl' after Professor Haushofer. Both men after whom the baby was named acted as his godfathers."
Lynn Picknett, Clive Prince, and Stephen Prior[1]

WOLF RÜDIGER HESS, THE ONLY SON AND CHILD of his father Rudolf and his mother Ilse Hess nee Pröhl, was barely a three and a half years old when his father flew on his now infamous flight in May of 1941 to Great Britain. It was only much later, in Spandau prison, that he saw his father again for the first time as a grown man, and from that point, during much of his adult life, he sought to obtain his father's release from Spandau on humanitarian grounds, and after his father's suspicious death until his own death in 2001 at the age of sixty-four, fought to overturn the suicide verdict of the official narrative, and to restore his father's honor. Whatever one may make of that quest, it is at least understandable.

As the surviving son of Rudolf Hess, and father of three children himself, Wolf Hess was naturally in touch with, and contacted by, many of the researchers of the Hess affair throughout his life, and himself published three

---

[1] Lynn Picknett, Clive Prince, and Stephen Prior, *Double Standards: the Rudolf Hess Cover-up* (London: Sphere, 2014), p. 61. If one gets only one book on the Hess Affair, then in this author's opinion, their book is *the* book to have. Its probing of the known details is thorough, their ability to unearth *new* details in the case is profound, and their synthesis and speculations are boldly, tightly and well-argued. As we shall discover, they unearthed a highly suggestive detail which has, as I shall argue subsequently, massive and contemporary significance and implications.

books on his father, two of which—*My Father Rudolf Hess* and *Who Murdered My Father, Rudolf Hess? My Father's Mysterious Death in Spandau*—we shall have occasion to cite in this book. In this chapter, our concentration will naturally be upon the latter, for Wolf Rüdiger and his lawyer, Dr. Alfred Seidl, who was also his father's lawyer at the Nuremberg Tribunals, noted many anomalies about the death of Spandau's famous Prisoner Number Seven, and attempted to bring them to the attention of the wider public.

Wolf Adolf Karl Rüdiger Hess,
November 18, 1937- October 24, 2001

Rudolf Hess with Wolf Rüdiger, possibly sometime shortly before the flight to Britain. Rudolf Hess's over-bite is evident in the picture.

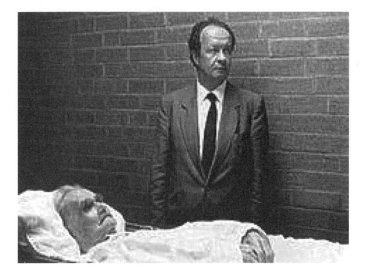

Wolf Rüdiger with his father's body.

A. Anomalies Noted by Hess's Son, Wolf-Rüdiger Hess

Like his father's nurse, Abdallah Melaouhi, with whom he was in contact, Wolf Hess did not believe the story that his father had committed suicide, and in *Who Murdered My Father, Rudolf Hess*, he attempted to outline his personal concerns and the reasons for them. Wolf Hess begins the first chapter of *Who Murdered My Father* by noting one glaring anomaly: the death certificate itself was signed only by British personnel, and yet, his father's death occurred in the month of August, during the *American* guard rotation.[2] It may be objected that as a British prisoner initially, and as Hess's medical needs were always attended to by the British Military Hospital, there was nothing unusual in this.

However, as will be seen, Wolf Hess raises a number of other issues which place this small fact into a rather larger and more serious context. Not the least of these is that he adds the important detail that as soon as the American governor of Spandau, Darold Keane, phone him in Munich, he and his lawyer, Dr. Seidl, boarded a plane and flew to Berlin the very next morning and attempted to gain entry to the prison, only to be told that they "were neither allowed inside the prison complex" nor were they allowed to view Wolf Hess's father, and that no further information was forthcoming.[3]

Hess and Seidl booked a hotel room, and Hess called the secret phone number of the prison and demanded to speak to Keane, who, "after some attempts to stall me,"[4] finally took the call and informed Hess that the prison governors were still in conference, and that he would be informed as soon as the press report was prepared for

---

[2] Wolf-Rüdiger Hess, *Who Murdered My Father, Rudolf Hess? My Father's Mysterious Death in Spandau* (Decatur, Alabama, Reporter Press: 1989 [Printed in Argentina at Talleres Graficos, Genesis, calle Murillo 2548, Buenos Aires]), p. 45.

[3] Wolf-Rüdiger Hess, op. cit., p. 47.

[4] Ibid.

release. He was told to stay calm and wait in his hotel for the call from Spandau.

"Finally," writes Hess, "the long awaited call came." But when it did, Hess and his lawyer began to observe the carefully crafted wording of the release might be concealing a crime:

> I was speechless at what I got to hear. Keane said: "I will now give you the report that we will release immediately afterwards to the press. It reads: 'Initial examination indicates that Rudolf Hess attempted to take his own life. On the afternoon of August 17, under the supervision of a prison guard, Hess went to a summerhouse in the prison garden, where he always used to sit. When the supervisor looked into the summerhouse some minutes later, he discovered Hess with an electric cord around his neck. Attempts were made at resuscitation, and Hess was taken to the British Military Hospital. After further attempts to revive Hess, he was declared dead at 4:10 p.m. The question whether this suicide attempt was the cause of his death is the object of an investigation including a thorough post-mortem which is still ongoing at this time.'"
>
> I hung up. Obviously neither a response nor small-talk were expected on the other end—both were quite superfluous. This was now the third conflicting official account of my father's death within 24 hours. *The first had spoken of the death in the British Military Hospital, the second of the death in Spandau prison.* So now it was a "suicide" in the prison's garden summerhouse. It was not yet to be the last version of his death![5]

Pausing to note the same frail health and physical weaknesses stressed by Melaouhi, Wolf Hess and Seidl began to question the explanations, not the least because in the "press announcement" there was no time of death itself, only an announcement of the time of the certification of death, leaving open the question, where,

---

[5] Wolf-Rüdiger Hess, op. cit., p. 48, emphasis added.

exactly, did Hess die? At Spandau, or at the British Hospital?

Then came yet another "clarification," this time from the Americans:

> In their Telex #241904 of August 24, 1987, the Berlin office of the American news bureau Associated Press put it this way: "Hitler's former Second-in-Command, Rudolf Hess, hung himself in the Spandau Prison for War Criminals with the extension cord of a reading lamp. *According to the latest details made available by the Allies on Monday evening, August 24, 1987, Hess (on Monday, August 17, 1987) wrapped around his neck part of the cord that was already attached to the **ceiling or wall** of the prison's garden summerhouse. He then apparently let himself drop off the bench on which he had sat."*[6]

It is worth pausing to consider this report, for as we have already seen, Rudolf Hess's habit was to sit in the summerhouse in such a fashion that he was visible through the window. Why then, as he was presumably wiring the cord for his suicide, was he not visible, and prevented by the guards? Note again the physical difficulties of an old man performing the task, which this press story appears to attempt to address by maintaining that the cord was *"already* attached to the ceiling or wall of the prison's garden summerhouse." But the statement, having attempted to address one physical difficulty, creates another, for Rudolf Hess then "Let himself drop off the bench on which he had sat."

This newly-created difficulty is revealed by the *next* Associated Press Telex:

> Shortly after—in Telex #241917—a further communication from the same news agency stated more precisely: "While sitting in the summerhouse, Hess had to *elevate his legs*. According to the details available, he left himself *fall sideways* with the cord around his neck. It is not known

---

[6] Ibid., p. 49, emphases added.

whether the cord broke in the process..." Immediately after (Telex #241938), even more details: "The Allies later indicated more precisely that the cord had been an extension cord. It had always been hung on the window latch when not in use. Hess is said to have looped the cable around his neck and then apparently dropped off the bench..."[7]

Again, it appears that the explanations are designed to meet objections to the suicide explanation based on Hess's frail health and arthritis: the cord is "already attached," and now, rather than being attached to the window latch *or the ceiling* it is now just the window latch. And Hess is no longer dropping off of the bench (which he might have had difficulty getting *on* to), he is now "falling sideways." But yet a new problem is created, for in order to do so, we are informed he had to "elevate his legs," a difficult proposition for an arthritic old man that was stooped over from the ailment, and who had to walk with a cane, and whose left thigh according to Meloaouhi was atrophied. Interestingly enough, notes Wolf Hess, the initial press release "containing the first mention of suicide was not signed by the Russians, but on the insistence of the British, the Americans released it to the public anyhow."[8]

B. The Pre-Planned Protocols for Hess's Death, vs. What Actually Occurred: The Autopsies Again

In June 1983, as it became evident that Prisoner Number Seven, already advanced in years and in increasingly deteriorating health, was nearing his mortal end, "the four Allied prison Governors had arrived at an agreement that established the measures that would be taken in the event of Rudolf Hess' death."[9] When the situation actually occurred, however, these agreed-upon protocols were quickly thrown out, and the British

---

[7] Wolf-Rüdiger Hess, op. cit., p. 50.
[8] Ibid., p. 61.
[9] Ibid.

"immediately seized the initiative."[10] While the matter of a joint autopsy conducted under the auspices of medical personnel of all four Allied powers in the governing structure of Spandau was *not* specified nor called for in those protocols, such a joint autopsy was only to be expected, and indeed, it *was* proposed after Hess's death. But every attempt to *pursue* this proposal was obstructed "by the angry insistence of the British,"[11] who thus assured that it would be a Briton—Dr. Cameron as we discovered in the previous chapter—who would perform the first and only official autopsy.[12]

There were other anomalies noted by Wolf Hess, one of which concerned the extraordinarily small dimensions of the garden house. It was *so* small that an "extension cord"—the alleged "suicide" weapon—simply was not needed for any of the electrical appliances in it.[13] His requests to obtain the testimony of his father's black American guard, Tony Jordan, simply went unanswered by the American authorities.[14]

But *one* request did meet with an unusual success, for Wolf Hess asked for, and received, not just a copy of Cameron's report, but an original, "signed by Professor Cameron and written on the stationary of the University of London's forensic medical institute, which he heads."[15] Wolf Hess, following the suggestion of Dr. Hugh Thomas, another British physician who had attended his father in the British hospital on one occasion, and with whom we shall have much to do later in this book, believes that Dr. Cameron in fact performed "two autopsies," or rather, one autopsy with two entirely different reports or versions of it, one for public consumption, and a much more secret one, intended only for certain British authorities.[16]

---

[10] Wolf-Rüdiger Hess, op. cit., p. 61.

[11] Ibid., p. 63.

[12] Ibid., p. 62.

[13] Ibid., p. 86.

[14] Ibid., p. 88.

[15] Ibid., p. 91.

[16] Ibid.

C. Was Rudolf Hess Suicidal?

One of the persisting questions in the Hess Mess is—if Hess knew something so dangerous that he had to be permanently incarcerated and then murdered—why not try to murder him earlier than actually happened? Wolf Hess attempts to provide an answer to this nagging question[17] by pointing out that earlier in the year of his death, on January 14, 1987, his father put in a formal requisition request to the four Allied governing powers for a pacemaker to be installed on his heart, indicating that "he was prepared to risk the 'possible dangers associated' with the operation."[18] His father, according to Wolf Hess, told him he had been suffering more cardiac arrhythmia and variable pulse-beats, and even heart attacks, all of which was disputed by two British medical experts, who had "supposedly been unable to ascertain any negative changes of my father's heart."[19]

But according to Wolf Hess, there was more going on that meets the eye:

> I have recounted the pacemaker-episode here not only to document by father's unbroken will to live, but also because his transfer, soon after, to the British Military Hospital would otherwise have been even more mysterious and inexplicable than it is. Within our family, we speak of it as the second attempt on my father's life....
>
> On Sunday, March 1, 1987, at 3:00 a.m., Rudolf Hess was transferred to the British Military Hospital because of bronchitis. There could be two explanations for this more than unusual time: 1) The British wanted to keep the matter out of the public eye and avoid awkward questions by the press; 2) they wanted to make use of the "blind spot," in the night of February 28 to March 1, between the French and Soviet guard periods, in order to place the blame on the Soviets for everything that would—or should?—happen.

---

[17] It will continue to nag us for the rest of this book.
[18] Wolf-Rüdiger Hess, op. cit., p. 113.
[19] Ibid.

One day earlier, on Saturday, February 28, 1987, our father had still written to us. The letter was peculiar in its unusual brevity and its content. It was not the first time that the handwriting had been shaky, but we could only wonder helplessly at the text. It read: "Dear Gräfelingers, for lack of subject matter, sincere greetings, Yours." If, on this evening before his coup-like transferal to the British Military Hospital, he lacked subject matter for a letter, then he could neither have been seriously ill nor informed about the imminent transferal.[20]

In other words, Rudolf Hess's cryptic letter to his family may have forestalled a "murder-by-medical-emergency."

1. A Prior Attempt on Hess's Life?
Or an Interrupted Mind Control Procedure?

But the situation grew even stranger, for Hess remained in the British hospital for some days, after Ilse Hess, Rudolf's wife, had received a telephone call from the prison telling her that Rudolf was in the British hospital suffering from bronchitis, but that there was no need for concern and that he would "surely be taken back to Spandau within 24 hours."[21] Four days, however, passed, until on the fifth day the German magazine *Stern* called the family, inquiring what news it had of Rudolf's pneumonia! Wolf Hess called the prison authorities and requested permission to see his father, which was granted by the British governor, Le Tissier...

... for the *next* week, and on a day that Wolf Hess could not take off from work! Hess's son then requested a *different* day off that week, and Le Tissier informed him to call back on March 9. When he did so, the British governor then informed Wolf that his father did not want to see him until the *end* of the month.[22]

---

[20] Wolf-Rüdiger Hess, op. cit., p., 115.
[21] Ibid.
[22] Ibid., pp. 116-117.

Frustrated by the run-around, and increasingly suspicious of the British prison authorities, Wolf Hess and his lawyer, Dr. Seidl, decided to go to Berlin anyway, and informed the press that they were coming. They were met by an avalanche of press, and a strong German police presence around the prison. Once admitted, they were confronted by all four Allied prison governors, and various interpreters and medical personnel. As it was March, the Soviets were in charge of the prison, and the Soviet governor suggested that the medical experts could update Hess and Seidl on his father's condition.

Wolf Hess and his lawyer refused, and insisted on seeing his father. At this point, the Soviet governor produced a document and placed it on the table. It was

> ...a sheet of paper of DIN A 4 format, bearing almost illegible writing with unclear and jumbled syntax, faulty spelling and punctuation. I could hardly decipher it: "I request that my son come to see me on the very last day of the month." No date, no salutation, no signature, only the familiar round stamp: Allied Prison Spandau Official" and two date stamps, one from March 9 and one from March 11, 1987. The latter had been crossed out with ball-point pen.
>
> We studied the document for a long time, astonished. "If my father really wrote this, he can only have done so in a state of almost total mental derangement," I said. Dr. Seidl confirmed that who-ever had written this was "not legally competent." So the document in question was "completely worthless." We insisted again on seeing the patient our-selves, immediately. Now the Russian demanded a written application to visit. I explained that I had already sent one two weeks ago, but had not received an answer yet. To which the Russian replied: "No answer is an answer too."[23]

After more back-and-forth between Hess, his lawyer, and the Russian governor, Wolf Hess was finally told that only a written request to see his father would be considered.

---

[23] Wolf-Rüdiger Hess, Op. cit., p. 118.

He immediately wrote out the application, and passed it to the Allied governors who, not expecting such stubbornness, retired to consider it. Eventually they returned, and informed him that the application for a visit had been turned down, but he *could* go to the door of his father's hospital room with the four Allied governors, and look at his father from the door![24]

What happened next, provides the first entrance into yet another mystifying aspect of the Hess Mess, and here it is necessary to cite Wolf Hess's account extensively:

The Governors and their entourage accompanied me to a special elevator which went to the so-called Rudolf-Hess-Suite of the British Military Hospital. The entrance to this elevator was guarded by British paratroopers with machine guns. Two of them went up with us. Upstairs, in the hall, there were more armed guards. We went to the room where my father stayed. Through an open door, I could see my father, about 10 feet away. The attendants had pushed two chairs together, sat him down on them like a string puppet and covered him with a blanket.

He looked frightening: pale, hollow-cheeked, eyes sunk deep into their sockets, flickering and looking unsteadily into a void. Yes, this figure matched the letter we had been shown. He was obviously not in full possession of his faculties. What had they done to him? I don't know for how long I stared at my father like that.

The French Governor went to my father and spoke to him, insistently, like one might speak to a child, or to someone who is not all there. He had a surprise for him, he said, his son was here and wanted to speak to him. My father interrupted the Frenchman, his voice sounded hollow and alien. No, he said, he didn't want to speak to his son now, not until month's end. He repeated this in the exact same words he had scribbled down on that paper. It was eerie. Was he drugged?

I couldn't take it any more (sic). Agreement or no, I had to do something. The Governors had left the room; I took a step forward, towards my father, and said loud and clear:

---

[24] Ibid., p. 119.

"Father, I am your son and am here to talk to you. Can you recognize me?" What would happen? Would the machine guns go into action? Would the commandants drag me out of the room? Nothing happened, they stood behind me as if in silent fascination.

My father showed no sign of recognition, his face was unchanged. He just repeated, as though memorized or forced, the one senseless sentence he had already expressed in writing. I repeated my question twice, a little louder each time. Then I gave up. We left. There was deathly silence, none of the Governors even said a word.[25]

Such behavior is characteristic of victims of mind-control experimentation and techniques, and it is not the last time we shall encounter that subject with the Hess Mess, for as we shall eventually discover, it is a *consistent and egregious feature* of the affair.

The strange episode was not over for Wolf-Rüdiger, for after the "encounter" with his drugged father, he was able to speak with a young British orderly. This individual

...had obviously not been instructed in any way and spoke to me frankly. My father, he said, spent all his time in a sort of *dazed half-sleep.*[26] He was no longer interested in anything; newspapers, television, books, he pushed them all away. *Real sleep alternated with a sort of daze.* He had tried to rouse him out of his apathy, but with hardly any success.

For me, *this conversation was an important and informative clue. Now I knew for sure that something unusual had been done to my father.* This was not just a matter of pneumonia or circulatory weakness, as the doctor had argued. He had described the effects of these on the brain of a 93-year-old as generally irreversible. But in fact, 14 days later, I found my father in almost splendid health—quite "his own self" again, one could say... *But for me, it was the ultimate proof that something was very wrong on March 12, 1987. My father's condition at that time*

---

[25] Wolf-Rüdiger Hess, op. cit., pp. 120-121.

[26] These words, as we shall eventually discover, are quite important as is the timeframe—1987—in which they were made.

cannot have had any natural causes, it must have been artificially induced.

Should our unexpected appearance in the British Military Hospital have interrupted an operation whose aim it was to secretly put my father to sleep?

Had we perhaps prevented a murder, at the last possible moment?[27]

Or had Wolf Hess interrupted a very *different* procedure, one designed to reinforce prior imprinted patterns of behavior? Had Wolf interrupted a *mind control* procedure? Strange and bizarre as this sounds now, subsequent facts long known to researchers of the Hess Mess will place this question and its corollary—*who* was imprisoned as Hess in Spandau—in a premier position of importance. As Wolf Hess notes, when he reported his observations of his father and his conversations with the British orderly to his lawyer, Dr. Seidl, the latter "left it open whether it was a matter of mind-altering drugs or injections, hypnosis or withholding of necessary medical care."[28]

2. The First Attempt at Murder-by-Medical Emergency: The Prostate Surgery Affair

As noted previously, Wolf Hess's family believed the March 1987 "bronchitis" affair to have been a *second* attempt on his father's life, or, as suggested by Dr. Seidl, an interrupted mind-control procedure. The occasion that Wolf Hess's family suspects was the "first attempt" on his life was the "prostate surgery" affair of 1979.

This incident was occasioned by the news that the Soviet dictator, Leonid Brezhnev, was considering a reversal of Soviet policy regarding Hess, allowing his release, much like Mikhail Gorbachev was to do a decade later.[29] As these possibilities were being pursued through diplomatic channels, unusually—or perhaps, predictably—

---

[27] Wolf-Rüdiger Hess, op. cit., p. 121, emphasis added.
[28] Wolf-Rüdiger Hess, op. cit., p. 122.
[29] Ibid., pp. 126-127.

Rudolf Hess suffered another medical "emergency" on September 4, 1979, shortly after Wolf Hess had just visited his father. According to Wolf Hess, on this occasion

> ... the British had practically kidnapped him, that is, taken him to the British Military Hospital. Neither the family nor the public had been informed of this coup. We only found out on September 10, through a press report, that Rudolf Hess had been taken to the British Military Hospital for a "thorough examination" and had since been transferred back to Spandau.
>
> All this was made even more mysterious by the way in which the then British Commandant, G.P.T. Marshall, tried per telephone on September 21, 1979, and then even per letter, to convince the family of the necessity of immediate surgery on Rudolf Hess' prostate—an operation which, he said, the recent examinations had indicated must not be delayed if uraemia was to be prevented. My father stubbornly resisted this operation. Despite the presence of the four Governors, I had warned him most insistently against agreeing to a dangerous operation if it was to be performed by surgeons from those political powers who through his continued imprisonment had shown so much inhumanity that nothing could be put past them. The British attempts to change his mind via my influence were thus useless.
>
> The fact that my father agreed with my opinion and stood firm presumably saved his life at that time and led to the failure of a plan that can be regarded with a high degree of certainty as the first attempt on Rudolf Hess' life. The man responsible—the British Commandant Marshall—was recalled from his position, ostensibly for health reasons. I suspect that in reality it was the Soviets who urged his dismissal after he had tried to cross their plans for the release of Spandau's last prisoner by means of an attempt at murder, disguised as prostate surgery.[30]

In other words, as far as Wolf-Rüdiger Hess was concerned, both Soviet attempts to reverse their position on Hess, and

---

[30] Wolf-Rüdiger Hess, op. cit., pp. 144-145.

allow his release, both those of Brezhnev in the late 1970s and of Gorbachev in the late 1980s, led in both instances to strange "medical emergencies" which Wolf Hess believes to have been disguised murder attempts. Notably, the attempt which finally succeeded avoided the medical aspect until the last minute: Hess was "suicided" either at Spandau, according to Wolf Hess, or at the British Military Hospital, where attempts were made, by the Allies' own statements in their press releases, to "resuscitate" him. As far as Wolf Hess was concerned, the murderers had to have already been in the prison in the morning, with the full collusion of the senior ranking American warders.[31]

This is not as far-fetched as it may sound, for that "full knowledge and collusion" does *not* necessarily imply that the senior American officers were privy to the *purpose* of the presence of additional strange personnel. A cover story could have been easily concocted to cover their presence.

And this brings us to Wolf Hess's final, and most sensational, disclosure:

D. The South African Affidavit

Referring directly to Abdallah Melaouhi's statements and affidavit to the German authorities, Wolf Hess observes that Melaouhi

> ...was so flustered by the sight of his charge lying motionless on the ground that he first of all attempted resuscitation and furthermore asked the two strangers if they knew how to perform heart massage. One of them readily bent down to my father and began to massage his chest. The pressure he exerted in doing so was so great that later, during the autopsy, nine ribs and the sternum were discovered to be broken. It is thus quite clear that no life-saver was at work here, but rather one of the two murderers.[32]

---

[31] Ibid., p. 93.
[32] Wolf-Rüdiger Hess, op. cit. p. 97.

But why was Wolf Hess certain that the "two strangers" of Melaouhi's affidavit were his father's murderers, beyond the strong convictions of Melaouhi himself in this regard?

The answer, while unverifiable, is worth citing from Wolf Hess's book extensively once again, for it contains a pattern that will be reflected in other evidence encountered later, and thus, once the supporting evidence for the pattern *is* encountered, *the following* information gains in credibility. There was "*another* affidavit regarding the events in Spandau on August 17, 1987," writes Hess.

My wife brought it back from South Africa, where she had called on a South African lawyer with contacts to Western secret services. Very little of it has reached the public to date. With Dr. Seidl's and my assistance, my wife was able to persuade the lawyer to phrase his testimony in the form of an affidavit before a judge. It is dated February 22, 1988, and reads as follows:

"I have been questioned about the details of the death of the German Reich Minister Rudolf Hess.

"*Reich Minister Rudolf Hess was killed on the orders of the British Home Office.* The murder was carried out by two members of the British SAS (22nd SAS Regiment, SAS Depot Bradbury Lines, Hereford/England). The military unit of the SAS (Special Air Service) is subordinate to the British Home Office—not the Ministry of Defence. The planning of the murder as well as its direction was carried out by MI-5(normally responsible for Great Britain's internal security; secret service actions outside of Great Britain fall under the jurisdiction of MI-6). The secret service action whose aim was the murder of Reich Minister Rudolf Hess was so hastily planned that it was not even given a code name, which is absolutely not customary.

"*Other secret services which had been privy to the plan were the American, the French, and the Israeli.* Neither the KSG (sic) and QU (sic) nor the German secret services had been informed.

"The murder of Reich Minister Rudolf Hess had become necessary because the government of the USSR intended to release the prisoner in July 1987 (in connection with Federal President von Weizsäcker's visit to Moscow), in which respect President von Wiezsäcker was, however, able to negotiate an extension with the head of the Soviet government, Gorbachev, until November 1987, *the next Soviet period in the guard cycle.*

"The two SAS-men had been in Spandau prison since the night of Saturday-Sunday (August 15-16, 1987). *The American CIA gave its consent to the murder on Monday (August 17, 1987).*

"During Reich Minister Rudolf Hess' afternoon walk, the two SAS-men lay in waiting for the prisoner in the prison's garden summerhouse and tried to strangle him with a 4 ½ foot-long cable; afterwards, a 'suicide by hanging' was to be faked. But as Reich Minister Rudolf Hess put up a fight and *cried for help*, which alerted at least one American guard solider to the attack, the attempt on the prisoner's life was broken off, and an ambulance of the British Military Hospital was called. The unconscious Reich Minister Rudolf Hess was taken to the British Military Hospital in the ambulance.

"I was given the above information personally, verbally, by an officer of the Israeli service on Tuesday, August 18, 1987, around 8:00 a.m. South African time. I have known this member of the Israeli service both officially and personally for four years. I am completely satisfied that he was sincere and honest and I have no doubts whatsoever as to the truth of his information. The absolutely confidential nature of his conversation with me is also beyond doubt."[33]

Because Wolf Hess does *not* provide the jurisdiction or court before which this affidavit was allegedly sworn, one must *assume* it to be true, and allow further evidence to be developed that might corroborate its core concepts.

The concepts themselves, however, if true, are breathtaking in their implications:

1) Rudolf Hess was indeed murdered;
2) The language of the affidavit, with its strange repetition of the phrase "Reich Minister Rudolf Hess," suggests that the alleged affiant, a lawyer, was trying to draw

---

[33] Wolf-Rüdiger Hess, op. cit., pp. 99-100, emphasis added.

attention *to a point of law* by his repeated and consistent reference to Rudolf Hess by his governmental title, i.e., Hess was the target of a *political assassination*, and was not simply the victim of a murder;

3) Once viewed as a political assassination, one must search not only for those with the means, motive, and opportunity for the crime, but also for those *sanctioning* it; according to the alleged affiant: these were:

a) The British, in the form of the Home Office;

b) The American CIA, which may be "shorthand" for the entire military-intelligence-national security complex;

c) The French secret services; and,

d) The Israeli secret service, the Mossad;

4) The implication of point 3), and sub-points a)-d) above, is that whatever secret Hess knew, or that Britain, France, the USA, and Israel *suspected* he knew, that secret was of major *international* implication, and not confined simply to Great Britain alone. However, since Hess himself had expressed to Melaouhi that a Russian reversal on its policy of non-release doomed him to death, as we saw earlier, this means it is likely that the Soviets *knew* that the Western Allies would likely murder him, and thus their release overtures may have been made cynically, forcing the West to do the dirty work. This implies that they either knew, or strongly suspected, the nature of this secret.

These considerations lead us to make one final observation whose full significance will reveal itself only much later:

E. A Brief Note on German Reunification

The *timing* of the Hess release plans by Gorbachev and German *Bundespräsident* von Weizsäcker alluded to in the above alleged affidavit suggests that his death, the last of the major Nazis alive, and the last to have possessed the title of *Reichminister*—Albert Speer having died in 1981—has something to do with German reunification that occurred a mere five years later, with the Berlin wall actually being torn down only two years after his death.

While this is a topic that must be taken up again in this book, once more details of the Hess Mess are known and explored in subsequent pages, it is worth noting here that Wolf Hess alludes to a vague and mysterious connection between his father and German reunification:

> The Russian attitude to the Hess case had always been mixed. I knew that in 1952, Stalin had offered Adenauer the reunification of Germany, with certain conditions, but the latter—as we know—did not even respond to the offer. Perhaps my father was to play a special role in the reunification. *He refused—like Adenauer,* but certainly for vastly different reasons.[34]

In my previous book, *The Third Way,* I detailed some of the machinations of that time period, including Stalin's strange reunification offer. At the time the Soviet dictator made this offer, no explanation was given on how West Germany would be able to expel the British, French, and American occupation forces, and this may have been a factor in the Adenauer government's calculations to simply ignore the Soviet offer; how indeed could Bonn accept such an offer, without perhaps triggering another major war?

But nowhere does one encounter with respect to those proposals any mention of Rudolf Hess in their connection. Wolf Hess's choice of words is, however, and to say the least, suggestive, and laden with more ponderous implications, for he is implying that the Soviet proposals had something to do with his father, and that they were *communicated to him,* doubtless during a month when the Soviets were in charge of Spandau, and that his father had turned the Soviet dictator down.

The Hess Mess just became even messier.

But again, we're still just getting started...

---

[34] Wolf-Rüdiger Hess, op. cit., emphasis added.

3
A BRIEF BIOGRAPHY

"We had come to realize that, despite the almost universal dismissal
of the Deputy Führer as a powerless has-been, he was the most
important man in the Nazi empire after—perhaps even including
Adolf Hitler. This made his flight to Britain in the middle of the war
an act of supreme significance."
Lynn Picknett, Clive Prince, and Stephen Prior[1]

BIOGRAPHIES ARE A STAPLE RESEARCH TOOL for anyone investigating the turbulent years of the rise of Nazism, and the unleashing of the Second World War. Brief searches under the significant names of World War Two leaders will produce a rash of titles for every individual; there are biographies of Chamberlain, Churchill, Roosevelt, Stalin, Hirohito, Hideki Tojo, Chiang Kai-shek, Benito Mussolini, Daladier, Laval, Antonescu, and of course, Adolf Hitler, not to mention biographies of their various military leaders; there are biographies of Marshals Petain, "Bomber Harris" and Dowding, of Generals Curtis LeMay and Patton and Galland and Guderian and (for real connessiuers of the operational art) Giovanni Messe; there are biographies of Field Marshals Montgomery, Auchinleck, Rommel, Rokossovski, Zhukov, Koniev, Kesselring, Keitel, Kleist and Kluge, Yamashita and Terauchi; there are biographies of Admirals Nimitz, Halsey, Yamamoto, Kimmel, Raeder, Tovey, Dönitz and Darlan. And when it comes to Nazis, there are biographies—even memoirs or diaries in some cases—of virtually everyone: Hitler, Himmler, Göbbels, Göring, Rosenberg, Heydrich, Bormann.

Yet one searches in vain for biographies on Hess or titles like "Hess: Hitler's Deputy" or "In the Shadow of the Führer," and Hess left no memoirs that could be made into "Life with Adolf in Landsberg Prison." There are, of course, plenty of books in which Hess plays a central role, but these are not books about *him*, but rather about whatever it was that led him on the strangest mission

---

[1] Lynn Picknett, Clive Prince, and Stephen Prior, *Double Standards: the Rudolf Hess Cover-up* (London: Sphere, 2014), p. xx.

of the twentieth century, and which then kept him in prison for the rest of his very long life.

In short, there are no biographies of Hess; there are only theories, and all of them are conspiracy theories, to boot.

A. Early Life and World War One (1894-1914)

Rudolf Walter Richard Hess was the eldest of three children, born on April 26, 1894, in Alexandria, Egypt, to a moderately well-to-do German merchant, Fritz Hess, and his wife Clara. Because of this circumstance, some believe that Alexandria's rich history within classical and ancient Egyptian culture was the matrix in which the future Deputy Führer acquired his interest in history, esoteric and occult subjects, the sciences and mathematics. Alexandria was also, of course, where Hess learned to speak Arabic.[2]

While the Hess family often vacationed in the summers in Germany where it owned a summer house, Hess's schooling until 1908 occurred in the German Protestant school in Alexandria. His father, Fritz, was grooming him to take over the family merchant business, and as such sent Rudolf to a boarding school in Bad Godesberg from 1908 to 1911, then to study business for a year at the *École supérieure de commerce* in Neuchâtel, Switzerland, before going to Hamburg to begin an apprenticeship with another company.[3]

Fate intervened with the outbreak of World War One in the summer of 1914, however, and in the autumn of that year, Hess, a Bavarian—enlisted in a field artillery regiment, transferring later to an infantry regiment. He quickly distinguished himself and was soon promoted to the highest non-commissioned officer rank (*Vizefeldwebel*), and received the Kingdom of Bavaria's Military Merit Cross.[4]

---

[2] Wolf Hess notes that his father was fluent in Arabic to the extent of having also learned more "colorful" colloquialisms. See Wolf Rüdiger Hess, *Who Murdered My Father Rudolf Hess?*, p. 22.

[3] "Rudolf Hess," https://en.wikipedia.ord/wiki/Rudolf_Hess.

[4] Ibid. It should be noted that under the arrangements of the founding of the German Empire in 1871 at Versailles, the Kingdom of Bavaria continued to be a more or less autonomous entity within the Greater Reich: Bavaria still had

B. Wounds: Hess becomes a Pilot (1914-1918)

With Hess's military service during World War One, however, we begin the encounter with yet another bit of bothersome "debris" in the Hess Mess, in this case, debris in the form of shrapnel and bullets, which will haunt the remainder of this book and, indeed, which haunts *any* researcher trying to make sense of the Hess Mess. This is the matter of the war wounds which he sustained during various battles of World War One both on the Western and Eastern fronts, for which he was awarded the Iron Cross, 2nd class.[5]

During his military service, Hess oddly shows up at most of the "hot spots" of the war, being present at the First Battle of Ypres in 1914 until his posting to the Somme front, and from thence, being posted to the Verdun front during the horrific battle which occurred there in 1916. It was there that Hess sustained his first serious battle injury from shrapnel in his left hand and arm. For a month Hess was on leave to recover, and then his regiment was shifted to the eastern front to a sector of heavy fighting in Romania.

Here he suffered two more wounds. The first occurred on July 23, 1917, when a splinter from a projectile hit his left arm. This wound was apparently not serious, and was dressed in the field and Hess returned to duty.

However, on August 8, 1917, while his regiment was attacking a fiercely-defended Romanian position, Hess was pierced by a bullet which, in one important account, "entered the upper chest near the armpit and exited near his spinal column"[6] and piercing and collapsing his lung in the process. Hess was sent on convalescent leave, first to Hungary and then subsequently back to Bavaria.

Hess was promoted to become an officer, a Lieutenant of the Reserve, but his career as an infantryman, with such a serious

---

its King, and still had its own military which, under the terms of the 1871 constitution, answered to the Kaiser directly as "Supreme War Lord and Commander of the Armed Forces."

[5] Many are under a misapprehension of what this military decoration meant. It was an award given for being wounded or having one's blood shed during military service. It is roughly analogous to the American "Purple Heart" decoration. During World War One it was obviously, and tragically, a fairly common decoration.

[6] "Rudolf Hess," https://en.wikipedia.org/wiki/Rudolf_Hess.

wound, was in doubt, and while convalescing Hess requested transfer to the air corps to train as a pilot. He was accepted, and trained for several months until June 1918, during the period of the final massive German offensives on the Western Front. He was ordered to report for duty with a Bavarian pursuit squadron (*Jagdstaffel*) in October of 1918, but saw little action as the armistice occurred the very next month. Hess was finally discharged that December.[7]

It was, however, a crucial period for Hess, for this instilled in him his love of flying and piloting, and he soon became a very skilled pilot.

Hess, commissioned as Lieutenant of the Reserve, 1918

---

[7] "Rudolf Hess," https://en.wikipedia.org/wiki/Rudolf_Hess.

Lieutenant Hess, training as a pilot, 1918, in front of a Fokker triplane

C. Post-War: From Putsch to Power (1919-1933)
1. The Haushofers, and Hess
a. Hess and the Freikorps von Epp

Hess returned from the front like millions of other demobilized German soldiers to find the home front economy in a shambles, and the various *Länder* (German state) governments in chaos and, oftentimes, in the hands of socialist radicals threatening to overthrow them, and agitating for a Bolshevik revolution in the central Reich government itself. This was particularly true in Bavaria, as we shall see.

Like many veterans, Hess joined the various paramilitary organizations that grew up in Germany, and particularly in Bavaria, as a result of this, the *Freikorps* (Free Corps). These were veterans' groups, largely of conservative political and economic leanings, that were determined, by force of arms if necessary, to prevent any Communist or Bolshevik revolution in Germany as had happened in Russia. In Hess's case, in 1919 he joined one of the most famous— or infamous—of these *Freikorps*, the *Freikorps von Epp*, commanded by former Bavarian General Franz Xaver Ritter von Epp.

General Franz Xaver Ritter von Epp (1868-1947)

Hess and some members of the Freikorps von Epp; Hess is seated in the front row on the left.

General von Epp was a power to be reckoned with in the post-war chaos in Bavaria, for as a former General officer in the Imperial Army, his *Freikorps* formed one of the nuclei of the private armies that would eventually be so associated with Nazi Party strong-arm tactics. Additionally, when Adolf Hitler was tasked to secretly infiltrate the nascent "German Workers Party" in Munich and spy on it in behalf of the postwar German military, the *Reichswehr*, it is possible that the assignment, which came ultimately from Berlin and army chief Colonel-General Hans von Seeckt, may have been conveyed to Hitler via General von Epp.

For our purposes, however, we see the first example of an emerging larger pattern of Hess forming relationships with organizations and individual persons of power after the war. In fact, Hess was consummately skillful in what would in today's terms be called "networking," and it is this pattern that calls into question the standard judgments that, by 1941, Hess was losing power in the Nazi Party and state. Quite the contrary, as we shall discover.

b. 1919: Hess, the Haushofers, "Geopolitics," and the Thulegesellschaft
(1) The Thulegesellschaft

1919 was a "joining" year for Rudolf Hess, for in that year he also enrolled in the University of Munich, and quickly established a reputation among his professors as having some aptitude for mathematics and physics.[8] Additionally, in that same year he was introduced to the infamous *Thulegesellschaft*, the "Thule Society," an anti-semitic, quasi-occult lodge in Munich, complete with its own private army, the *Thulekampfbund*, that met in five rooms which it leased at the Munich hotel, *Vier Jahreszeiten* (Four Seasons Hotel), by a *Freikorps* friend, and a member of the organization, who invited Hess along to a meeting in February, 1919.

> Hess was stunned. Each of the five large rooms that he entered was lavishly adorned with swastikas and large, oak-leaf-crowned daggers superimposed on shining swastika sun-wheels. The men wore bronze pins with a swastika on a shield crossed by two spears; the women, pins with plain gold swastikas. Members greeted one another with *"Heil und Sieg"* ("Hail and victory!"). Hess met Rudolf Baron von Sebottendorff, the founder and head of the Thule Society and its armed wing, the Kampfbund-Thule. He at once joined both organizations.[9]

No sooner had Hess joined the Thule Society and its private army, the *Thule Kampfbund*, then it became the target, in April, of the Bavarian Spartacists, the radical socialist and Communist revolutionaries throughout Germany, who likewise had their own

---

[8] W. Hugh Thomas, in his famous and controversial book, *The Murder of Rudolf Hess* (New York: Harper and Row, Publishers, 1979), notes that Hess while in the Lutheran boarding school in Bad Godesberg displayed quickness and intelligence, and that he was "good at maths, physics, engineering, and astronomy" in addition to showing a special aptitude for history. (p. 53).

[9] Holger H. Herwig, *The Demon of Geopolitics: How Karl Haushofer "Educated" Hitler and Hess* (Lanham: Rowman and Littlefield, 2016), p. 72. Herwig's book fills a much-needed gap in studies of this period, and particularly of General Karl Haushofer and his son, Dr. Albrecht Haushofer, and their geopolitical theories. Herwig devotes much time to an analysis of the relationships of the Haushofers and their theories to other geopolitical thinkers of the era, including Sir Halford MacKinder. For students of the history of geopolitics, this is a valuable book.

private armies. On April 26, 1919, one of these, the "Schwabing Soviet" raided the headquarters of the Thule Society at the Four Seasons Hotel, and "found a treasure trove: the society's card index, its membership lists, dozens of anti-Semitic pamphlets, charts showing the deployment of Egelhofer's Red Army,[10] and a cache of weapons.["11]

A few days later, on May 1, Sebottendorff's *Thule Kampfbund* retaliated, recovering much of the stolen material, which simply subsequently —and some would say, suspiciously—vanished in the aftermath of this first clash of private armies that came to be called the "Battle of Munich."[12] This raises certain questions, for as a result of the disappearance of its records, the sources of knowledge—or rather, *source* of knowledge—about the *Thulegesellschaft* remains Baron von Sebottendorff himself and his "highly self-inflated memoir, *Before Hitler Came*. Therein he claimed credit as having been the 'inventor' of National Socialism and Adolf Hitler's 'precursor.'"[13]

The relationship between Hitler and the Thule Society has always been a point of contention. In the absence of the records of the society, we have only Sebottendorff's own claims, and these have been viewed with some suspicion. The bottom line is, there is no documentary evidence that Hitler himself ever joined the society.

Hess, however, *did*, and the behavior of the Nazi regime *after* it took power certainly leaves the impression that Hitler and Hess were concerned to obscure the connection between the National Socialist Party and the *Thulegesellschaft*, for Sebottendorff was arrested after his book was published. Its three thousand initial copies quickly sold out, and a second printing of five thousand copies was quickly confiscated by the Bavarian government and Sebottendorff was again arrested and sentenced to three months in prison. He obtained his release by promising to the Bavarian

---

[10] Yet another "private army."

[11] Herwig, op. cit., p. 72.

[12] Ibid.

[13] Ibid. The actual German title of Sebottendorff's book was *Bevor Hitler Kam*. The book was published in 1933.

A Brief Biography

Minister of Justice, the Nazi Hans Frank—a former Thule member!—that he would leave Germany.[14]

Well might Hitler and Hess have attempted to silence Sebottendorff, for in his book he provides a list of members of the society, a "veritable *Who's Who* of early National Socialists."[15] Among these were Dietrich Eckart, the poet who is alleged to have urged "Follow Hitler; he will dance, but it is I who have composed the music"; the economist Gottfried Feder, whose economic theories of debt-free money bypassing central banks became a cornerstone of the Nazi Party platform,[16] and of course, Rudolf Hess. Additionally, Sebottendorff claimed that "virtually every senior military commander in Bavaria"[17] was closely associated to the *Thulegesellschaft*. For Herwig, the significance of the Thule Society is that it is contrary to Hess's and Hitler's own "official narrative," which has Hitler and Hess meeting for the first time when Hess attended his first meeting of the Nazi Party in *Hofbräuhaus* beer hall in Munich, and heard Hitler speak for the first time. Herwig believes it is more likely that the two met at a Thule Society meeting in 1919,[18] and the possibility cannot be ruled out.

---

[14] Herwig, op. cit., p. 73.

[15] Ibid.

[16] As I noted in *Babylon's Banksters*, Feder's theories were actually implemented in modified form by the Nazis once they took power, by the issuance of labor-treasury certificates, the so-called "Feder notes," that were denominated in *Reichsmarks* and spendable domestically as currency. See my *Babylon's Banksters: the Alchemy of Deep Physics, High Finance and Ancient Religion* (Port Townsend, Washington: Feral House 2010), pp. 32-34.

[17] Herwig, op cit., p. 74.

[18] Ibid.

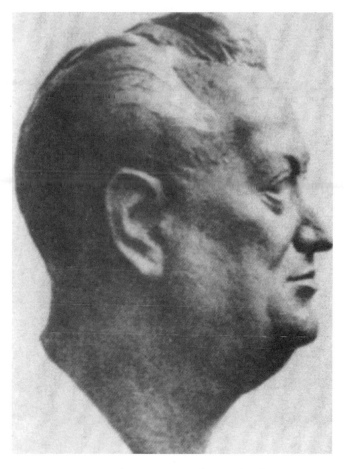

Bust of Baron von Sebottendorff

Thule Society Logo

It would be an oversight if, in reviewing the association of the Nazi Party and of Hess with the Thule Society, no mention was made of its core doctrines and beliefs, for these as we shall discover may have some relevance in unravelling the Hess Mess.

The founder of the Thule Society, Rudolf von Sebottendorff, was born Rudolf Glauer, son of middle class Prussian parents. Like Hess, Sebottendorff spent much time in Egypt and Turkey, where he studied the Giza complex and the doctrines of esoteric Islam.[19] During these studies at one point Sebottendorff even called himself "a Muslim Brother" as well as an "Odinist."[20] Glauer became "von Sebottendorff" while in Turkey, where he claimed he had been adopted by the patriarch of the family, Baron Heinrich von Sebottendorff. The family never challenged and actually endorsed the claimed relationship, though it appears that the claim to nobility was never formally recognized by Kaiser Wilhelm II.[21]

Once back in Germany von Sebottendorff founded the Thule Society, borrowing heavily from the racist doctrines and beliefs of Lanz von Liebenfels and Guido von List, doctrines which also included a "revisionist history" of an ancient very high civilization, from which the Aryans were descended.[22] This was blended with the claims of ancient lore, that the Aryans descended to Earth at the poles (usually the North Pole), and dispersed themselves throughout the planet, marrying the "lesser" humans already on the planet, and thus "corrupting" their race.[23]

---

[19] Nicholas Goodrick-Clarke, *The Occult Roots of Nazism: Secret Aryan Cults and Their Influence on Nazi Ideology* (New York: New York University Press, 1992), pp, 135, 138.

[20] Joscelyn Godwin, *Arktos: The Polar Myth in Science, Symbolism, and Nazi Survival* (Kempton, Illinois: Adventues Unlimited Press, 1996), p. 50.

[21] Goodrick-Clarke, *The Occult Roots*, p. 140.

[22] For a summary of this history, Goodrick-Clarke's work is the best. See particularly p. 145. Also see my *Reich of the Black Sun: Nazi Secret Weapons and the Cold War Allied Legend* (Kempton, Illinois, Adventures Unlimited Press, 2004), pp. 161-180. Joscelyn Godwin calls Guido von List, Lanz von Liebenfels, and von Sebottendorff the three "godfathers" of the "Nazi" version of the Thule doctrine.(See Godwin, op. cit., p. 48)

[23] This idea of miscegenation and a "corruption" of an otherwise "pure" race was also a large component of List and von Liebenfels' doctrine. It is worth mentioning that Godwin points out earlier precursors of the "polar descent and migration" theory, including the Frenchman Jean-Sylvain Bailly (1737-1793) who, consulting ancient texts and coordinating their claims to actual astronomical data, concluded that the polar descent and migration might have been true. (See Godwin, op. cit. pp. 27-29, particularly p. 29)

The influence o the Thule Society on the formation and evolution of the National Socialist German Workers' Party (*National Sozialistische Deutsche Arbeiters' Partei*, or N.S.D.A.P.) was thus, in terms of some of its core doctrines, immense; "it may," writes Goodrick-Clarke, "justifiably be regarded as a ginger group and predecessor of the National Socialist German Workers' Party."[24]

One influence in particular was Sebottendorff's doctrine of the "Temple of Halgadom," an "empire of all the Germans" between the Rhine and Vistula rivers, and eventually including all "Germanic peoples," the "other descendants of Thule": Norwegians, Danes, Swedes, Dutch, Britons and French.[25] As we shall discover below, this is remarkably similar to the doctrine of *Lebensraum* of Hess's geopolitics professor at the University of Munich, Professor General Karl Haushofer.

All of these considerations become terribly important when one understands that the influence of the Thule Society and its doctrines on the Nazi party were *possibly mediated directly by Hess himself*, for it was Hess who, after all, became Hitler's "Deputy," in charge of running the day-to-day affairs of the Nazi Party itself, and maintaining its doctrine and ideology.

This in turn implies something of possible significance for the Hess Mess, for it means that Hess was familiar not simply with the "run-of-the-mill" occult doctrines typical of the Western esoteric tradition, but with much more peculiar doctrines—twisted doctrines—on the fringes of that tradition via his membership in the Thule Society. The potential significance lies in the fact that the occult influence on various Nazi leaders was suppressed at

---

[24] Nicholas Goodrick-Clarke, *Black Sun: Aryan Cults, Esoteric Nazism, and the Politics of Identity* (New York: New York University Press, 2003(, p. 114. Goodrick-Clarke also observes that there is some evidence that the alleged Vril Society was an offshoot of the Thule Society, and that it was in the matrix between the two that the claims to have "psychically contacted" the Aldebaran system arose. With that, the myth of a polar "Thule" or *ultima Thule* – the Arctic "touch down" point for the ancestors of the ancient Ayrans—became not merely interplanetary, but interstellar. (See pp. 166-167). Godwin mentions that as early as 1914, a conference was held in the town of Thale in the Harz Mountains of Thuringia, attempting to unite all pan-Germanic and anti-Semitic secret societies in Germany around the doctrine of Thule, i.e., of an interplanetary origin of the Aryan race, its descent to Earth at the poles, and its subsequent migrations.(See Godwin, op. cit., p. 50).

[25] Godwin, op. cit., p. 50.

Nuremberg by the Allies, lest it be used as a component in "insanity" defenses.[26]

There is, however, a potentially deeper significance, for it has been suggested "that Rudolf Hess's quixotic flight to Britain was the last attempt of the old Thule Society—long dissolved, or driven underground—to affect world politics in the face of a Führer who had escaped their clutches and completely deformed their visions."[27] While this may sound incredible, one has only to examine its basic implicit premises to see that it is not, for the statement is asserting that:

1) a faction existed within Germany and within the Nazi Government itself which opposed the policies of Hitler; and that,

2) this faction was influenced by occult doctrines tied to the Thule Society, the most prominent of which is the doctrine of Thule itself, i.e., the idea of "Aryan descent" from off planet to the polar regions, and subsequent migration from there.

When these considerations are coupled with the observation that the Nuremberg Tribunal prosecutors forbade the introduction of any evidence of an occult connection into the trials, then the conclusion cannot be avoided that perhaps their fears of an "insanity defense" might itself be a kind of cover story for something else, a secret they were desperate to preserve: the relationship of Hess to Antarctica.

Indeed, Joscelyn Godwin himself, in his classic study *Arktos: The Polar Myth in Science, Symbolism, and Nazi Survival*, has to wonder about the wisdom of the Tribunal in suppressing this evidence. "One would know much more about the political and even the occult machinations of this period, so integral to an understanding of the twentieth-century's greatest tragedy," he writes, "if Hess had been encouraged to speak *instead of being held incommunicado in Spandau prison for over 40 years.*"[28] This is quite

---

[26] Picknett, Prince, and Prior, op. cit., p. 35.
[27] Godwin, op. cit., p. 57.
[28] Godwin, op. cit., p. 52, emphasis added.

correct, for under the regulations of Spandau, none of its Nazi inmates were permitted to speak with visitors about politics, history, or anything to do with the Third Reich, and after the others' release and eventual deaths, this left Hess alone. The implications of Godwin's observations are thus profound, and one cannot help but suspect that lurking in between his carefully worded statement lies the suspicion that *Hess's continuing imprisonment might have had something to do with his occult interests, and his membership in the Thulegesellschaft and his possible belief in these doctrines.*

(2) Hess, the Haushofers, and "Geopolitics"

While the occult influence on Nazism, and on Hess, was palpable enough for the Allies to ban consideration of it at Nuremberg, the specific details of that influence have always been subject to interpretation and debate. The situation is much less ambivalent when one turns to a consideration of the influence of Hess's geopolitics mentor while he was a student at the University of Munich, Professor General Karl Haushofer, for it was Haushofer who was Hess's "gray eminence," and who, via Hess, exercised an enormous influence on Adolf Hitler's geopolitical vision and ambitions.[29] Haushofer's son, Albrecht, also became a geopolitical guru to Hess, achieving his doctorate in geography and becoming a leading light and lecturer at Berlin's elite Geographical Society.[30]

---

[29] See Picknett, Prince, and Prior, op. cit., pp. 30, 43.

[30] It should be noted that, at the time, "geopolitics" was not a discipline in which one could obtain an advanced academic degree. In this respect, "geography" often encompassed "political geography," which was Professor General Haushofer's term for what we now call "geopolitics." For Haushofer, "political geography" meant the relationship between a nation-state—particularly a great power—and its "physical space" and how the latter determined, or should shape, its foreign policy.

Professor General Karl Haushofer (1869-1946)

Dr. Albrecht Haushofer, General Haushofer's eldest son (1903-1945)

Professor Doctor General Karl Haushofer, left, and his prize student, Rudolf Hess, right, ca. 1919-1920, after Hess's matriculation at the University of Munich

Karl Haushofer was well-acquainted with, and well-suited for, a life of "military academia," for his father had been a professor of economics, and Haushofer himself entered military service in the Bavarian Army in the field artillery, completing three courses in Bavaria's War School, Artillery School, and Bavaria's War Academy. Notably, he married his wife Martha, whose father was Jewish, in 1896. This small fact will assume some importance when we turn to contemplate Hess's actions and character once the Nazis assumed power.

Haushofer's abilities were quickly recognized, and he became part of the Imperial German Army's General Staff, and by 1903 was an instructor in the Bavarian army. Crucially, in 1908 the German Army dispatched him to Tokyo as a military observer and consultant to the Imperial Japanese General Staff, where Haushofer instructed his Japanese counterparts in tactics and artillery operations. It was during this period that Haushofer became fluent in Japanese. This accounts for Haushofer's later practice, in private letters to his son Albrecht, of referring to leading Nazis with Japanese codenames.[31] Haushofer returned with his wife to Germany in 1910, and during an illness and leave from the army, completed his doctorate from the University of Munch, writing a thesis on Japanese geopolitics. During World War One, he attained the rank of major general and commanded a brigade on the Western front.[32]

(a) MacKinder, Kjellén, the Heartland, and "Lebensraum"

After the First World War, Haushofer became a professor of geography at the University of Munich where he began to elaborate and perfect his conceptions of geopolitics, and to chart a course via those concepts for Germany's restoration as a military and great power. Two geopoliticians were particularly crucial in Haushofer's own unique elaboration of geopolitical theory.

The first was, of course, the British geopolitician, the "godfather" of geopolitics, Sir Halford Mackinder. Mackinder's geopolitical vision, at the cusp of the outbreak of World War One, and throughout the war and after, was not only consistent, but eerily similar to the geopolitical difficulties now emerging in the early twenty-first century, with the formation of the BRICS bloc of nations clustered around the strategic alliance of Russia and China, and the increasing tensions between the American and British bloc on the one hand, and the German-led European Union on the other. It is worth citing Holger H. Herwig's summary of Mackinder's prescient views in full:

> Mackinder painted with broad brushstrokes. He divided the world
> into three major camps—the land power of the "pivot area,"

---

[31] Holger H. Herwig, op. cit., p. 157.

[32] "Karl Haushofer," https://en.wikipedia.org/wiki/Karl_Haushofer. German generals' ranks are often confusing to people more acquainted with British and American ranking systems. The German rank of *Generalmajor* is actually not a two-star general, but a one-star general, equivalent to a brigadier in the British and American ranking systems. *Generalleutnant* or lieutenant general is thus a two-star general, and not, as in the American system, a three-star general. *General der Artillerie/Infanterie/Kavalerie* would be the three-star equivalent, and *Generaloberst* or Colonel General is equivalent to a four-star general.

encompassing today's Russia, Iran, and the central Asian republics; an inner or marginal crescent, consisting of Germany, Austria, Turkey, India and China; and an outer or insular crescent, peripheral to the "geographical pivot," consisting of the sea power of Britain, South Africa, Australia, the United States, and Japan. He categorized the first group as "nomads (later robbers) of the steppe"; the last, as "pirates from the sea." His concern as a British patriot was that there had been *a paradigm shift in transport and distribution. Railroads had replaced ships as carriers of the world's goods.* They were faster, easier to build, more dependable, and able to penetrate even the remotest hinterland. Ever more, national wealth was counted not in seaborne trade and commerce but rather in rail-hauled pig iron, steel, coal, sulfuric acid, dynamos, engines, tools, dyes, and the like. Political power, Mackinder warned his countrymen, was now the product of "geographical conditions, both economic and strategic," and the "relative number, virility, equipment, and organization of complete peoples." At heart, he was a determinist: the tectonic forces of geography in large measure decreed historical development. "Man and not nature initiates," he once stated, "but nature in large measure controls."

Mackinder's nightmare vision was one of the grafting of German industry, knowledge, and technology to the vast land and natural resources of the Russian colossus. He described the latter as "a continuous land, ice-girt in the north, water-girt elsewhere, measuring 21 million square miles, or more than three times the area of North America." If there came into being a contiguous Russo-German block" could the "outer crescent" of Britain, Canada, the United States, South Africa, Australia, and Japan long survive?

World War I did little to dispel Mackinder's fears. By 1919, he warned that the physical parameters of the "geographical pivot" might even be enlarged to include all the "regions of Artic and Continental drainage," this is, eastern Europe and Siberia. This vast expanse, inaccessible to sea power, would be opened up and exploited by railroads and airplanes. "Let us call this great region the Heartland of the Continent." Therewith, a catchy term had been coined, one that would find great resonance in Germany in the 1920s. And while Mackinder refused to have the label "geopolitician" attached to himself, his German counterparts would have no such qualms.[33]

---

[33] Holger H. Herwig, op. cit., pp. 116-117, emphasis added.

Viewed from this perspective, the two World Wars were but two separate and discrete acts in one World War designed to prevent that German-Russian Eurasian bloc from forming; Mackinder was, in effect, telling his fellow-countrymen that while they may have just won the first round of the World War, they were already losing that war over the long term. Indeed, Mackinder's vision is often misunderstood, for what he was *also* saying was that the world was in a major geopolitical and economic *paradigm shift*, a shift *away* from the paradigm that had prevailed since the Renaissance and the beginning of the Age of Exploration, that age which was also the beginning of a global *sea-based* economy, where power accrued to the chief sea power. By Mackinder's time and according to his lights, that era was *beginning to end*, and a new integrative economy was being formed, based not on the *seas* of the world's great oceans, but based on *land* and *connected trade via land*. In *that* power structure, the principal world powers would be *land* powers, and sea power would be largely ineffective.

All of this General Haushofer, and through him, Hess, absorbed completely. But there was another crucial influence on Haushofer, and therefore on Hess. This was the Swedish geopolitician Rudolf Kjellén of the University of Uppsala. It was Kjellén who provided much of the technical terminology for the emerging concepts of geopolitics.[34] Haushofer read Kjellén's book *Contemporary Great Powers* in 1917. In this book, Kjellén:

> ...divided the globe into four true "world powers" (Britain, Germany, Russia, and the United States) as well as four lesser "great powers" (Austria-Hungary, France, Italy, and Japan). More, he argued that the world was constantly in a state of flux. "Vigorous, vital states with limited space"—read Germany—were held together neither by laws nor constitutions but rather by "the categorical imperative of expanding their space by colonization, amalgamation, or conquest." It was heady reading in a time of global war and expansive war aims.
>
> Haushofer next immersed himself in Kjellén's *The State as a Living Organism*. Karl immediately recognized its cardinal importance. For there, in black and white, were the terms that

---

[34] Herwig, op. cit., p. 117.

explained so much of what he had been reading in the works of German geographers. First and foremost, Kjellén gave the vague field of "human geography" its future title: *Geopolitik* (geopolitics).[35]

For General Haushofer and his son Albrecht, these concepts required a complete "rethinking" of German imperial policy.

From this process of "rethinking" German geopolitics and goals, Haushofer elaborated a concept which he called *Lebensraum*, the "living space" in which a nation and its people existed and lived, and this *Lebensraum* was defined by the interplay of that nation's economics, politics, natural resources, military strength, its "position on the map"[36] as well as by much subtler factors such as culture and ethnicity. From this consideration of the German *Lebensraum* Haushofer concluded two things: first, Germany's imperial policy prior to World War One was completely wrong: there was no need for a confrontation with Great Britain nor for Germany to build such an incredibly large navy in order to acquire, and sustain, colonies. This led to Haushofer's second conclusion: Germany, in order to remain a Great Power, would have to increase its *Lebensraum* to encompass what effectively had been the old Holy Roman Empire, i.e., the areas of Holland, Austria, Bohemia, the Tyrol, and western Poland would have to be incorporated into the Reich in order to ensure that all ethnic Germans were in a common *Lebensraum*. From there, the Reich would have to expand to the East.

The importance of Haushofer's vision cannot be over-emphasized, for via his influence on Hess, and through Hess on Hitler, one finds the origin of the idea which will dog Hitler's diplomacy after the outbreak of World War Two, and which will become a central component in how one interprets the infamous flight of his Deputy Führer to Britain: with Haushofer's geopolitics, we are chin to chin with one of the central pieces of debris in the Hess Mess. It is because of the above two fundamental theses that Adolf Hitler attempted, repeatedly, to reach out and offer a negotiated peace to Great Britain, from September of 1939 to May of

---

[35] Herwig, op. cit., p. 117.
[36] Picknett, Prince, and Prior, op. cit., p. 32.

1941. The British Empire was not, Hitler repeatedly stated, Germany's natural enemy.

Crucial to these overtures, as we shall discover, were the Haushofers' numerous contacts within the upper reaches of British Society, including people who, like Haushofer, viewed the future as belonging to Russia and the USA, *unless the two principal economic and military powers of Europe untied to prevent it*. Indeed, Haushofer foresaw the need for a "united Europe," a federation of the European powers, led by Germany.[37] These contacts included Albrecht Haushofer's friendship with a key actor in the Hess Mess, the young Duke of Hamilton.[38]

c. The Spartacist Coup, the Counter-coup, and the Beer Hall Putsch

The crucible in which the Haushofers' influence over Hess and Hitler was forged were the events prior to, during, and immediately after the Nazi attempt to seize power in Bavaria in November, 1923, the so-called Beer Hall Putsch. This event is one of the most *mis*understood events in standard historiography, and consequently, in most people's understanding of the event. The popular understanding is, in this instance, almost diametrically the opposite of the reality.

As was previously seen, in the turbulent post-war years of 1919-1920, the socialist-communist revolutionaries within Germany—the so-called Spartacists—raided the Thule Society, stole its documents, and, in what was *not* previously discussed, captured and murdered some of its members, one of whom was the Prince von Thurn-und-Taxis, a scion of one of Germany's oldest noble and banking families.[39] This gives a measure of the powerful influences at work with the Thule Society, which because of the donations of such wealthy patrons, had been able to purchase a nearly defunct newspaper called the *Völkischer Beobachter* (The People's

---

[37] Picknett, Prince, and Prior, op. cit., p. 32.

[38] Ibid., p. 33.

[39] For those tracing such things, the Thurn-und-Taxis family gained their wealth via special postage and taxation charters from the Holy Roman Emperors. The Italian branch of the family is named "della Torro i Tasso."

Observer), which became the official organ for the Thule Society and then subsequently for the Nazi party.[40]

As we noted previously, the Thule Society struck back forcefully via its own *Kampfbund* and in connection with the *Freikorps von Epp*, and recovered its documents. But the tensions and street battles between the radical left and right continued, to the extent that conservative elements in Bavaria,[41] fed up with the growing slide of the Reich government to the left, attempted to seize power in Bavaria via Gustav Ritter von Kahr, who was made a councilor of Bavaria, given dictatorial powers, and who began to court elements of the German army and Bavarian state police. The goal was to break Bavaria out of the German Reich and restore its complete independence as a sovereign nation, the status it had prior to the proclamation of the German Empire in 1871.[42]

*It was because of this threatened **break** with the German Reich that Hitler, Hess, and the Nazi leadership acted,* for they were not trying to seize power in Bavaria to *break* with "Greater Germany," but rather the contrary, they were trying to *prevent* that break. As Picknett, Prince, and Prior aptly put it, "(Hitler) could not let Bavaria leave the German union, for this would effectively put his plans for a Greater Germany into reverse. He had to act before it was too late."[43]

Here an interesting pattern emerges, a pattern of the delicate dance of power between Hitler, Hess—who would become Hitler's

---

[40] Nicholas Goodrick-Clarke, *The Occult Roots of Nazism*, pp. 148f. notes that one of the major contributors to the purchase of the newspaper was Georg Feder, the economist and theorist of "debt free money" for the Nazi Party. During the period of hyper-inflation, what kept the Thule Society and Nazi party running were infusions of stable cash in the form of foreign donations in US dollars and Swiss francs.

[41] To understand the full measure of the political crisis in Germany at that time, it's worth mentioning that Lenin himself sent representatives and "experts" in revolutionary tactics to Bavaria to assist and secure the revolution there. See Martin Allen, *The Hitler/Hess Deception: British Intelligence's Best-Kept Secret of the Second World War* (London: Harper Collins Publishers, 2003), pp. 4, 8

[42] Picknett, Prince, and Prior, op. cit., p. 50. Picknett, Prince, and Prior understand the mechanics and politics behind the Beer Hall Putsch better than most historians and certainly better than the popular view that the Nazis, in the Putsch, were attempting to make Bavaria independent. Accordingly their presentation will be followed closely here.

[43] Ibid.

"Deputy Führer" within the Nazi Party itself after the seizure of power—and Göring, who would become Hitler's designated successor in offices of *state* itself. While Göring was at that time the head of the *Sturmabteilung*, the notorious SA "Brownshirts," and therefore the boss in charge of any "wet works" that needed to be performed during the attempted counter-coup, it was *Hess* to whom Hitler entrusted secret orders to round up the ministers of the Bavarian state itself,[44] which Hess was successful in doing. Indeed, this is not often reported in accounts of the Beer Hall Putsch, but it is nonetheless true. As the coup collapsed, Hitler was captured and put on trial for treason (while von Kahr, of course, was not). Göring fled to Sweden, and Hess fled to Austria where he was to remain for five months, until, upon learning of Hitler's shockingly light sentence, he returned to Munich, stood trial, and was sentenced to prison.

d. Landsberg Prison: Hitler, Hess and **Mein Kampf**

Hitler and Hess both served their time in the same prison, Landsberg prison, and were given adjoining cells which in turn shared a cell that was converted into a comfortable, almost salon-like work area. It was here that their strong personal relationship was forged, and it was here that Hess and Hitler were regularly visited by General Karl Haushofer. It was Landsberg that, in Picknett's, Prince's and Prior's apt words, "redefined" Hess's role:

> ...establishing him as Hitler's confidant, muse, and mentor. There was no question of his being Hitler's lackey. If anything, at least at this time, the reverse was true. Far from being kept in the dark about Hitler's plans, Hess himself shaped many of them. The two men were their own charmed inner circle, from which the likes of Hermann Göring were excluded. A visitor to Landsberg commented on Hess's manifestly growing influence over Hitler and their deepening friendship: "Hitler enjoyed repeating his friend's slogans. (It is interesting that they were *Hess's* slogans, not his own.) It was obvious to everyone that a very close relationship exited between the two of them. For the first time I

---

[44] Picknett, Prince, and Prior, op. cit., p. 52.

heard them use *du*." Hitler had taken to calling his friend by the affectionate diminutive "Rudi" or "Hesserl."[45]

Landsberg was thus a pivotal turning point in the Hess-Hitler relationship.

One myth that grew during the Landsberg period and that was sustained both by Hitler, by Hess, and by party propaganda itself ever afterward, was that Hitler had dictated his "magnum opus," the infamous and infamously turgid *Mein Kampf* to Hess, who obediently typed the first manuscript as Hitler expostulated on his ideas.

But the reality is the exact opposite, particularly in those few lucid passages in the work, which were not the ravings of Hitler the thwarted artist, but of Hess, the multi-lingual university student of Haushofer, himself a regular visitor to the two frustrated putschists. For starters, Hitler's original title for the work was *Four and a Half Years of Struggle against lies, Stupidity, and Cowardice*, which hardly rolls very easily off the tongue. It was Hess who "insisted he change it to *Mein Kampf (My Struggle)*, which at least had the virtue of brevity."[46]

But there's more, for one of the earliest English language translators of *Mein Kampf*, James Murphy, had actually worked in Berlin for one of the many bureaucracies controlled by Hess prior to the war. Murphy left no doubt of who had ghost-written much of the more "conceptual" parts of Hitler's manifesto:

> Those chapters of *Mein Kampf* which deal with the propaganda and organization of the Nazi movement owe their inspiration to Rudolf Hess and most of the actual composition was done by him. He was also responsible for the chapters dealing with *Lebensraum* and the function of the British Empire in the history of the world.

---

[45] Picknett, Prince, and Prior, op. cit., p. 53. In the German, there are two words for addressing someone else as "you," "Sie" the formal usage, equivalent to our English pronoun "you," and "du," equivalent to our now-archaic pronoun of familiar or intimate address, "thou." While the niceties of courtesy and etiquette are no longer as attached to these usages as they used to be, prior to the war they were still very present in German culture, and the intimate and familiar address "du" also connoted equality.

[46] Ibid. p. 54.

His younger brother Alfred, often assured me of this. For a time we used to see each other almost daily in Berlin.[47]

After the war at Nuremberg, when inquiries were made on precisely this point of the relationship between Hess and Hitler, and who was actually the inspiration of certain passages of the book, General Haushofer stated that it was actually Hess, not Hitler, who had dictated some passages of the work.[48]

Hess, standing on left and leaning down, his wife Ilse seated on the left and holding Wolf Hess, and Adolf Hitler, seated on the right, at the Hess's.

Like Hitler, Hess was released from Landsberg after having served only a few months of his sentence, and from this point until the Nazi assumption of power, it is a testimony of the closeness of Karl Haushofer, Rudolf Hess, and Adolf Hitler that when Hess

---

[47] James Murphy, *Who Sent Rudolf Hess?* (London: Hutchinson, 1941), p. 9, cited in Picknett, Prince, and Prior, op. cit., p. 54.

[48] Picknett, Prince, and Prior, Op. cit., p. 54. This should be contrasted to Wolf Hess, who believed that Hitler was the primary contributor, and that his father's role was primarily as scribe and editor.

married his wife Isle Pröhl in 1927, that it was Haushofer and Hitler who served as his groomsmen, and when Wolf Hess, Hess's son was born approximately a decade later, that it was again Haushofer and Hitler who stood as godfathers at his christening.

Rudolf Hess, left, Adolf Hitler and a young Wolf Hess, center, and Ilse Hess, right.

D. The **Stellvertreter:** Hess's Power within the Nazi Regime
1. The Nuremberg Indictment and Hess's Power

It is difficult to give an exhaustive accounting of the actual power that Hess held in the Nazi state prior to his flight to Great Britain in May, 1941 even by enumerating the many bureaus, agencies, intelligence services, and liaison connections between them all, that he controlled. Not only this, but as Party chief, he literally had control over most bureaucratic appointments in the Nazi state. But Hess also knew the ways of the symbols of power, and knew them well. It was he, in fact, who began the "Führer cult" within Nazism, for prior to the Putsch and their incarceration in Landsberg, Hitler had simply been "Herr Hitler." After this period, however, and due to Hess's constant manipulations of language, Hitler became *der Führer*, and of course, all the Thule Society symbolism became the protocols of the party, from endless *Sieg Heils* to the swastika.[49] During the final campaign to woo the German industrialists and bankers to financially support the Nazi cause in the final political campaign of 1932, it was also Hess, in conjunction with Hjalmar Schacht, who had helped put the "sophisticated face" to Nazism.[50]

However, one gets a measure of the vast power that Hess possessed by reading the Nuremberg Tribunal indictment against him:

> The defendant Hess between 1921 and 1941 was a member of the Nazi Party, Deputy to the Führer, Reich Minister without Portfolio, member of the Reichstag, member of the Council of Ministers for the Defence of the Reich, member of the Secret Cabinet Council, Successor designate to the Führer after the defendant Göring, a General in the SS and a General in the SA.[51]

The term *Stellvertreter*, which is often translated as "Deputy" of the Führer, is actually a stronger term than can be rendered into English, and Hess's relationship to Hitler and Göring has been the source of some confusion because of this, since many view Göring's being designated as Hitler's successor as head of state and government (Führer) as a demotion of Hess in the pecking order of the Nazi hierarchy. The term, however, in its etymology, suggests something far more powerful: a place-holder or personal emissary. Perhaps the best analogy would be to an apostolic nuncio, an ambassador simultaneously not only of the papal *office*, but also of *the person holding it*, a kind of "plenipotentiary" or, if one wants to be "Ottoman" about it, a "Grand Vizier."

Thus it is important to remember that Hess as *Stellvertreter*, was literally "place taker" or personal representative for Hitler in

---

[49] Picknett, Prince, and Prior, op. cit., p. 68.

[50] Ibid.

[51] International Military Tribunal, vol. 1, p. 31, cited in Picknett, Prince, and Prior, op. cit., p. 11.

the Party hierarchy. This made him the de facto head of the operational day-to-day management of the Party, of its various intelligence agencies, and bureaucratic appointments. Hess, like Stalin earlier in the Soviet Union, was in a position equivalent to "General Secretary of the Communist Party," and while the position of *Stellvertreter* did not continue after his infamous flight to Britain, in effect, the *power* of that position did, when Bormann took over from his former boss the control of all party functions as Party *Reichsleiter*.

Because of this powerful position, Hess's signature thus appears on German legal documents, including actual legislation itself, during this period, signing on behalf of the party as a kind of witness to, and for, Hitler. This fact, as Picknett, Prince, and Prior point out, was at the core of the Nuremberg Tribunal's prosecution's case against Hess, for during its presentations, "the emphasis remorselessly lay not only on Hess's culpability, but on his power within the Third Reich up to 1941. The prosecution spent a great deal of time and effort establishing the extent of his responsibility and the fact that *nothing could happen in Germany without his knowledge and approval.*"[52] The reason for this? Quite simply, because in the Nazi state, nothing could, nor should happen without the Party's knowledge and approval, which Hess, as Hitler's personal "place holder" or Deputy, provided. This will become quite the crucial point in part two of this book.

Indeed, prior to 1941 and Hess's flight to Britain, one could wonder just to what extent Hess, with his party bureaucracy— which, let it be noted, included *his* secretary, Martin Bormann— was really the "brains" of the operation. Picknett, Prince, and Prior point out that even the American journal *Foreign Affairs*, mouthpiece of the American "deep state" apparatus, The Council on Foreign Relations, wondered at that time if Hess was not the ultimate "intellectual creator of Adolf Hitler to the extent that a piano creates music."[53]

---

[52] Picknett, Prince, and Prior, op. cit., p. 13, emphasis added.
[53] Konrad Heiden, "Hitler's Better Half," *Foreign Affairs*, 1951, p. 73.

2. The Moral Ambiguity of Hess, and the Hess-Bormann Relationship

As noted above, there was no regulation or law enacted in Nazi Germany without Adolf Hitler's, and Rudolf Hess's, signatures; virtually nothing happened without Hess's knowledge and quiet involvement. This means, of course, that Hess's signature was on the infamous Nuremberg Race Laws. Yet, Hess acted as, and was viewed by many as, the conscience of the Party, objecting to some of the harsh measures meted out during the *Reichkristalnacht* violence against Jews. Additionally, Hess protected General Haushofer's "half Jewish" wife throughout his tenure as *Stellvertreter*, and this seems to have been somehow continued after his departure to Britain.

However, it also means that Hess is at the epicenter of several threads of covert activity, both diplomatic, and in terms of secret research, including, as we shall discover, the German a-bomb, and Hitler's plans for settling the "Jewish question," and, as we shall argue in part two, Göring's 1938-1939 Antarctic expedition. Here, as we shall discover, other researchers have uncovered something truly astonishing, but have not properly understood (or perhaps, as is more likely, not been willing to state) its true significance.

We have also seen that in Haushofer's thinking, and therefore in Hess's and Hitler's, the British Empire was not viewed as the natural enemy of Germany. Yet, while Hess shared this view to such an extent that he flew to Great Britain on an ostensible peace mission, it was also Hess who opposed Hitler's *Haltbefehl*, the "halt order" issued to the Wehrmacht at Dunkirk, which permitted the British Army to escape almost certain annihilation. It was Hess who, on the contrary, urged Hitler to finish off the British Army.

Similarly, it was Hess and his secretary, Martin Bormann, who urged the action in the "Night of the Long Knives" in taking out the leadership of the SA, the Brownshirts; it was Hess who spotted Bormann's talent, and made him his own right hand man within the party machinery, particularly of the party's own intelligence services, and the liaison office between the party and the Reich's intelligence and security services, the so-called Hessamt or "Hess

Bureau."[54] It was Hess who cynically placed Bormann as his eyes and ears within Hitler's inner circle itself.

We are now in a position to evaluate the central core of the Hess Mess, his flight itself, his motivations for undertaking it, his subsequent imprisonment in Great Britain, and the many details other researchers have uncovered, and the scenarios and hypotheses they have advanced to explain all of it. To do this will require probably the longest single chapter I have ever written, for each facet must be examined again and again from several points of view, and each hypothesis evaluated. Before we take that plunge, it should be recalled that Spandau Hess, Prisoner Number Seven, confided a document to his Tunisian nurse, Abdallah Melaouhi, that at one point in his imprisonment in England, he was not permitted to smoke, when pre-flight Hess in Germany did *not* smoke at all. We should also recall (1) Hess's commitment to the Thule Society and its doctrines, (2) his fascination with "occult" matters, and (3) the implication of Joscelyn Godwin's remarks that perhaps Hess's continued imprisonment might be somehow related to those occult, and occulted, concerns. As we shall discover, there *is* evidence that Hess's mission was about far more than just a simple "peace plan," or rather, that he brought a *comprehensive plan for Britain's consideration, one touching on all these subjects, from atomic bombs to the "Jewish question," from European peace and order, to Antarctica, for consideration.*

Buckle in, because this will be a long, and bumpy, flight.

---

[54] Jochen von Lang, *The Secretary: Martin Bormann, the Man Who Manipulated Hitler*, pp. 66-67, 77-80. The Hessamt functioned as Hess's personal vetting agency within both the party machinery and the Reich bureaucracy, thus becoming a kind of parallel bureaucracy to all the functions of the state, in a manner quite similar to the party machinery of Communism in the Stalinist Soviet Union. See pp. 89, 128.

4

FLIGHT OF FANCY, PEACE PROPOSALS, DOUBLES DILEMMAS, DIFFICULTIES WITH DUKES, AND NONSENSE AT NUREMBERG

"It is perhaps because of the many aspects of the affair that sensible academics have chosen to leave it well alone. It is far from a simple story."
John Harris and Richard Wilbourn[1]

VIRTUALLY EVERYTHING IN THE HESS MESS has a double aspect, if not a triple or even quadruple one, admitting of a multitude of interpretations, depending on how one interprets each detail of the case, and which hypotheses one adopts to explain them.

Before the end of this chapter, we will have bumped into the Cambridge Five, the notorious Soviet spy ring that included Philby, Burgess, and Blunt; the brother of Ian Fleming of James Bond fame, Peter Fleming, the British Royal Family and the Dukes of Hamilton, Windsor (the abdicated King Edward VIII), and Kent, younger brother of King George VI, and the Duke of Bucceleuch; the notorious SS general Reinhard Heydrich and a few Luftwaffe generals (Udet and Galland), and a British doctor who caused a firestorm of controversy when he published a book maintaining that Spandau Hess was not Hess at all. In other words, Hess may have ceased being Hess altogether and may have been replaced at some point, either by an actual physical double, or, at the other end of the spectrum, a mental one, an "alternative personality" brought about either by increasing mental deterioration, or caused by more malicious means, or (after all, this is the Hess Mess), both. And for those favoring the *Doppelgänger* hypothesis, there is every possibility that the double—if there was one—might *himself* have undergone mental deterioration via natural or deliberate causes, and in turn, had to have his "Hess personality" reinforced from time to time by "artificial means." All of this only serves to emphasize,

---

[1] John Harris and Richard Wilbourn, *Rudolf Hess: A New Technical Analysis of the Hess Flight, May 1941* (Stroud, Glocestershire: The History Press, 2014), p. 11.

once again, the importance of the One Question: why all the decades-long fuss?

If this sounds like mind control, that's because it is, but if this sounds too impossible to be even *remotely* connected to the Hess Mess, then brace yourself, for there is no other way to approach this first of a long list of "problems" in the Hess Mess other than to plunge into the deep end.

A. Nonsense at Nuremberg, and Difficulties of Doubles
1. Foretastes of MK-Ultra: Allen Dulles and Hess at Nuremberg

In 1979, British physician W. Hugh Thomas published a book that, in retrospect, has to be considered to be at the very heart of the Hess Mess. That book was *The Murder of Rudolf Hess*, and in it, Thomas argued that the prisoner in Spandau Prison was not Rudolf Hess at all, but a double, and from this context, Thomas spent much of his book trying to fathom what the whole Hess Mess was really all about. That book touched off a storm of controversy continuing to this day. Thomas argued his case because, on one brief occasion, while serving in the British military in Berlin, he had the opportunity briefly to see the infamous prisoner without his shirt on, during a routine medical examination at the British Military Hospital.

Hess, he maintained, showed no scars of the war wounds he had suffered in World War One. In fact, we have already seen hints that Spandau Hess may have been a double, for recall his complaining to his nurse, Abdallah Melaeouhi, that during a certain period of his confinement in England, he was not allowed to smoke, and the real Hess, like his beloved Führer Adolf Hitler, did not smoke. Such behavior anomalies were a major focus of Thomas' book, and have become a major focus for anyone investigating the Hess Mess.

But Thomas was not the first.

Far from it. The first people to observe that something was "off" about Hess were those who encountered him at Nuremberg, where his behavior was nothing less than a performance, and a nonsensical one at that. His former colleagues, especially *Reichmarschall* Göring, clearly indicated they thought something was "wrong," and, for that matter, so did Hess's Allied captors, and particularly, the Americans.

One of those Americans who had his suspicions about Hess was none other than Allen Dulles, OSS station chief in Zurich during the war, former advisor (with his brother, John Foster) to President Wilson at Versailles, a partner of the prestigious Wall Street law firm of Sullivan and Cromwell, and, of course, future director of the CIA, and future member of the Warren Commission. Dulles, in what Picknett, Prince, and Prior quite aptly qualify as "the most telling episode at Nuremberg,"[2] called upon his friend, psychiatrist Dr. Donald Ewen Cameron, to examine Hess.

This one fact should make anyone's "suspicion meter" shoot into the red zone, for Dr. Ewen Cameron is notorious for his role in the CIA's "mind control" program, MK-Ultra, having developed the technique, alluded to earlier, of "psychic driving," whereby he hoped to erase one personality from an individual, and substitute another. Cameron, in short, was one of the "pioneers" working in the field of mind control

At this juncture, matters become even *more* complicated:

In the words of Gordon Thomas, in his study of the military and intelligence uses of psychiatry and psychology, *Journey into Madness* (1993):

"Dulles first swore Dr Cameron to Secrecy, and then told him an astounding story. He had reason to believe that the man Dr. Cameron was to examine was not Rudolf Hess but an impostor; that the real Deputy Führer had been secretly executed on Churchill's orders. Dulles had explained that Dr Cameron could prove the point by a simple physical examination of the man's torso. If he was the genuine Hess, there should be scar tissue over his left lung, a legacy from the day the young Hess had been wounded in the First World War. Dr Cameron had agreed to try to examine the prisoner."

He was never to make that examination. The next day, when Hess was brought to him, he was handcuffed to a British Military Police sergeant, who refused point blank to remove the handcuffs so that

---

[2] Picknett, Prince, and Prior, *Double Standards: the Rudolf Hess Cover-up*, p. 9.

89

Cameron could take the prisoner's shirt off—or even unbutton it—
to look at his chest.[3]

Why would Allen Dulles have chosen Dr. Cameron for such a task,
much less have confided in him his suspicions that (1) "Nuremberg
Hess" was a double, and (2) the real one had been executed on
orders from Churchill?

Picknett, Prince, and Prior note that there is a conceptual link
between Cameron's later techniques of "psychic driving" during his
MK-Ultra research for the CIA, and the work of British psychiatrists
L.G.M. Page and R.J. Russell, who first published a paper about
similar techniques in 1948, a paper summarizing "many years of
intensive experimentation."[4] In other words, Dulles needed
someone he knew to be familiar with the British work, and its
possible use on "Nuremberg Hess." In Cameron's hands, the
techniques pioneered by the British psychiatrists would be taken to
new levels, one implication of which was that an amnesiac, quasi-
sonambulistic state could be induced by cocktails of drugs, and
prolonged sleep, during which patients—or rather, victims—were
highly susceptible to suggestion, including the inducement of false
memories.[5]

These considerations raise yet a further possibility: was
"Hess"—either his double or the real individual—possibly used as a
"mind control" experiment subject for the express purpose of
sending a Manchurian candidate *back* to Nazi Germany, to
assassinate top Nazi leaders? In fact, Picknett, Prince, and Prior,
note that a meeting occurred in Great Britain in 1944 where this
possibility was proposed.[6] The implications of this meeting are
profound, for it suggests (1) that "Hess"[7] was already the deliberate

---

[3] Picknett, Prince, and Prior, op. cit. p. 9, citing Gordon Thomas, *Journey into
Madness: Medical Torture and the Mind Controllers* (London: Bantam Press, 1988),
pp. 167-168.

[4] Picknett, Prince, and Prior, op. cit., p. 444.

[5] Ibid., p. 445.

[6] Ibid., p. 446.

[7] "Hess": we will now, from time to time, have to refer to this individual as
"Hess," in quotation marks, to denote the uncertainty of whether or not we are
dealing with the real Hess, or a double, in order to emphasize the nature of the
hall of mirrors we are now entering.

subject of such mind-control techniques, and (2) that those techniques were being used to create the "Manchurian Candidate," the perfect, mind-controlled assassin and spy.

At this juncture we must pause for yet another reason, and consider the strange orthography of referring to him as "Hess." From time to time, we shall now have cause to refer to this individual as "Hess," in quotation marks, to denote the uncertainty of whether or not we are dealing with the real Hess or a double, in order to emphasize the nature of the hall of mirrors we are now entering. Picknett, Prince, and Prior are quite alive to this problem in a way that most Hess researchers are not, for the double problem compounds the difficulties at almost every step of analysis. For example, they point out that

> If it was the real Hess, then the doctors had tampered with his memory in order to eradicate what would otherwise prove to be— at least to the Churchill legend and the Establishment—the aspects with the most potential to embarrass and undermine. They would have attempted to erase from his mind issues connected with the Duke of Hamilton, the Royal Family and anything else that might have seriously rocked their boat.
>
> If it was a double at Maindiff Court, the intention would have been more ambitious. But could they actually make the double believe he was really Rudolf Hess? Perhaps. But the human mind is far too complex and tricky for that to be a safe and reliable option, and there could have been no guarantee that any apparent success would be lasting. It is, however, possible though the use of drugs and hypnosis to reinforce suggestions that bypass the brain's critical faculties.[8]

The need for constant "reinforcement" of these induced memories and patterns of behavior might explain why the British government constructed an entire "Hess suite" in its military hospital in Berlin. Indeed, Picknett, Prince and Prior suggest this possibility earlier in their ground-breaking work, when they ask how long, and why, a double would keep up a pretense for so long.[9]

---

[8] Picknett, Prince, and Prior, op. cit., p. 447.
[9] Ibid., p. xxviii-xix.

But we are getting ahead of ourselves, and hence it is necessary to return to the Allen Dulles-Ewen Cameron element of the Hess Mess to observe another highly important question that Picknett, Prince, and Prior raise, but do not attempt to answer. "How did Dulles," they ask "arrive at the notion that the Hess in Nuremberg was a double, and that the real Hess had been killed on Churchill's orders?"[10] How, indeed, did Dulles know?

There are, I suspect, two possible routes for this knowledge, and neither are mutually exclusive. One route would be via the financial and intelligence contacts through his law firm, Sullivan and Cromwell, and its deep ties to the American and British financial elites. These contacts would certainly have extended to his acquaintance, William McKittrick, American president of the Bank of International Settlements in Basel, Switzerland, during the war, where both men were posted. The BIS, even alone and apart from any contacts Dulles would have through Sullivan and Cromwell, would have been a possible conduit for such information, since it maintained close business ties between the Allied Powers and Nazi Germany throughout the war, even enabling business transactions between corporate and financial interests whose nations were at war.

This raises the other pipeline of possibility, for Dulles also had cultivated many contacts with high-ranking Nazis toward the end of the war, including a number of contacts in the SS, such as through SS General Wolff. Dulles could even count Walter Schellenberg, head of the *Sicherheitdienst*, or SD, as a distant acquaintance through his network of contacts in the Third Reich. They could also have informed him of their suspicions vis-à-vis "Hess," for as we shall discover, the Hess Mess engulfs many high ranking Nazis, even casting its shadow over the notorious Reinhard Heydrich, of the RSHA (*Reichsicherheithauptamt*, or "National Security Agency").

There is, of course, a final possibility, and one which no one to my knowledge has researched or mentioned. It has *no* evidence in support of it that I have been able to unearth, but on the other hand, it is suggested by a string of very odd synchronicities and the balance of probabilities implied by them. That fact is simply that no

---

[10] Picknett, Prince, and Prior, op. cit., p. 9.

one, to my knowledge, has ever inquired whether or not Dr. Donald Ewen Cameron, Dulles' confidant at Nuremberg in the Hess Mess, and later a leading scientist involved in the CIA's MK-Ultra Mind Control programs when Dulles was CIA Director, was related to Dr. James Malcolm Cameron, the British forensic pathologist who conducted the "Hess" autopsy (and, as we saw previously, a possible secret autopsy). Both men, after all, have the same last name, and more importantly, both men were associated with Scotland, Ewen Cameron being born there in the small town of Bridge of Allan, *and James Malcolm Cameron attending the University of Glasgow for his medical studies, where Ewen Cameron also received degrees in "psychological medicine." The fact that both men are associated with the University of Glasgow, and that both of them studied medicine there, and have the same clan surname, is enough to suggest that Allen Dulles' pipeline into the Hess Mess might have been directly from the family of British pathologist who would ultimately perform the official autopsy.* In this respect it should be noted that James Cameron was born in 1930, and died in 2003, making him 11 years old when Hess parachuted into Britain, so the speculation must remain speculation, of a very high order at that.

2. "Hess's" Strange, Buffoonish Behavior at Nuremberg: "Brain Poison" and "Hess's" Jewish-Bolshevik Mind Control Conspiracy

Whatever Allen Dulles' pipeline of information about the Hess Mess might have been, there were *other* important indicators that "Hess" himself was a mess, not the least of which was the strange behavior he exhibited, and the strange statements he made, at Nuremberg. As will be seen, a pattern of statements and behavior emerges in Nuremberg that was presaged by behavior and statements he made after his capture by the British, and which was continued—off and on—during his years as Prisoner Number Seven at Spandau. This pattern consisted of strange remarks made in passing, without thought or further comment, calling into question "Hess's" identity, along with much more deliberate statements by "Hess" asserting memory loss and memory *"reacquisition."* We have seen already one such statement that Hess made "in passing," in the letter he entrusted to his nurse, Melaouhi, complaining of not being able to smoke during his confinement at Maindiff, in England.

This is not the only such statement.

Lieutenant Colonel Eugene K. Bird was the American commandant of Spandau prison until he was dismissed from that command in 1972 for having consulted with "Hess" about his memoirs. In his book, *Prisoner #7: Rudolf Hess: The Thirty Years in Jail of Hitler's Deputy Führer*, Bird reproduces several entries from Hess's "Nuremberg diary." One of these entries for October 13th, 1945, reads "Goering tried for an hour to refresh my memory—in vain. He told me that when I flew to England I should have left a letter behind for the Führer." While this comment is ambivalent and capable of more than one interpretation—was "Hess" dissembling to Göring and only *pretending* he did not remember that in fact he *had* left a letter for Hitler prior to his flight, or did "Hess" really *not* remember the letter?—it highlights once again the problem: is "Nuremberg Hess" the real Hess or not? If the real Hess, was his memory lapse genuine, or only faked, as he himself would later claim in his now well-known and infamous statement to the Tribunal? Or was it a "double" who simply had not been adequately "programed" to remember all details? (And if the latter, why even risk it?)

That speech to the Nuremberg Tribunal Hess was never able to deliver *in toto*, but he did make copious notes for it, which Col. Bird reproduces in his book. In that speech, Hess intended, at least in part, to recount his recollection and version of his confinement in Britain. Before introducing the comments themselves, Bird writes this:

> His terms had been rebuffed, even laughed at. Hess, at this time, became convinced there was only one possible answer to this "craziness" on the part of others: they were all either hypnotized or secretly drugged by some evil power. The evil power was, in his mind, the dread coalition of Jews and Bolsheviks.[11]

He then introduces "Hess's" prepared remarks:

---

[11] Ibid., p. 23.

"I had the impression," Hess remembers, "that most of the people who came to me for the first time had first been detained with tea or a meal before they were brought to me. This was also the case with Lord Simon when he visited me for a long conference on the orders of the British Government. He had the typical glassy and dream-like eyes.

"From my observations it can be gathered that people who are in this abnormal state of mind can be forced to put others in the same state. Field-Marshal Milch has said that he had the impression the Führer was not normal in the last years. I would say that the expression of the Führer's face and his eyes *had* changed in the last years; there was an expression of cruelty in it, if not of insanity.

"I am aware that what I have to say about what happened to me in my imprisonment in England will at first sound unbelievable."[12]

After writing more about a period of painful constipation which he believed to have been brought about by the British secretly drugging him, "Hess" goes on to make even more sensational claims:

The suffering was indescribable. If they had shot me or killed me with gas or even let me starve, it would have been humane in comparison. They began to add acids to the food as well. I found out by leaving a fork in the food; within a few hours the fork was covered with verdigris. The doctor was very embarrassed by this experiment. After meals I could often only sit, or walk bent with pain. In my desperation I scratched chalk off the walls, hoping this would have a neutralizing effect. But it was in vain.[13]

With "Hess" being such a mess, one must always be cautious in weighing his allegations and interpreting them, except, on this point, "Hess" was always consistent: he believed the British were secretly drugging him.

---

[12] Lt. Col. Eugene K. Bird, op. cit., p. 23. Bird notes that "Hess" had written this "in his 'closing statement' he prepared for delivery at the Nuremberg Trial. But he was cut short by the Court and only some of it was delivered."(p. 23, n.)

[13] Ibid., p. 24.

In this case, the comment about "acid" is illuminating in the light of other claims by "Hess" that he was suffering amnesia and that he was being given "brain poison," for "acid" in this case might be a careful reference to LSD, a drug which was later to play a role in the CIA's mind control experiments. While LSD was still a very "new" drug in "Hess's" time, and thus it is questionable whether he would have been familiar with it or its effects, it is intriguing to note that regular LSD use *has* been associated with constipation.

The "acid-and-constipation" allegations, however, were not the end of "Hess's" mind control fantasias. Indeed, they may not have been fantasias at all, but may have contained some element of truth. This is certainly implied by Dulles' remarks to Dr. Ewen Cameron, but it is also implied by some of "Hess's" other remarks. In November 1941, after his capture by the British, "Hess" was at dinner with his doctors. This event, we shall consider again, but from a very different context. We introduce it here to highlight the strangeness of "Hess's" remarks and behavior at Nuremberg. It was at this dinner that he first alluded to looming amnesia; he was, he said, having difficulty remembering things, even things that had happened only a short time previously. Two weeks later, he informed his British doctors his memory had failed completely, and he was to remain in this state "for almost two years. The doctors had little doubt that it was real."[14]

But in his "Last Word" statement for the Military Tribunal in Nuremberg, Hess expanded, and in the expansion, one finds the subject of mind control being suggested once again:

"My memory failed quite a lot.... At the same time, I was constantly asked strange questions about my past. *If I answered them correctly, they were disappointed. If I was not able to answer them, they were obviously pleased. So I proceeded to increasingly feign a lack of memory. They explained that they could bring back the memory with an injection.* Since I had to remain constant in my "loss of memory," I could show no mistrust, and agreed. I had been told that the injection would be followed by a narcosis in which questions would be asked me that were supposed to con-nect the conscious with the sub-conscious. It was clear to me that they wanted to test in this way if the loss of memory was real."[15]

---

[14] Lt. Col. Eugene K. Bird., op. cit., p. 24.
[15] Ibid., pp. 24-25.

"Hess" finally agreed to this procedure on May 7, 1944, and was injected with the drug Evipan.

What followed next was sheer theater, or was it? The transcript of the session, which Col. Bird reproduces in his book, reads like someone unable to remember his identity (perhaps, of course, because "Hess" wasn't Hess):

2210 hrs Dr. Dicks (psychiatrist) enters and stands by Hess's bed.

2110 hrs Dr Dicks tells Hess: "You will now be able to recall all the names and faces of your dear ones. Your memory will return. We are all here to help you..."

2112 hrs Groans.

Dr Dicks: What's the matter?

Hess: Pains! In my belly! Oh if only I were well. Bellyache. Water! Water! Thirst!

D: Remember your little son's name?

H: I don't know.

D: Do you remember your good friend, Haushofer...

H: No.

D: Willi Messerschmitt?

H: No (groans). Bellyache! Oh God!

D: ... And all the stirring times with Adolf Hitler in Munich.

H: No.

D: You were with him in the fortress at Landsberg.

H: No.

D: You will recall all the other parts of your past.

H: Recall all the other parts.

D: Recall all the great events of your life.

H: All the great events...

The session ended at 2215 hrs and the doctors noted afterwards: "At no point did the patient make a spontaneous remark: the sole unprovoked utterances were groans. This was followed by repeated exhortations that here were all his old doctors eager to help him, but he sat up and said: "Water please, and some food."[16]

But "Hess" later claimed, in a letter written to his mother from Nuremberg on July 5, 1947, that he knew the whole time what had been going on, and in a letter to his wife Ilse from Nuremberg, he

---

[16] Lt. Col. Eugene K. Bird, op. cit., pp. 25-26.

stated it was all "a great piece of play-acting," and that he had been feigning his insanity because he was hoping to be sent home.[17] This was not an irrational hope, as it turns out, for under the terms of then-existing international law, insane people we not to be held prisoner, but returned to their countries.

Later, at Nuremberg, the insanity-feigning was to serve a different purpose. By February 1945, as the war in Europe was coming to its inevitable conclusion, "Hess's" memory had fully returned, when "Hess" confessed to his British captors and physicians that his memory losses and amnesia had all been faked on his part, a conclusion that Dr Dicks dissented from. Acknowledging "Hess's" full memory recovery, Dicks wrote "I cannot accept his own statement that the memory loss never existed. There was at that time a true partial dissociation of the personality, which permitted the patient to 'take in' what was going on around him but caused difficulty of recall. It is a case of preferring to have duped us to having shown temporary weakness."[18]

But at Nuremberg, "Hess" had a very *different* version of what had happened to him; writing in his "Last Statement," he stated:

> Slowly my memory returned fully, *even though the brain poison was given to me for at least two years.* The latter was the reason that I continued to pretend to have a loss of memory. I kept this up until after the beginning of the proceedings,[19] since I suspected that otherwise I would never be admitted to the proceedings and would never have the chance to make by exposure to the public. Only after the danger appeared that *I was not in a state to take part in the proceedings and would have to be excluded, did I admit my manoeuvre. But since I was given a brain poison on each possible occasion in Nuremberg I again took to "feigning a lack of memory" in an increasing manner.* Only at the moment I began to make my closing statement did I let my memory "return."[20]

So, was "Hess" able to fool his British doctors in spite of being drugged (as he alleged), and as at least on one occasion he actually

---

[17] Ibid., p. 26.
[18] Lt. Col. Eugene K. Bird, op. cit., p. 27.
[19] "Proceedings," i.e., the Nuremberg Tribunals.
[20] Ibid., p. 27, emphasis added.

was, and possible on other occasions, as his complaint about constipation would indicate? Or was his claim of feigning amnesia *itself* a part of the programming of which he was complaining?

Before we consider "Hess's" infamous speech at Nuremberg claiming he was feigning his memory loss, not only in Britain, but in Nuremberg itself when he was confronted, face to face, with General Haushofer and Hermann Göring himself, and claimed he could remember neither man, we need to take note of some other strange occurrences at Nuremberg involving "Hess." Picknett, Prince, and Prior state that Airey Neave, the process-server on the Nuremberg defendants, recounts that "Hess" once responded to "an officer who called his name: 'There is no Rudolf Hess here. But if you are looking for Convict Number 125, then I'm your man!'"[21]

A Rogue's Gallery at Nuremberg: on the front left, Hermann Göring uses papers to cover his mouth while he is laughing at "Hess," in the front center. On the front right, former Foreign Minister Joachim von Ribbentrop appears to be staring in disbelief at "Hess." In the back row, former Grand Admiral Dönitz, in sunglasses, is glaring at "Hess." As will be seen later, this picture and the odd "seating" arrangement, may have some synchronous symbolic significance, since all four men are implicated in the Nazi Antarctic Expedition. In any case, it is not known at what point in the proceedings this picture was taken, but it may very possibly have been after one or the other of Hess's infamous "statements."

---

[21] Picknett, Prince, and Prior, op. cit., p. 10.

Göring clearly gave indications that he knew "something" was going on with "Hess," for at one point during a recess in the proceedings, when all the prisoners were together in a room, he alluded to a "great secret" that "Hess" should reveal. The former *Reichmarschall* again repeated this in the actual tribunal court room dock itself during a break, needling "Hess," who was seated next to him throughout the proceeding: "By the way, Hess, when are you going to let us in on your great secret? ... I make a motion Hess tell us his big secret in the recess. How about it, Hess?"[22] Picknett, Prince, and Prior imply that Göring's emphasis on "Hess's" surname might suggest that he suspected "Hess" was not Hess.[23]

Returning now to the Tribunal itself, "Hess's" lawyer, Dr. Alfred Seidl, whom we have encountered in earlier chapters, attempted to defend his client on several grounds, contesting the legality and standing of the Tribunal, the conflict of interest in having Soviet judges present on the court sitting in judgment of his client, and finally, contesting whether or not his client, "Hess," was even competent to defend himself, since he could not remember anything.[24] After all, recall that by this point, "Hess" had been interviewed by American psychiatrists, and had been confronted

---

[22] Picknett, Prince, and Prior, op. cit. p. 10, citing G.M. Gilbert, *Nuremberg Diary* (London: Eyre and Spottiswoode, 1948), p. 89.

[23] Ibid.

[24] Wolf-Rüdiger Hess, *Who Murdered My Father, Rudolf Hess?*, pp. 11–12. Dr. Seidl, who wrote the foreword to this book and who was defense counsel for "Hess" at Nuremberg, notes on p. 11, in his foreword, that as a signatory to the Molotov-Ribbentrop pact, whose secret protocols divided Poland between Germany and the Soviet Union, the Soviet Union "acted as legislator, prosecutor, and judge. In other words, it was judge in its own case. It is a general held juridical maxim that this ought not to be permissible." Dr. Seidl goes on to quote extensively from the October 5, 1946 issue of the famous British weekly magazine *The Economist*, which pointed out the same legal and moral ambiguity of the Tribunal: "Such silence, unfortunately, proves that the Nuremberg court was an independent court only within certain restrictions. In a proper criminal trial, it would be most remarkable if a judge in a proceeding against a murderer were to leave out of consideration testimony about an accomplice's part in the murder because the testimony revealed that the judge himself had been the accomplice. That no one in the Nuremberg Trial considers such a concealment to be out of the ordinary shows just how far removed we are from anything that could be called 'rule of law' in international matters."(p. 12)

face to face by both Göring and Haushofer, whom he claimed he could not remember.

However, as Dr. Seidl rose to begin the defense of his client, yet another turn in this bizarre circus unfolded. Dr. Seidl, through no fault of his own, was completely unprepared for it, nor were, for that matter, the judges of the court and the other defendants in the dock. On November 27, 1945, "Hess" wrote at length in his Nuremberg diary, what happened:

> The psychologist said to Goering that my stomach and abdominal cramps were psycho-somatic in origin. Soon afterwards Goering said to me that the cramps were "hysterical" and that this was the opinion of the German doctor as well. I replied that he would one day learn the truth. My defence counsel said at the end of today's hearing that the decision would probably be taken on Friday as to whether or not I was fit to stand trial. That the decision would presumably be that I was not. I asked him to point out that I felt myself and regarded myself to be fit to stand trial, and wished to continue to take part in the court proceedings. Counsel and Goering thereupon exchanged knowing looks.
>
> Four o'clock in the afternoon, a special session to decide the question whether I am fit to stand trial. One minute before the start, I said to my counsel that I had decided to say that my memory had returned. He turned away in some perturbation and said: "Do as you wish." Whereupon he started delivering a summing-up which lasted about an hour. He argued against my fitness to stand trial because without memory I would not be in a position to defend myself or to provide him with the necessary information to enable him to defend me. Although he was bound to add that I myself regarded myself as being fit to stand trial. He goes on endless reading out from the medical reports. I send him a message saying that the whole matter could be shortened by letting me speak. He takes no notice of this but goes on speaking for a long time. After that the prosecuting counsel talk one after the other, likewise at great length, in the course of which they suggest that I may be exaggerating my condition and alleged loss of memory. They likewise read extracts from the medical reports and quote from massive law-books. The judges also have their say and argue to and fro regarding the consequences of my loss of memory and its effect on my fitness to stand trial. One of the judges points out to the American prosecutor Jackson that I

apparently wish to be cross-examined. Jackson replies that he does not believe this wish to be genuine and presumably counts on the arguments of the defence counsel in favour of unfitness to stand trial to be stronger than my alleged wish.

After about two hours of argument, the President of the Tribunal submits that I ought perhaps to be allowed to speak.[25]

Eventually, of course, "Hess" was allowed to speak, and his remarks caused, then and now, a further interpretive problem (besides that of who was really uttering them):

Mr. President, I would like to say this: at the beginning of this afternoon's proceedings I gave my counsel a note that I am of the opinion that these proceedings could be shortened if they would allow me to speak myself. What I say is as follows:

In order to anticipate any possibility of my being declared incapable of pleading, although I am willing to take part in the rest of the proceedings with the rest of them, I would like to give the Tribunal the following declaration, although I originally intended not to make this declaration until a later point in the proceedings.

My memory is again in order. The reasons why I *simulated loss of memory were tactical.* In fact, it is only that my capacity for concentration is slightly reduced. But in consequence of that, my capacity to follow the trial, my capacity to defend myself, to put questions to witnesses or even to answer questions—these, my capacities, are not influenced by that.

I emphasize the fact that I bear the full responsibility for everything that I have done or signed as signatory or co-signatory. My attitude, in principle, is that the Tribunal is not competent—is not affected by the statement I have just made. Hitherto in conversations with my official defence counsel I have maintained loss of memory. He was, therefore, speaking in good faith when he asserted I lost my memory.[26]

The court, records "Hess" later in his diary, listened in shock, with some judges' mouths actually open in disbelief, while the Press box broke out into laughter as it ran out of the courtroom to file its reports.[27]

---

[25] Lt. Col. Eugene K. Bird, op. cit., pp. 42-43.
[26] Ibid., p. 43, emphasis added.
[27] Lt. Col. Eugene K. Bird., op. cit., pp. 43-44.

As far as his defense counsel, Dr. Seidl, and Göring and the rest of the defendants were concerned, "Hess's" speech was *proof* of his incompetence to stand trial, and indeed, it may have been a desperate ploy on his part to evade trial. The Tribunal did not share this view, however, and "Hess" as we know, stood trial and was sentenced to life in prison.

Then, after all this, the circus took its final turn, when on the day of closing statements, "Hess" made his final statement to the Tribunal, and as it would turn out, his last public statement, ever. In it, he once again alluded to the subject of "mind control," and that his, and some of the other defendants' behavior, had been externally induced:

> He talked of the "predictions" he said he had made before the start of the trial... predictions that people would make false statements on oath; that some of the defendants would act strangely. *He spoke of former political trials where the defendants actually clapped in frenzied approval when their death sentences were passed.*
>
> *It all pointed to the same evil influence: the secret force that made men act and speak "according to the orders given them."* When he had rambled on for some 20 minutes, the President of the Court interrupted to say that defendants could not be allowed to make lengthy statements at that stage in the proceedings. He hoped Hess would soon conclude.
>
> Hess did. "I was permitted to work for many years," he intoned, "under the greatest son whom my country has brought forth in its thousand-year history. Even if I could, I would not want to erase this period of time from my existence...
>
> "No matter what human beings do," said Rudolf Hess finally, "I shall some day stand before the judgement seat of the Eternal. I shall answer to Him, and I know He will judge me innocent."[28]

Those were the last, and conveniently unrepentant, words that the world ever heard from "Hess," probably the world's "most mentally examined patient."[29]

---

[28] Ibid., p. 50, emphasis added.
[29] Lt. Col. Eugene K. Bird., op. cit., p. 100.

3. Picknett's, Prince's, and Prior's Assessment of "Hess's" Nuremberg Speeches

These statements would all be perfectly dismissible if one had not already encountered the likes of Allen Dulles and Dr. Ewen Cameron lurking in the mix, not to mention Dulles' alleged words to Cameron that he suspected "Hess" was a double. Nor should one forget the actual British drugging session in 1944, trying to "recover" the lost memories of "Hess," and his strange, hypnotic "replies." Looked at a certain way, this session could easily have been not a "programming" session but rather, a *testing* session, to see if the programming "took." We have, of course, not yet proven nor even argued the case that "Nuremberg Hess" (or any *other* Hess) was a double. By referring to him as "Hess" we are, once again, leaving the question open.

But the allusion to mind control suggests that something sinister was indeed going on at Nuremberg, and "Hess" —or whoever—was trying to draw attention to it, albeit, clumsily. It is worth reviewing Picknett's, Prince's, and Prior's evaluation of "Hess's" closing Nuremberg statement. On any surface reading,

> It was a rambling monologue in which he blamed the atrocities committed by German concentration camp guards, and even Hitler's actions, on unknown mind controllers.

Before we continue with their words, stop and let this sink in for a moment: "Hess" was, in effect, saying that the entire war, and all of its atrocities, was an example of some *worldwide* "mind control phenomenon," which in his Nazi hysteria, he was blaming on Jews and Bolsheviks. But if one leaves the Jews and Bolsheviks out of it, this is, nevertheless, a breathtaking statement to make, and let it be noted, "Hess" warned the Tribunal that, indeed, his remarks would seem incredible. Continuing with Picknett, Prince, and Prior:

> However, close study of the content suggests that, while at times confused and unclear, the defendant at Nuremberg was trying to convey a message. (It should be noted that the president of the tribunal ordered Hess to end his defence speech on the grounds that the defendants were allowed a maximum of twenty minutes.

Reading Hess's actual words from the trial proceedings—even allowing for hesitancy and slowness of speech—it is difficult to make them last much more than ten minutes.[30]

In other words, the subject of "mind control" was a subject that the Tribunal—or at least, its president, who was British—did not want to be addressed at any length.

This is not, however, where Picknett, Prince, and Prior leave it, for they note that "Hess" began his speech, by predicting odd behavior from defendants, and alluding to the "show trials" of Stalin's 1930s purges, where defendants did indeed seem to be in a trance, behaving completely contrary to their self-interest. At this point however, Picknett, Prince, and Prior note a detail that was omitted in Bird's account, for "Hess" then states in his speech before the Tribunal that while confined in Britain, he had been given access to pre-war issues of the Thule-Nazi Party official newspaper, the *Völkischer Beobachter*. This is an extremely *odd* oddity, since "Hess" was prohibited from having access to *any* newspapers or news at all, British, German, or otherwise. Their question, at this point, is "Could this have been part of the schooling of a double?"[31]

It is also worth mentioning that "Hess," while at Nuremberg, refused to allow his wife Ilse to visit him or to bring his growing son, Wolf Rüdiger, to visit, writing to her that it would be an affront to his dignity. Indeed, "Hess" would not allow his family to visit him until the 1960s at Spandau, many years after the end of the war.

"Hess's" speech, however, contained even more oddities, and here it is best to allow Picknett, Prince, and Prior to speak for themselves, and at length, for their assessment of the speech is central to that nagging One Question at the center of the Hess Mess:

> Hess goes on to suggest that the German concentration camp guards, and the scientists who experimented on the inmates, were under a similar form of control as the Moscow defendants, and even that Hitler's reported mental abnormalities in the final years were due to an external cause. He then describes how he began to

---

[30] Picknett, Prince, and Prior, op. cit., p. 448.
[31] Ibid.

think along these lines because of the behavior of his guards and doctors in Abergavenny:

"Some of them—these persons and people around me—were changed from time to time. Some of the new ones who came in place of those who had been changed had strange eyes. They were glassy and like eyes in a dream. This symptom, however, lasted only a few days and then they made a completely normal impression. They could no longer be distinguished from normal human beings."[32]

Again, note that "Hess" is alleging some sort of "mind control" experiment is taking place, one of truly international extent, for it is, by his confused lights, occurring not just in the Soviet Union, and not just in Nazi Germany, but in Great Britain as well, with his own doctors and guards apparently subject to some sort of "procedure" prior to becoming involved with him.

Picknett, Prince, and Prior note that these "confused ramblings about 'mental influence' were an attempt to argue that Hitler and the Nazis were not responsible for their actions."[33] But in their view, this is not really the intention of "Hess's" remarks, because his real goal is not justification of Nazi atrocities, but rather, simply to persuade the Tribunal that "such things are possible," because, on their view, "he is building up to some revelation concerning himself."[34]

It is difficult and problematical to dismiss their assessment, because "Hess" himself stresses the importance of the subject, time and time again, not only in his speech at Nuremberg, but as we shall discover, elsewhere as well:

After giving his examples he stresses the importance of what he is going to say next:

"Obviously it would have been of the utmost importance if I had stated under oath what I have to say about the happenings during my own imprisonment in England. **However, it was impossible for me to persuade my defence counsel to declare himself willing to put the proper questions to me**... But it is of the utmost importance that what I am saying be said

---

[32] Picknett, Prince, and Prior, op. cit., p. 449.
[33] Ibid., p. 449.
[34] Ibid.

under oath. Therefore I now declare once more: I swear by God, the Almighty Omniscient, that I will speak the pure truth, that I shall leave out nothing and add nothing... I ask the High Tribunal to give all the more weight to everything which I declare under oath, expressly calling God as my witness."

Having stressed at such length the importance of what he is about to say next, Hess then begins his revelation: "In the spring of 1942..." *It is at this point that the president interrupts,* telling him that he is at the end of his allotted twenty minutes.[35]

While my own reaction to "Hess's" speech may not be the same as the reader's, I cannot help but record my impression that one senses a certain desperation in his words, an urgent need to convey information, perhaps even a warning, to the Tribunal and, through it, to the world.

But whether or not "Hess" was desperately trying to save himself, it does at least appear that he was trying to say something, for another strange question occurs in connection with his remarks: why would Dr. Seidl *not* wish to question "Hess" about his mind control ideas and allegations, particularly when, at that time, such ideas would have been considered absurd. Even today, when the evidence of patents and studies has at least rendered the topic "discussible," people are reluctant to do so, especially in courts, where the technology is a direct epistemological challenge to existing theories of evidence. But questioning "Hess" on his remarks, he may have been able to mount an insanity defense.

Thus, in "Hess's" case, such an airing of his views might actually have *helped* the case that Seidl—not "Hess"—wanted to make, namely, that he was *not* fit to stand trial.

However, what would have happened had he done so? Here it is worth noting that Picknett, Prince, and Prior point out one extreme difficulty with the "double" or *Doppelg*änger hypothesis: the British government, by allowing a "double" to stand trial was taking an extraordinary risk that the whole charade might be exposed in open court, thus risking an airing, in open court, not only before the world press, but before the personnel of the other three Allied

---

[35] Picknett, Prince, and Prior, op. cit., pp. 449-450, italicized emphasis in the original, boldface emphasis added.

powers, France, the U.S.A., and U.S.S.R., whatever it is that they were trying so hard to conceal and obfuscate. The second risk was allowing the double—or the real Hess—to continue for life in prison, where the programming of either the double or the real Hess might break down at any moment.[36]

In this context that they observe that the only physician unqualifiedly urging that "Hess" was *not* fit to stand trial was Lord Moran, personal physician of Winston Churchill, who had literally pushed himself into the three-man British team of physicians at Nuremberg and who, they note, omitted all reference to his diagnosis of "Hess's" unfitness for trial from his memoirs. "Strangely enough," they state, "if Hess had not stood trial because of insecurity, he would not have gone free. Instead, he would have been incarcerated in a top-security mental institution somewhere in Britain (as he was still in British custody). Is this why Churchill's man alone argued for such a diagnosis?"[37]

This question also raises questions about Dr. Seidl's defense, and why he did not want to put questions to "Hess" about his mind control allegations. It also raises into sharp relief the possibility that "Hess" was not *intended* to stand trial, but rather, be returned to Britain, where he would be incarcerated for a time before being removed more permanently; in this respect, only recall that "Spandau Hess" maintained that the Soviet reversal on his release was in fact a death sentence, and that the British would never allow him to leave Spandau alive. If that *was* the intention, then "Hess" thwarted it by the speech he gave, insisting that he stand trial.

The "nonsense in Nuremberg" highlights the fundamental question, who was "Hess"? Was the "Hess" in Nuremberg, or later, in Spandau, the Hess who took off from Germany in May 1941? The nonsense in Nuremberg thus leads, directly, to the other questions and hypotheses in the Hess Mess that we must now confront directly: the doubles dilemma, his flight of fancy itself, and what he—or rather, what researchers argue that he—hoped to accomplish by it, which leads to the peace mission and "lure" hypotheses, and to the Difficulties with the Dukes of Hamilton, Windsor, and Kent.

---

[36] Picknett, Prince, and Prior, op. cit., p. 450.
[37] Ibid.

B. More about the Doubles Dilemma
1. War Wounds, Missing Scar Tissue, and Magic Bullets

That "Hess" in Nuremberg—and therefore subsequently in Spandau—was a double is a hypothesis that was first put forward and argued before the public in W. Hugh Thomas' now classic book *The Murder of Rudolf Hess*. The controversy has raged ever since its publication in 1979, for Thomas presented a number of compelling "details" to buttress his main argument.

In Thomas' case, that controversy has raged largely because he maintained that it was the Nazis who substituted a double for Hess from their "stable of doubles,"[38] having learned of his secret "peace plan" proposal and determination to fly to Britain to negotiate with an alleged "peace party" in the upper strata of British society and politics. The substitution was made, Thomas argued, because high-ranking Nazis such as Himmler and Göring were eager to remove a powerful rival from the equation. Accordingly, Hess's plane was shot down and another plane, with a double, was substituted.[39] While most researchers, including the present author, reject this particular detail of Thomas' theory, it will nonetheless be reviewed thoroughly here because there are details in Thomas' elaboration that imply a significant political dynamic at work in the background of the Hess Mess. If it is true that the *one* book to own concerning the Hess Mess is Picknett's, Prince's, and Prior's *Double Standards: The Rudolf Hess Cover-up*, it is equally true that Thomas's book more than any other provoked the world-wide interest in the Hess Mess, and triggered the articles and books about the case that followed it.

Like everyone else who has ever investigated the Hess Mess, Thomas himself admitted that the whole affair was "disturbingly enigmatic," and pointed out that ever since "Hess's" parachute landing in Scotland on May 10, 1941, his behavior was one of the biggest mysteries. He refused, as we have noted previously, to see his wife or son at Nuremberg and indeed, did not allow them to visit him in Spandau until 1969. Pressed to identify Haushofer,

---

[38] Rebecca West, "Introduction," in W. Hugh Thomas, *The Murder of Rudolf Hess* (New York: Harper and row, 1979), p. 4.
[39] Ibid., p. 3.

Göring, or even his two secretaries by the psychologists in Nuremberg, he could not do so.[40] As we shall see, for Thomas, such anomalous and erratic behavior became supportive evidence in his main argument that "Hess" was not Hess at all, but someone else, a very clever double, from *someone's* "stable of doubles."

Such behavior, however, was *not* the issue that opened the Pandora's Box of the "Doubles" hypothesis and all the dilemmas it posed. Thomas had not shown much interest in the Hess Mess until, while serving in the British military as a physician, he was posted to Berlin as a "Consultant in General Surgery to the British Military Hospital."[41] Realizing that this meant Spandau prison's infamous Prisoner Number Seven might come under his care at some point, Dr. Thomas began to familiarize himself with "Hess's" medical file, compiled by the British Army psychiatrist J.R. Rees, who kept a meticulous record of "Hess's" bizarre behavior in Great Britain.[42]

It was in this file that Dr. Thomas learned about "Hess's" wounds that he suffered during World War One, with the shrapnel hit at Verdun, and the far more serious bullet wound on the Romanian front a year later. At this point, the mystery began, for completely unaware of Allen Dulles' suspicions about Nuremberg's "Hess"—after all, they had not yet been written about!—Dr. Thomas then discovered something quite odd in "Hess's" medical file, written by Captain Ben Hurewitz, "Hess's" examining American doctor when he was first brought to Nuremberg after the war. What was missing from Hurewitz's otherwise meticulous report was any mention of scaring that would have resulted from the bullet wound Hess suffered while on the Romanian front.

In September of 1973, Thomas finally was able to see Hess in the British Military Hospital for a routine examination, when "Hess" was completely naked. "I looked in bewilderment," he writes.

> I saw at once the two small linear scars reported by Hurewitz, and also a small scar on one wrist; *but apart from these marks there was no trace of any former wound.* For an instant I froze in

---

[40] W. Hugh Thomas, op. cit., p. 13.
[41] Ibid.
[42] Ibid., p. 14.

disbelief. Then I put out a hand and held the dressing-gown, in the pretence of helping but in reality to have another, longer, absolutely clear view of his torso. Neither chest nor arms carried any wound-scars whatever. Satisfied with my scrutiny, I let the dressing-gown go and muttered something like *"Es tut mir Leid'* (I'm sorry). No. 7 probably thought I was just being clumsy in helping him on with the gown.

For the rest of the evening I felt stunned. This man had *not* been shot in the chest during the First World War, or at any other time. Nor had he been wounded in the arm. Perhaps, I thought, there was a persistent mistake running all through his records. Perhaps Rudolf Hess never *had* been wounded... .[43]

Before "Hess" returned for a follow-up visit later that month, Thomas had time to review the X-rays that were taken of "Hess," and sure enough, there was no evident bullet scaring or damage to be seen on the picture. For Thomas, the conclusion was beginning to be inescapable: "For thirty-two years the world had believed he was Rudolf Hess. Yet now I knew that unless the historical records were wrong, he could not be."[44]

When "Hess" returned later that month for the follow-up visit, Thomas made certain he would be present throughout the entire examination. "Hess" was in a good mood, communicating with Thomas, "making pleasant small-talk in his excellent English."[45] X-rays were once again taken, and Thomas remained with "Hess" as the pictures were developed and examined. What happened next is worth recording in Thomas' own words:

> Then someone called out that the films were all right, and that No. 7 could get dressed. At once he slipped off his shirt—still sitting on the edge of the table—and began to pull on the warmer dressing-gown. As he did so, I again had a clear view of his chest. I stepped forward and pointed at it, saying in a friendly, straightforward voice, *"Was ist passiert mit den Kriegsunfallen? Nicht hauttief?"* ("What happened to your war-wounds? Not even skin-deep?")

---

[43] W. Hugh Thomas, op. cit., p. 21, emphasis in the original.
[44] Ibid., p. 22.
[45] Ibid., p. 24.

The question had a startling effect. The patient's manner changed instantly. From being in a sunny, cheerful mood, he turned chalk-white and began to shake. For an instant he stared at me in what appeared bewilderment or even utter disbelief. Then he looked down and avoided my eyes. After what felt like ages he muttered, *"Zu spät, zu spät"* ("Too late, too late").[46]

At this point, the reader is probably wondering why no *other* physician had noticed the discrepancy between "Hess's" World War One wounds and the *lack* of scarring on Prisoner No. 7. If "Hess" *was* a double, did this mean that all of his French, British, American, and Russian doctors, since Nuremberg were in on one of the greatest secrets of the century? Or did it mean something else entirely? And if "Hess" *was* a double, why was no attempt made to "duplicate" the scarring effects on the *Doppelgänger*? This could have easily been done under anesthetic.

Thomas began to dig, and discovered the original records of Hess's military service and wounds during World War One. This record lists his wounding by a piece of artillery shrapnel near Fort Douaumont, one of the French fortresses at Verdun, and scene of some of the bitterest combat during that battle. Here, Thomas discovered another anomaly, for the wound Hess suffered at Verdun was not, apparently, minor, for it required a full month in a military hospital, a stay of time representing a "substantial wound."[47]

But when he examined the war record for the wound to his left lung on the Romanian front in 1917, Thomas discovered just how serious the wound must have been for Hess had to spend four months, moving from military hospital to military hospital until he arrived back in Germany, but when he was finally discharged, he was discharged into the reserve, and spent two more months convalescing. Then, as further proof of the seriousness of the wound, Hess was discharged altogether from the infantry—reserve or otherwise—by being awarded the "Dull White Battle Wound Badge," effectively a sign that he could no longer physically function at the peak performance needed for the infantry.[48] In fact,

---

[46] W. Hugh Thomas, op. cit., p. 24.

[47] Ibid., pp. 28-29.

[48] W. Hugh Thomas, op. cit., pp. 29-30.

while Hess maintained himself in as healthy condition as he could, for the rest of his life he would complain of shortness of breath on long walks, or climbing hills, a natural result of a serious wound to the lung.[49]

In any case, Hess needed surgery in order to repair the damage to this wound, and, as Thomas points out, this surgery itself would have left scarring, visible both on his skin and in chest x-rays, and the surgical repair additionally would have required incisions of at least four inches in length. None of these were visible on "Hess," or "Hess's" x-rays.[50]

This left Thomas with two logical possibilities: Spandau "Hess" (and therefore, Nuremberg "Hess") was not Hess, or his war record had been falsified.[51] Dr. Thomas naturally shared his suspicions with the Hess family, Frau Hess and her son Wolf, and while Frau Hess was under no doubt that the man in Spandau *was* her husband, she did confirm that he had indeed suffered a severe wound—a *Lungen Durchshuss* or "shot through the lung" that had left scars on the front and back of his body[52]—during the First World War.

2. Anomalous Corroborating Behavior and Other Miscellanies

Hess's war wounds—and "Hess's" apparent lack of them—formed the core of Thomas' argument that the prisoner in Spandau was a double. In addition to this, however, Thomas pointed out certain examples of anomalous behavior by "Hess" that made sense if his *Doppelgänger* hypothesis were true. For example, the real Hess was not only *not* a smoker, as we have pointed out previously,

---

[49] Ibid., p. 31. In addition, Thomas found what must surely be the oddest synchronicity in the whole Hess Mess (one of those "You've got to be kidding" moments), for the Romanian Royal army, he discovered, used an 1893 Mannlicher rifle of 6.5mm caliber! (cf. p. 30) Perhaps this weapon managed to fire a "magic bullet" too, a bullet leaving no bullet-track of scar tissue through Hess. Perhaps this was the bullet that was discovered in pristine condition on the hospital bed in Parkland Hospital in Dallas, Texas, on Nov 22, 1963, having not only been allegedly shot through Kennedy and Connally, but perhaps Hess as well. (Sorry, I just couldn't resist.)

[50] Ibid., pp. 31-33.

[51] Ibid., p. 34.

[52] Ibid., 35.

he was also a vegetarian. Yet, once he had been apprehended by the British in Scotland and taken prisoner, "Hess" the "vegetarian" was seen gobbling up salmon on one occasion with his British captors.[53] Additionally, Thomas notes that in 1969, when "Hess" finally allowed his family to visit him for the first time since he took off on his infamous flight to Scotland, his wife Isle made what, for her, was merely an "in passing" observation but which may be very significant, for she observed her husband's voice had become deeper.[54]

Thomas comments as follows on this small, but important, observation:

> Whether she realized it or not, Frau Hess had stumbled on a physical near-impossibility. Any normal man's voice *rises* with age, rather than deepens. Physical processes associated with ageing inevitably push the timbre up rather than down. Only if the man has a disease of the vocal chords called myxedema, which causes a thickening of the tissues, can his voice drop in old age.[55]

One of the numerous problems with the Double Hypothesis was "Hess's" numerous letters home, which he began to compose while in confinement in England, and which naturally continued after his return to Germany at Nuremberg, and later, at Spandau. In these letters, "Hess" makes copious detailed references to things only known to his family. This fact, many would argue, means that "Hess" was in fact Hess.

But Dr. Thomas points out a disturbing pattern with these "letters home":

> At first sight the numerous references to family affairs and friends seem to constitute obvious proof that the writer of the letters was Hess himself. Yet if the correspondence is studied in chronological order, a striking pattern soon emerges. A very high proportion of the events and people mentioned occur first in earlier letters which the prisoner had receivced from Germany: almost everything he says about his former life is an echo of

---

[53] W. Hugh Thomas, op. cit. p. 20.
[54] Ibid., p. 172.
[55] Ibid., pp. 172-173.

something already written by another correspondent. It would take a computer analysis to work out precisely what proportion he himself initiated, but even without going into that amount of detail it is clear that his modest amount of original material could easily have been mastered by an intelligent double.

The pattern becomes even more curious when considered in the light of his methods of receiving and answering mail. As several of the men who looked after him in Mytchett and Maindiff still testify, he showed absolutely no enthusiasm or emotion when a letter came from Frau Hess, but would often leave it lying about unopened for several days. When he did rouse himself to reply, he would spread out numerous earlier letters on a large table, together with many small scraps of paper on which he had made notes, and thus, furnished with several dozen reminders, he would write his answer.[56]

However, anomalous behavior is not the only type of corroboration of the Double Hypothesis.

While we have not yet examined Hess's flight to Scotland itself, where we will encounter still more messy details in the Hess Mess, it is worth noting that Hess, according to the standard narrative of the flight, used someone *else's* flight suit when he left Augsburg, Germany, in his twin-engine Messerschmitt 110. That flight suit belonged to Helmut Kaden, "who had written his name in full on the inside pocket. The suit worn by the man who came to Scotland bore no name at all (the garment is still in Spandau Gaol where I myself have inspected it)," Thomas maintained.[57] This, of course, is one of the key reasons that Thomas believed that Hess was killed, and the *Doppelgänger* substitution was made by the Nazis, long before "Hess" reached Scotland. Again, while this author does *not* subscribe to this particular aspect of Thomas' scenario, it must be mentioned because other researchers have very different explanations for what might have happened, manifesting once again that at every step and detail of the Hess Mess, several interpretations are possible.

Finally, Thomas points out a disturbing comparison between Rudolf Hess, the pilot, sitting in the cockpit of a Messerschmitt 110,

---

[56] W. Hugh Thomas, op. cit., pp. 136-137.
[57] Ibid., p. 93.

and "Rudolf Hess" the potential double: the real Hess had a very real, and visible, gap between the upper incisor front teeth; "Nuremberg" Hess did not:

Hugh Thomas' comparison photos of the real Hess, left, in flight suit, showing his famous overbite, and the gap between the upper incisors, and Nuremberg "Hess," on the right, where the "gap" appears to be not between the upper incisors, but between the upper left incisor and canine.

There were yet other behavioral anomalies noted by Thomas that when viewed in conjunction with all the other evidence of missing war wound scars, the wrong flight suit, and different dental characteristics, seemed to synch the case for a double that he was making. All of the psychiatrists knew the real Deputy Führer was not only a vegetarian, but, having been raised as an upper middle class German, had very fastidious eating habit" and impeccable table manners, the man in their captivity ate "enormous quantities of all kinds of indifferent food, including beef and chicken curry, at a positively alarming rate," the "Hess" in British captivity hardly had the table manners of:

...a strictly-brought-up German of the upper middle class. He sat slumped at meals with his elbows splayed out sideways on the table; he tore bread into great chunks, drained his soup by raising the plate to his lips, and shoveled solid food into his mouth like a boy racing for a second helping.[58]

Additionally, the "Hess" in British captivity did not know anything about tennis, whereas Hess himself, born in Alexandria, Egypt, grew up around the game, and according to Frau Hess herself, "played tennis well and with enthusiasm."[59]

A picture is worth a thousand words.
A goofily smiling Nuremberg "Hess" with a skeptical-looking Göring in the dock at Nuremberg. It is worth remembering that pre-flight pictures of Hess seldom show him smiling because of his overbite.

3. Picknett, Prince, and Prior Weigh in on the Doppelgänger Dilemma

As might be expected Thomas' theory of a *Doppelgänger* was not universally accepted. Certainly Frau Hess and Wolf Rüdiger

---

[58] W. Hugh Thomas, op. cit., pp. 118-119.
[59] Ibid., p. 119.

never accepted it, maintaining until their deaths that the man in Spandau was indeed their husband and father. Others, while accepting the theory, challenged Thomas' scenario that the double was substituted by the Nazis during "Hess's" flight to Scotland. This, as we shall see when we examine the flight itself, is problematic in the extreme.

Picknett, Prince, and Prior not only did not dismiss the Double Hypothesis, they uncovered new information and—pardoning the pun—doubled down on it. Acknowledging that the problem with *any* double theory is getting the double to accept Rudolf Hess's fate, they nonetheless accept that "Thomas is on to something. However, his theory is much less plausible when it comes to providing a motive for using a double, and when the substitution was made."[60]

Thomas claimed that Hess's original flight was to Sweden, but Göring, getting wind of the plot, ordered Hess shot down. At this point, the Nazis, who just happened to have a Hess double who was also a pilot(!), and who was also carrying his wife's Leica camera, as the real Hess most certainly was, waiting at Alborg, Denmark, then had the double fly to Scotland. To "synch" this difficult scenario, Thomas points out that the British doctors examining Hess in Scotland make no mention of Hess's war wound to his left lung, though they *did* note some small "calcified area" in the "upper right zone," a detail that is, as we shall see, highly significant, and indicative that it was, indeed, the *real* Hess who abandoned his Messerschmitt 110 and parachuted into Scotland.[61]

The chief difficulties, beyond the obvious "logistical" require-ments of Thomas' scenario, are to provide a motivation as to why Göring and Company would should Hess down, and why the British, once they knew they had a double on their hands, would play along with the Nazis in the farce from that point on. Indeed, one of the obvious *puzzlements* about the Hess Mess *is* the fact that on this one point—Hess himself—the Churchill and Hitler governments were entirely agreed on two points: prior to the flight, Hess was the third most powerful Nazi in Germany, a man of reason, of some education and culture and sophistication, the

---

[60] Picknett, Prince, and Prior, op. cit., p. 368.
[61] Ibid., pp. 368-369. 4

"conscience" of the Nazi party; both British and German propaganda agreed. But after the flight, Hess was insane, stupid, and of no consequence, a complete reversal of public propaganda in a matter of mere days!

For Picknett, Prince, and Prior, and indeed for many other researchers who have concluded that, double or not, the Hess mission was about trying to negotiate a peace between Great Britain and Nazi Germany, the "lone madman narrative" was a convenient narrative to disguise the fact that elements of the British Royal family had been involved on the British side of his "peace mission" scheme.[62] That involvement, of course, adds a new element to the Hess Mess that makes it even more problematic: was, and *is*, is *this* the real reason that aspects of the affair remain classified to this day? We shall explore this question more completely in the next chapter, but for the present, it is worth noting that this royal involvement, at whatever level, is the reason most authors give for the continued cover-up.

a. The Actual War Wounds, and the Implication:
The Real Hess Parachuted into Scotland

As was seen previously, Prisoner Number Seven, "Hess" had two autopsies performed on him, the first by J. Malcolm Cameron, and the second private autopsy arranged by Wolf Hess. Neither of these autopsies mentioned any scarring commensurate with Hess's World War One wound to his lung.[63] The only scaring visible and mentioned in both autopsies was a small scar over the heart, which resulted from a suicide attempt of "Hess" while in British custody and confinement at Maindiff Court, which, as Picknett, Prince, and Prior point out, only proves that the man in Maindiff and the man in Spandau were the same,[64] but it falls short—in the absence of a scar to the left lung—of proving that both were the real Hess.

Thomas's *Doppelgänger* theory spurred the British Foreign Office to "prove" that Spandau's Prisoner Number Seven was indeed Rudolf Hess. Or at least, in the estimation of Picknett, Prince, and

---

[62] Picknett, Prince, and Prior, op. cit., p. 296
[63] Ibid., p. 360.
[64] Ibid.

Prior, "they tried hard" to do so, for over a year after "Hess's" suspicious death in Spandau, the Foreign Office announced

> ...that there was: 'a fibrous, irregular roughly circular old scar typical of an exit wound... in a posterior position on the left side of the chest.'

But the "proof" was no proof at all, and raised even more unsettling questions:

> As this was over a year after Prisoner Number Seven's death and burial, the 'finding' seems a trifle suspicious. Why hadn't this information been provided when they had the body? And if this description is correct, why had no previous examination noticed the scar?
> ....
> Clearly, Hess's medical records at the British Military Hospital where he had been treated for over twenty years did not record either the front or back scar. Either they were astonishingly inefficient, or the scars simply did not exist.

At this juncture, Picknett, Prince, and Prior point out that one glaring problem has dogged the "war wounds-*Doppelgänger*" argument from the outset, namely, *prior to the actual discovery of Hess's military record in Bavarian archives in 1989*[65]—*ten years **after** the appearance of Thomas's book—**no one** knew exactly where the entrance and exit wounds really were, and hence no one really knew where to look.*[66]

What was known of the wounds *prior* to this point were *summaries* from other files, and, of course, "Hess's" statements themselves. What the actual Bavarian records state, however, is that the bullet entered Hess in the upper left armpit, proceeded at an angle downward, grazing the top of his lung, and exiting under his shoulder blade.[67] This is a crucial point, for Wolf Rüdiger Hess informed them that after he had read Dr. Thomas' book, he asked "Hess" about that bullet wound, to which his father replied that

---

[65] Picknett, Prince, and Prior, op. cit., p. 358
[66] Ibid., p. 361. The discovery, of course, was used to discredit Thomas' *Doppelgänger* theory but, if anything, seemed to make it even more certain.
[67] Ibid., p. 362.

while he could not see the wound on his back, he could see the wound *on his chest*.[68] "It seems," they quip, "that not even 'Hess' himself knew where the scar was supposed to be."[69] Of course, this would be another argument that "Hess" was *not* Hess.

But there is more.

Somehow Prisoner Number Seven was able to read a newspaper article about Thomas' book shortly after it came out, in spite of strict regulations at Spandau that absolutely nothing about Hess or Hitler could enter the prisoner's "reading list." When the French pastor visited Prisoner Number Seven after this, he was informed by "Hess" that "a bullet had passed right through his chest, brushing the heart and exiting under the left shoulder blade."[70] But once again, this only serves to raise the question once again of whether "Hess" was a *Doppelgänger*, because the path of the bullet, according to the Bavarian archival discovery in 1989, was *not* through the chest, but through the *armpit*, and did *not* graze the heart.

As if the Hess Mess could not absorb any more mystification, there is the matter of his British dental charts, one from September 1941 from "Hess's" stay at Mytchett Place, and the other, from April 1943 from Maindiff Court. While the "fillings and bridgework are similar, though not identical,"[71] a glaring problem emerges with the fact that the 1941 chart records a crown and a gold tooth which are missing from the 1943 chart. Such a discrepancy could be the result of mere sloppy record keeping, as Picknett, Prince, and Prior observe,[72] or it could be the result of very accurate recording-keeping, and hence, also be an oversight on the part of British intelligence which forgot to "scrub" this incriminating fact from the

---

[68] Picknett, Prince, and Prior, op. cit., p. 361.

[69] Ibid. One can imagine—though Picknett, Prince, and Prior do not describe Wolf's reaction—how the knowledge of the real placement of his father's war wounds might have affected him, having learned to love a man who may *not* have been his father, and to fight for his release for years, to pay for private autopsies, and then to bury him with full Lutheran funeral services as a member of the family. I emphasize *this* aspect of the cruelty to highlight, in yet another way, the One Question at the heart of the Hess Mess.

[70] Ibid., p. 362.

[71] Ibid., p. 366.

[72] Ibid.

records. But in either case, as Picknett, Prince, and Prior aptly put it: "we find records that should demolish the doppelgänger theory do not."[73]

b. The Secret Measurement of Hess for a Duplicate Uniform: Substitution and Assassination Theories

Not all the anomalous behavior that seemed to confirm that at some point after his arrival in Britain, one was dealing with a *Doppelgänger*, came entirely from "Hess." Some of it came from the British themselves, and of these episodes, none is more suggestive than the "affair of the second uniform."

When Hess parachuted into Scotland, he was quickly taken into custody, and from there, eventually wound up for a brief period in the Tower of London, before spending approximately two years in confinement at Mytchett Place, prior to being moved to Maindiff Court, where he spent the rest of his years in British captivity. We shall have more to say about these periods and places in due course, but for the moment, our focus is on the brief period when Hess was in the Tower of London, a period about which little is known.

The "suggestive" episode occurred when Charles Fraser-Smith, the man after whom the gadget-wizard character "Q" in the James Bond films is modeled, was contacted by MI5 to assemble textiles and tailors to make an exact copy of the Luftwaffe captain's uniform that Hess had donned for his infamous flight. Informed that Hess had been drugged in the tower and that they would have to measure him quickly, Fraser-Smith and his team took all the measurements. Besides being proof of the fact that Hess *was* drugged on more than one occasion, the question inevitably arises as to why British intelligence would need an exact copy of Hess's Luftwaffe uniform.[74]

Fraser-Smith himself speculated that the British intelligence services were possibly contemplating sending a double *back* to Nazi Germany to penetrate the Nazi high command, and who better to do this than a double of the Deputy Führer himself? For Picknett,

---

[73] Picknett, Prince, and Prior, op. cit., p. 366.
[74] Ibid., p. 296.

Prince, and Prior, this event also has another implication, namely, that the idea of substituting a double had already occurred to MI-5 and MI-6 shortly after Hess arrived.[75] In later life Fraser-Smith went further, maintaining that high level doubts always existed in MI-6 about whether or not the prisoner in British custody was, in fact, Hess. And as Picknett, Prince and Prior also note, a double would also explain why the British prohibition of photographs of their infamous prisoner was so rigorously enforced.[76]

There is, however, another possibility for why British intelligence was keen to create a Hess Double, namely, the threat of assassination attempts, either from the various governments-in-exile in Great Britain, or by the Nazis themselves. Additionally, the British may have wanted to convey the impression that Hess, or "Hess," was "cooperating." In this respect, Picknett, Prince and Prior record that while one Hess was in Mytchett Palace, another was retained in the Tower of London, and actually—and very secretly—taken to a meeting in Whitehall with none other than Churchill himself! And this was *not* apparently the only meeting between the two.[77]

One cannot discount the assassination possibility, for Picknett, Prince, and Prior also record the fact that the notorious SS General and "Reichprotektor" of Bohemia, Reinhard Heydrich, composed a memorandum to the Nazi Foreign Minister Joachim von Ribberntop (who, let it be noted, would be seated with "Hess" in the dock at Nuremberg, along with Göring). In his report, Heydrich told Ribbentrop that his agents had informed him that Hess was being held in Scotland at a villa.[78] While this is not the place to investigate these Hess-in-Scotland reports nor their significance to Picknett's, Prince's and Prior's theory, it does attest to the fact that the Nazis were attempting to monitor his whereabouts.

Before we can review their scenario in more detail, however, we must now turn, finally, to address the matters of Hess's flight, the motivations for it, and his capture.

---

[75] Picknett, Prince, and Prior, op. cit., p. 370.
[76] Ibid.
[77] Ibid., p. 371.
[78] Ibid., p. 356.

C. The Flight of Fancy and Hess's Capture
1. The Strange "Shoot Down" Order and Conveying the News of Hess's Flight to Hitler
a. The Hess Flight in Some Standard Histories

In standard histories of the Second World War, the May 10, 1941 flight of Deputy Führer Rudolf Hess to Great Britain is mentioned only cursorily, if at all. It is a curiosity, the insane mission of an insane man to stave off disaster for Germany and Europe. Yet, even in those brief accounts, one senses that something is amiss. For example, in Leonard Mosley's biography of Hermann Göring, *The Reich Marshal*, after briefly mentioning Hess's occult interests and membership in the Thule Society,[79] his role in the Beer Hall Putsch, subsequent flight to and return from Austria,[80] we are then informed that Hess had misgivings about Hitler's immanent invasion of the Soviet Union, *Unternehmung Barbarossa*, misgivings that, notes Mosley, the *Reichmarschall* also apparently shared.[81]

For Hess, as we shall eventually discover, Barbarossa was indeed one of the motivations that impelled him to make his now infamous flight to negotiate a peace with Great Britain. But Hess's motivations were fundamentally military in nature; he was not so much opposed to *Barbarossa*, but to undertaking the risky strategy while Britain was still in the war, with the potentiality of an American entry into the war looming.

In the midst of this cursory treatment, we are informed that Luftwaffe General Adolf Galland, in command of the Luftwaffe's air defenses over Germany and Western Europe, was concerned about *Barbarossa* as well, and concerned that the only major Nazi leader who shared his misgivings was Rudolf Hess. After this revelation, Mosley continues:

> On May 10, 1941, Hess suddenly took off from Germany in a purloined Messerschmitt 110 and flew to England. A subsequent communiqué announced that "he harbored the illusion that he

---

[79] Leonard Mosley, *The Reich Marshal: A Biography of Hermann Goering* (Garden City, New York: Doubleday and Company, Inc., 1974), p. 53.
[80] Ibid., p. 98.
[81] Ibid., p. 298.

could bring about peace between Germany and England by a personal intervention."

Galland decided in his own mind that Hess had heard about the plan to invade Russia, and had made a desperate attempt to prevent the two-front war that would follow.[82]

The implication of all of this is that Hess's flight was a more-or-less spontaneous affair, ill-thought-out and sloppily planned, a desperation mission to prevent a desperate situation.

Then in a footnote, Mosley adds:

Shortly after Hess's flight, Galland was ordered by Goering to put up his fighters and intercept the Deputy Führer. "The order I received was mad," said Galland. It was impossible to find a plane at that hour, as darkness was falling. "Just as a token, I ordered a takeoff. Each wing commander was to send up one or two planes. I did not tell them why. They must have thought I had gone off my head." Hess bailed out over Scotland and was made a prisoner-of-war. His peace overtures got nowhere.[83]

Implicit in this short treatment are three questions: *(1) When did the Reichmarschall become aware of Hess's flight, (2) How was he made aware of it, and (3) What was his motivation for the shoot-down order?*

The last question assumes greater significance when we recall that Göring, according to Mosley, harbored the same misgivings about the wisdom of *Barbarossa* as did Hess: a two-front war was, with American entry a looming possibility, an extremely risky strategy. But if Britain *exited* the war, then an American entry, and ability to *prosecute* a war with Germany became equally problematical to America without the forward bases of deployment that Britain could provide.

In other words, why would Göring, always a practical military man, *want* to stop Hess and his peace mission, assuming he knew the purpose of Hess's flight?

As General Galland noted, Göring's order came *too late* for an interception to have much of a chance of success. Was Göring

---

[82] Mosley, op. cit., p. 299.
[83] Ibid., p. 299n.

perhaps giving the order to cover his own involvement in a much larger plot? We shall return to this possibility much later.

One gains a few more suggestive details in John Toland's celebrated two volume biography of Hitler. There we are informed of the close relationship between Hess and the Haushofers, and Hess and Hitler, and the famous professor of geopolitics' visits to both men while they were serving time in Landsberg Prison for their roles in the Beer Hall Putsch. All of this, of course, is to stress Hess's membership in Adolf Hitler's inner circle.[84]

Again, we are informed of Hess's opposition to *Barbarossa* so long as England was in the war, but gone are the suggestions his flight was an entirely *ad hoc* spontaneous affair. Rather, we are informed not only of secret meetings between Hess and General Haushofer and his son Albrecht to discuss the feasibility of peace overtures to Great Britain,[85] but we are additionally informed that Hitler himself gave tacit approval for the idea, and that Albrecht Haushofer then utilized his pre-war contacts and friendship with the Duke of Hamilton to contact the Duke to propose a meeting between him and Hess.[86]

Toland then outlines how Hess had practiced flights in the twin-engine Messerschmitt 110, and persuaded the head of the company, Willi Messerschmitt himself, to add two 700 litre drop tanks to the wings and special radio equipment to the two-man cockpit. Additionally, *we are informed that Hess obtained a very secret map of the Luftwaffe's air defense and forbidden flying zones from Hitler's personal pilot, Hans Baur.*[87]

This anticipates the question that many readers by now have probably been asking: How is it that Hess took off from Augsburg in southern Germany in a fast twin-engine fighter on an unauthorized flight, then managed to evade German radar and air defenses—then state of the art—to fly to Great Britain where, again, he apparently was able to bail out before being shot down by

---

[84] John Toland, *Adolf Hitler*, Volume I (Garden City, New York: Doubleday and Company, Inc., 1976), pp. 131-132, 168, 208-209, 393.

[85] John Toland, *Adolf Hitler*, Volume II (Garden City, New York: Doubleday and Company, 1976), p. 757.

[86] Toland, Volume II, pp. 757-758.

[87] Ibid., p. 759.

the Royal Air Force in response to activating British air defenses, *also* state-of-the-art!

Answer, Hitler's pilot provided him with maps!

This fact, coupled with Göring's phone call to Galland, now raises the prospect that Hess had "assistance" in his flight—very covert assistance—from inside Hitler's highest command structure to a more definite possibility.

As for the flight itself, it is best to allow Toland to present it in his own words, for this version is more or less the version of the standard narrative, and hence the version that most people—insofar as they are aware of Hess's flight at all—have come to understand it:

> Hess rose early on the morning of May 10, a Saturday, and, upon learning that the weather forecast was good, he made arrangements for the flight. Never had he been more gallant to his wife. After tea he kissed her hand and then stood gravely at the door of the nursery, "with an air of one deep in thought and almost hesitating." She asked him when he was returning and, told it would be Monday at the latest, she bluntly said, "I cannot believe it. You will not come back as soon as that!" She guessed he was bound for a meeting with someone like Pétain but he feared that she had guessed the truth. He "turned hot and cold in turns" and, before she could say anything more, he dashed into the nursery to take a last look at their slumbering son.
>
> At 6 P.M., after giving his adjutant a letter for Hitler...

This is the letter, the reader will recall, that Nuremberg "Hess" recorded in his diary that Göring told him he should have written!

> ...Hess took off from the Augsburg airport and headed for the North Sea. Abruptly, contrary to the weather report, the cloud cover vanished and for a moment he thought of turning back. But he kept going and found England covered by a veil of mist. Seeking shelter, he dived down with full throttle, at first unaware that a Spitfire was on his tail. Outdistancing the pursuer, he hedgehopped over the dark countryside at more than 450 miles an hour, narrowly skimming trees and houses. Baur had always claimed Hess was the type of pilot who liked to fly through open hangar doors and it was in this barnstormer's spirit that he aimed at the mountain looming ahead. It was his guidepost and he literally climbed up the steep slope and slid down the other side, always keeping within a few yards of the ground. Just before 11 P.M. he turned east and picked out a

railway and small lake which he remembered were just south of the duke's residence. He climbed to 6000 feet, a safe height from which to parachute, and switched off the motor. He opened the hatch—then suddenly realized he had overlooked one step in his elaborate training: "I had never asked how to jump; I thought it was too simple!" As the ME-110 plummeted, he recalled a friend mentioning the plane should be on its back. After a half roll, he found himself upside down, held inside by centrifugal force. He began to see stars; just before passing out, he thought: "Soon the crash must come!" Regaining consciousness, he saw the speed gauge indicate zero. He flung himself out of the plane, pulled at the parachute ring. Fortunately, while unconscious, he had automatically brought the plane out of its semi-looping curve to finish almost perpendicular on its tail. And so, to his amazement, he found himself safely in mid-air.

He hit the ground, stumbled forward and blacked out a second time. He was found by a farmer, marched off to the Home Guard and brought to a barracks in Glasgow. Insisting that he was one Oberleutnant Alfred Horn, he asked to see the Duke of Hamilton.[88]

And that, more or less, is the version everyone has come to believe (overlooking the fact that 450 miles per hour was beyond the actual top speed of a ME-110, especially at low altitude!).

But what about the letter he had given his adjutant prior to taking off from Augsburg? Toland notes that this was delivered to Hitler the following Sunday morning at his Berghof mansion on the Obersalzburg. Hitler was in conference when Martin Bormann's brother interrupted the meeting and informed Hitler that Hess's aide wanted to see the Führer. After some confusion, Hess's letter was delivered, and Hitler "put on his glasses and began to read indifferently but as soon as he saw the words 'My Führer, when you receive this letter I shall be in England,' he dropped into a chair and shouted so loudly he could be heard downstairs, "Oh, my God, my God! He has flown to England!"[89] Hess added that he had kept the whole thing secret, because had he been forthcoming with his plan, Hitler "would have forbidden it," but that he was attempting to bring to pass an end to the war with England, which Hitler had never wanted. Then, closing, Hess stated "And if, my Führer, this project—which I admit has but very little chance of success—ends in failure and the fates decide against me, this can have no

[88] Toland, Volume II, pp. 759-760.
[89] Ibid., p. 760.

detrimental results either for you or for Germany; it will always be possible for you to deny all responsibility. Simply say I am crazy."[90]

Hitler then became a frenzy of action, ordering his aids to phone Göring, and get Bormann and Ribbentrop to the Berghof, and immediately placed Hess's adjutant under arrest. At this juncture, Hitler inquired to Luftwaffe General Ernst Udet, present for the conference, whether or not a ME-110 could even reach Britain; Udet replied "No."[91] Again, this is a hint that something is amiss with the standard narrative, for very obviously, Hess's 110 *did* reach England, and Udet, as a Luftwaffe General, would have known that a one-way flight was at least possibility with drop tanks or even re-fueling.

For the rest of the day, according to the standard narrative once again, Hitler raged and fulminated, fearing that Hess's flight would be interpreted by Germany's Axis partners Italy and Japan that Germany was trying to procure a separate peace. Finally, after some debate—a debate which took place *without* the expert input of propaganda minister Goebbels—a communiqué was prepared that simply stated that Hess had commandeered an aircraft against orders, and that he was missing, and had presumably crashed. The communiqué also stated that a letter had been left behind showing "traces of a mental disturbance which justifies the fear that Hess was a victim of hallucination."[92]

This of course was a propaganda blunder of the first order, since it implied that one of Nazi Germany's top leaders was insane, and that the *rest* of the leadership had not detected it![93] Within a few hours of the German press statement, the British followed with one of their own, stating that Hess had come to Great Britain. Beyond this, there were no more details, but it did force the Germans to "update" their previous statement, and in the process, they made matters much worse. In a new release issued on Tuesday, September 13, 1941, they stated:

---

[90] Toland, Volume II, p. 761.
[91] Ibid.
[92] Ibid.
[93] Ibid., p. 763.

As is well known in party circles, Hess had undergone severe physical suffering for some years. Recently he had sought relief to an increasing extent in various methods practiced by mesmerists and astrologers, etc. An attempt is also being made to determine to what extent these persons are responsible for bringing about the condition of mental distraction which led him to take this step...[94]

With that, the "standard narrative" comes to an end: Hess, via contacts to the Haushofers, flew to Britain to negotiate a peace for which, according to his own letter to Hitler, he held out little chance of success. He was denounced as insane by both the Nazi and later the Churchill governments, and remained to rot in confinement for the rest of his (many) days.

Except, in Toland's version it is suggested that Hitler gave the mission his tacit approval. Hence, his rage and fulminations on "learning" of the mission from Hess's letter was a bit of very convincing theater.

In this respect Toland mentions one more strange incident indicative, perhaps, that Hitler knew more about the Hess flight than he ever let on. During a meeting with a Frau Bruckmann to console her on the recent death of her husband, an unusual exchange occurred; Hitler's words were not those of a man raging against Hess:

"We all have our graves and grow more and more lonely, but we have to overcome and go on living, my dear gracious lady! I, too, am now deprived of the only two human beings among all those around me to whom I have been truly and inwardly attached: Dr. Todt (builder of the Westwall and Autobahn) is dead and Hess has flown away from me!"

"That is what you say now and to me," reportedly replied Frau Bruckmann, who had a reputation for frankness, "but what does your official press say? Year after year we all go to Bayreuth and are deeply moved, but who understands the real meaning? When our unhappy age at last produces a man who, like the Valkyrie, fulfills the deeper meaning of Wotan's command—seeks to carry out *your* most sacred wish with heroism and self-sacrifice—then he is described as insane!" She expected the Führer would retort

---

[94] Toland, Volume II, p. 762.

sharply but he remained quiet and thoughtful. "Is it not enough, what I have said to you—and to you alone—about my real feeling?" he finally said. "Is that not enough for you?"[95]

This strange episode paints Hitler's response to the Hess flight in dramatically different colors than the usual narrative, for it suggests that in some deep way he never recovered from the personal loss, and that it affected the day-to-day governance of the Third Reich. This, as we shall come to see during our subsequent review of Hess's relationship to his secretary, Martin Bormann, may not be as odd as it initially sounds.

For the present, however, we must remain focused on Hess's flight, and its details.

I have employed these two standard and well-known biographies to highlight something very important in the "standard narrative," for not only is Hitler's emotional closeness to Hess on display, his own role and foreknowledge—even in that standard narrative!—is open to question and debate. Additionally, as we have seen, we have a clear indication that Reich Marshal Göring himself had some sort of prior foreknowledge.

W. Hugh Thomas zeros in on Göring's orders to Galland and fleshes out its bizarre nature even more. In his memoirs published in 1953, Galland, according to Thomas, reveals additional details that call Göring's role into sharp relief, for *early in the evening* of May 10, 1941, Galland received a telephone call from Göring,

> ...who sounded "very agitated" and ordered Galland to take off immediately with his entire wing. When Galland pointed out that there were no reports of any enemy aircraft flying in, Georing shouted, "Flying in? What do you mean by flying in? You're supposed to stop an aircraft flying out! *The Deputy Führer has gone mad and is flying to England in an Me 110. He must be brought down.*"[96]

Note that according to Galland, Göring had *specific* information that Hess was flying a Messerschmitt 110, and that he had ordered

---

[95] Toland, Volume II, pp. 764-765.
[96] W. Hugh Thomas, op. cit., p. 47, emphasis added.

Galland to bring him down, in effect, ordering Galland to shoot down Hess.

But Thomas highlights just how bizarre this phone call really was, and the questions and implications that it raises:

> To Galland, it seemed that "someone had made a last-minute attempt to pull the emergency cord of a fast train speeding over the wrong points." He described the whole incident as "one of the most mysterious affairs" of the war. That seems to me an understatement. To be rung up suddenly by the Reichsmarschall commanding the air force and ordered to shoot down the Deputy Leader of the country must have been an astonishing experience, and Galland's published account of it is far from satisfactory. Yet when I tried to interview Galland to glean more information, it was made clear to me that my inquiries were not welcome.
>
> Goering's telephone call on the evening of May 10th, 1941, is in itself extremely suspicious. **Next day, when summoned to Hitler's mountain headquarters, the Berghof, he pretended to know nothing about Hess's departure. Yet, according to Galland, he did know about it. Not only was he aware of Hess's flight on the evening of the 10th, he had positively ordered the Luftwaffe to shoot the Deputy Führer down. This alone argues the existence of a plot. How did Goering know that Hess was about to do a bunk? Who had told him? How *long* had he known? On whose orders, or with whose consent, did he command the Deputy Führer's assassination? So desperate an action would surely have needed the direct approval of Hitler himself. Yet Goering did not even tell the Führer what was happening, let alone seek his consent. And why, when Goering did call Galland, was he in such a panic? His haste suggests that he feared part of the plot had misfired.**
>
> The timing of the telephone call also seems odd. Galland says it came only about ten minutes before dark. Yet on the north coast of Germany darkness did not fall until after nine p.m. that evening. By nine p.m. Hess—supposing he had carried straight on—would have been at least ninety minutes, or some 300 miles, beyond the coast, and far beyond the reach of any fighters based on the Continent. If Goering knew the time of Hess's take-off, he must have realized this. There would therefore have been no

point in telephoning just before dark. Could the call have come through much earlier than Galland relates?[97]

Indeed, could the call have come through much earlier, *or did Göring in fact place the call when Galland says he did, but for very different reasons than Thomas surmises? Was Göring perhaps trying to cover his tracks by issuing an order to shoot down Hess* **when he already knew it would be impossible to do so**, *in case his involvement in a plot with Hess should be discovered?*

In spite of the fact that Göring and Hess were rivals, there is enough to suggest this possibility might be true. In order to see this possibility, however, it is necessary to examine the flight itself.

2. The Flight Itself and Its Implications: British and German Air Defenses

The most recent detailed studies of the Hess Mess and the infamous flight at the center of it are Peter Padfield's *Night Flight to Dungavel,* and John Harris' and Richard Wilbourn's *Rudolf Hess: A New Technical Analysis of the Hess Flight, May 1941.* Padfield's book also has the advantage of being one of the few books that remembers that Rudolf Hess was actually a Nazi, and not simply a "martyr for peace" as revisionist literature often portrays him. The Harris-Wilbourn book has the advantage that it is one of the few books to subject Hess's Messerschmitt 110 to a thorough examination of its performance characteristics, and to subject the flight itself to careful analysis. Both books examine the problems posed by the British and German air defenses and the implications of those problems for collusion with Hess from high-ranking elements in both countries, and both books also offer widely divergent theories of the motivations for the flight. For the authors of both books, the Hess flight was *not* the spontaneous affair of "the lone madman." It was an international conspiracy of the highest order, involving powerful elements within both the United Kingdom and Nazi Germany.

---

[97] W. Hugh Thomas, op. cit., pp. 47-48, italicized emphasis in the original, boldface emphasis added.

*a. The Strategic Positions of Britain and Germany in the Spring of
1941 and the Oft-Overlooked Factor: The Atomic Bomb*

The Hess flight was motivated at least in part by the strategic
position in which both Germany and Great Britain found
themselves in early 1941. On the German side, on paper, everything
looked good: Germany was master of Western Europe from the
Pyrenecs to the Norwegian Arctic. In Eastern Europe Germany and
her allies Italy, Bulgaria, and Hungary had overrun pro-British
Yugoslavia, and unceremoniously ejected British forces from Greece
and Crete. Yet, as preparations for Operation Barbarossa moved
forward, the Churchill government continued to woo America to
enter the war. Sooner or later, Berlin knew this would happen.
Time was on Britain's, and not Germany's, side.

On the British side of this equation, things looked no better, for
the above reasons, and more besides. Britain simply was not strong
enough to prosecute a successful war against Germany on its own.[98]
The string of losses placed the Churchill government under severe
pressure, for it had essentially two choices: it could hold out until
American entry, thus virtually dooming the British Empire as the
dominant world power and ensuring its replacement by the U.S.A.,
or it could preserve the Empire at the cost of a negotiated peace
with Germany.[99]

Like many other researchers into the Hess Mess, however, John
Harris and Richard Wilbourn, whose book *Rudolf Hess, A New
Technical Analysis of the Hess Flight, May 1941* we shall review in
this section, point out yet a third problem faced by the Churchill
government. The British Royal Family "were half German, and saw
Germany as a natural ally, albeit preferably without Hitler as leader.
They were certainly in the 'those with much to lose' camp."[100] In
actuality, as we shall see, the Royal family were the tip of the
iceberg of a pro-peace party in Britain, a party that had some
representation in the British peerage, and in the various organs of
government.

---

[98] John Harris and Richard Wilbourn, *Rudolf Hess: A New Technical Analysis
of the Hess Flight, May 1941* (Stroud, Glocestershire: The History Press, 2014), p. 33.
[99] Ibid., p. 34.
[100] Ibid.

Hess and the Penguins

It is the existence of a peace faction both in Germany and in Great Britain that most researchers—including this author—believe was the ultimate context in which the Hess flight, and resulting Mess, occurred, as both sides covertly attempted to contact and negotiate. Harris and Wilbourn, however, suggest other motivating factors, including the Nazi A-bomb, and Hess's knowledge of it, for after all, as has already been discovered, up to the time of his flight virtually nothing was done in the Third Reich that Hess did not know about, Harris and Wilbourn suggest

> If the Germans believed that they were close, did this underpin Hitler's confidence in winning what was seen by many as an unwinnable war with Russia? We believe it significant that Hitler (and Hess) chose to play on this uncertainty. When Hitler attended the Reichstag on 4 May 1941, just six days before the Hess flight, he observed that '... the scourge of modern weapons of warfare, once they were brought into action, would inevitably ravage vast territories.'
>
> As will be described later, *when Hess was in captivity, if he wanted attention, he too would speak of the bomb.* He knew the British would want to know the reality of German nuclear production. *Hess knew that there was no German nuclear bomb and he may have wondered if there ever would be.* Did he know that Hitler was not holding any aces?[101]

However, as I argued in my very first book of "revisionist history" of the Nazi Period, *Reich of the Black Sun: Nazi Secret Weapons and the Cold War Allied Legend,* there is enough evidence to argue that the Nazis were *much* farther along in their atomic bomb project, perhaps even achieving tests of actual bombs in October of 1944, and then again in March of 1945.[102] As I also argued in that book, an actual existing atomic bomb project, one moreover achieving some success, *does* rationalize Hitler's confidence in his invasion plans for Russia, and also rationalizes his otherwise irrational and

---

[101] Harris and Wilbourn, op. cit., p. 31, emphasis added.
[102] Joseph P. Farrell, *Reich of the Black Sun: Nazi Secret Weapons and the Cold War Allied Legend* (Kempton, Illinois: Adventures Unlimited Press, 2005), see pp. 18-20, 70-80 for the October 1944 test, and pp. 80-88 for the March 1945 test.

inexplicable decision to declare war on the USA as his armies were freezing before the gates of Moscow.[103]

If these arguments are true, then Harris' and Wilbourn's observations, based as they are on that postwar Allied legend of German nuclear incompetence, changes color completely, for it adds *additional military and political pressure on the Churchill government, and additional pressure on the British peace faction to come to an agreement.* The atomic bomb, in other words, may be a key hidden factor to the Hess Mess that is seldom considered. Once one factors it in, however, the "negotiations" no longer have quite the aura of make-believe, and the air of desperation one senses on both the British and German sides finds additional grounding. Harris and Wilbourn also point out, quite correctly, that the British were monitoring German progress as closely as they could, monitoring that eventually led to the commando attack on the Norsk heavy water plant in Norway.[104]

As I point out in *Reich of the Black Sun*, there is a consideration that makes this atomic bomb context for the Hess Mess quite plausible, for in October of 1944, at approximately the same time as the first alleged Nazi nuclear test in the Baltic, the British government secretly placed its entire constabulary and emergency fire and medical services in the country on secret high alert. The reason? They had intelligence of a possible German atomic bomb attack.[105]

The atom-bomb relationship to the Hess flight is not without its own contextual corroboration, for Hess was also the Commissar of All Technologhical Matters and Organization within the Third Reich, and thus, he knew more than almost anyone at that time the full extent of the Third Reich's black projects world.[106] This important post will, as we shall see, bear important implications when we consider little-known aspects of the Hess Mess.

These considerations are important for two reasons; Harris and Wilbourn suggest that Hess's arrival was the *last* thing that Churchill wanted, since it put the Prime Minister and his

---

[103] Farrell, op. cit., pp. 154-155.
[104] Harris and Wilbourn, op cit., p. 31.
[105] Farrell, op. cit., pp. 72-73.
[106] Picknett, Prince, and Prior, op. cit., p. 138.

government in a very awkward position, for it made it look like he could be double-dealing the USA, on the one hand trying to woo an American entry into the war, and on the other, covertly negotiating a peace with Nazi Germany. Churchill, in other words, was placed in exactly the same position vis-à-vis his potential allies by the Hess flight as Germany was placed vis-à-vis *its* allies, Italy and Japan. The fear was that the flight would give new strength to yet another "peace faction," the American isolationists.[107]

(1) A Speculation on the "Lure" Hypothesis

Harris and Wilbourn point out that the contemporary American reaction to the Hess flight was summed up by two magazine articles, one in *Liberty* magazine from July 1941, and the other in an article in 1943 in *American Mercury*. Both articles maintained that Hess was *lured* to Great Britain by British intelligence,[108] the implication being that there was no "peace party" nor realistic hope that a negotiated peace with the Churchill government was possible.

One difficulty with the "Lure" hypothesis often pointed out by investigators of the Hess Mess is that if Hess *was* lured to Great Britain, why did Britain not seek to capitalize on the propaganda value of his capture much more than it did? If anything, the British reaction was inexplicably muted and low-key. It is my suspicion, however, that the "Lure" hypothesis itself is as much a fiction, or, as we would call it today, a "spinning" of the event, a legend created to reassure America that Britain was not double-dealing and to extricate the Churchill government from the diplomatic difficulty caused by the Hess flight.

---

[107] Harris and Wilbourn, op. cit., p. 13.

[108] Ibid., pp. 11-12. It should be pointed out that Abdallah Melaouhi's book on the Hess murder hypothesis includes the entire *American Mercury* article in its appendices.

(2) Churchill's 1942 Address to the House of Commons: Conspiracy Confirmed

By 1942, the USA had, of course, entered World War Two with the Japanese attack on Pearl Harbor, and Hitler's declaration of war on the USA two days after the attack. Buoyed by the new alliance with the USA and the Soviet Union, Churchill at last answered a question about Hess on the floor of the House of Commons. This crucial exchange is a pivotal feature of Harris' and Wilbourn's argument, and hence, we reproduce it in full:

> The Prime Minister: Surely the (honourable) Gentleman is not the man to be frightened of a Whip? The House of Commons, which is at present the most powerful representative Assembly in the world, must also—I am sure, will also—bear in mind the effect produced abroad by all its proceeding. We have also to remember how oddly foreigners view our country and its way of doing things. *When Rudolf Hess flew over here some months ago he firmly believed that he had only to gain access to certain circles in this country for what he described as 'the Churchill clique.'*
>
> Mr. Thorne(Plaistow): Where is he now?
>
> The Prime Minister: Where he ought to be—to be thrown out of power and for a Government to be set up with which Hitler could negotiate a magnanimous peace. The only importance attaching to the opinions of Hess is the fact that he was fresh from the atmosphere of Hitler's intimate table. But, sir, I can assure you that since I have been back in this country I have had anxious inquiries from a dozen countries, and reports of enemy propaganda in a score of countries; *all turning upon the point whether His Majesty's present Government is to be dismissed from power or not.*[109]

Harris and Wilbourn quite correctly point out that this speech—more revealing than Mr. Churchill perhaps cared to admit—is "the beginning of the conundrum" for he is clearly revealing the motivation of the Hess flight, namely, "to gain access to the certain

---

[109] Harris and Wilbourn, op. cit., p. 14, emphasis added, citing Hansard's, no reference given.

circles that could remove Churchill and his government from power."[110]

3. "Sealing the Deal":
a. Harris and Wilbourn's Examination of the British Constitution

As this juncture, Harris and Wilbourn supply a nuance to their version of the Hess Mess that is worth very careful consideration, for they point out the obvious fact—known to all Hess Mess researchers—that by the time of his flight to Scotland, *several* contacts had *already* been made been made between the German and British "peace parties," and that several discussions had *already* secretly taken place, in Sweden, Switzerland, and Spain. From this obvious fact, however, comes a stunning thesis: "Hess was not flying to add to the detail—that had already been agreed. He was flying in *to seal the deal* and his arrival was to demonstrate his commitment—at the highest level."[111] Like other researchers, they also believe that Hess's selection of *Scotland* rather than *England* as the ultimate destination was precisely because of these prior covert contacts between Hess and the German "peace party" and the Duke of Hamilton, Scotland's highest ranking peer, who, as such, could provide Hess with entre to the Royal Family.[112]

Did this have any chance of success?

Indeed it did, and the reason lies in the British Constitution itself, which Harris and Wilbourn take great pains to explicate, for their thesis that Hess came not for further *discussion and negotiation* but rather to *"seal the deal"* rests upon a close and tightly-argued examination of that constitution. This is, indeed, one of the most brilliant parts of their book, which is filled with many brilliant observations and arguments. The British Constitution, as most people are aware, is not a "written document," but rather has evolved from various covenants, conventions, precedents and courses of performance over time. One of these "courses of performance" well-established in British constitutional practice is that the Monarch "should act upon ministerial advice."[113] This

---

[110] Ibid.
[111] Harris and Wilbourn, op. cit., p. 22, emphasis added.
[112] Ibid., p. 15.
[113] Ibid., p. 35.

precedent, however, has been a very moot point of discussion and debate, as one may imagine, and there *were and are* cases in recent British history where the Monarch acted independently from the ministerial advice of his or her own government, and actually *created* British policy.

In this regard they cite perhaps the most famous case of all: King Edward VII, Queen Victoria's son, who in 1903 made his famous trip to Paris, beginning the British diplomatic offensive that turned France—long a continental nemesis—into a British ally. This initiative was almost wholly Edward VII's, made after quiet discussion with various key members of the British peerage. Other examples were the threat of a Monarchial veto during the parliamentary debates over Irish home rule in the years immediately prior to World War One, and finally, the role of the Monarchy in placing Stanley Baldwin into the premiership in 1923.[114]

More importantly, however, there are "the 'reserve powers the sovereign has accumulated over the years. They are rarely used and, indeed, *only ever considered in times of constitutional crisis.*"[115] These reserved powers of the Crown ultimately stem from the 1688 settlement during the era of the "Glorious Revolution," and as part of the common law do not become "extinct merely through lack of use."[116] Harris and Wilbourn expand on the nature of these powers and their relationship to the Hess Mess as follows:

> Amongst others, the powers included *the appointment and dismissal of ministers; the summoning, prorogation and dissolution of Parliament; royal assent to bills;* the appointment and regulation of the civil service; the commissioning of officers in the armed forces; and directing the disposition of the armed forces in the UK. In foreign policy: *the making of treaties; declaration of war;* deployment of armed forces overseas; recognition of foreign states; and *the accreditation and reception of their diplomats.* So in a time of constitutional crisis, the King or Queen could, in theory, act virtually independently of the government of the day.

---

[114] Harris and Wilbourn, op. cit., p. 35.
[115] Ibid., emphasis added.
[116] Ibid.

> *This is the reason that Hess was obtaining books on the British Constitution* in April 1941. He could request the monarch to invoke royal prerogative, dismiss the prime minister and, presumably, appoint in his place a prime minister who would act in accordance with the King's wish—to make a peace treaty with Germany.[117]

Harris and Wilbourn, on this basis, then argue that these constitutional considerations form the context from which Hess's motivations must be interpreted, for he was *not* trying to negotiate with the Duke of Hamilton, or, for that matter, any other peer, but rather, because peers had right of access to the Monarch, was attempting to use that connection to be introduced to King George VI, whom he hoped would invoke this constitutional process, and dismiss "the Churchill clique."[118] The conclusion that they draw from this is that, contrary to popular views, Hess was "quite able" under the British constitution to achieve an overthrow of the British government of Winston Churchill.[119] It was to be, in effect, another "Churchill-Halifax moment," for after all, it was George VI who made the decision to appoint Churchill using precisely the royal prerogative, and not Lord Halifax, to the premiership in May of 1940.[120]

---

[117] Harris and Wilbourn, op. cit., p. 35, all emphases added. Harris and Wilbourn point out that this enumeration of the reserve Crown powers and prerogative were the result of a study commissioned by the Blair Labour Government of 2003.

[118] Ibid., p. 36. They point out that the right of peers to access to the monarch is a principle acknowledged by Blackstone, the famous Oxford scholar of British jurisprudence. See p. 37.

[119] Ibid., p. 38.

[120] It should be noted that, in that instance, George VI *did* heed the "ministerial advice" of the then exiting Prime Minister Neville Chamberlain, who advised the King to choose Churchill over Halifax. In what is a strange irony, however, Churchill was also sympathetic to the previous King, Edward VIII, who was pressured to abdicate the throne in favor of his brother over his desire to marry the American divorcee, Wallis Simpson, which, eventually, he did. Edward VIII was, in turn, also known for his sympathies with the Nazi regime, and after his abdication, as Duke of Windsor, he and his new wife actually met and dined with the Hesses in Munich!

141

b. The Haushofer Letters:
The German Side: No Peace with Churchill;
The British Side: No Peace with Hitler

As we have already seen, the Deputy Führer had a close relationship with General Karl Haushofer and his son Albrecht, under whose tutelage Hess then mediated their geopolitical ideas to Hitler. It was the Haushofer-Hess peace faction in Germany that carried on the secretive discussions with the British peace faction via the Haushofers' extensive network of connections to it. In the preparations for Hess's flight, the "peace mission" was extensively discussed between the three men in a series of private and personal letters and memoranda. These documents form the core, in virtually all Hess Mess research, of the "Peace Plan Hypothesis" of the Hess flight.

In a September 3, 1940 letter to his son Albrecht, General Haushofer recounts a meeting that he had just had with Hess, revealing that severe attacks against Britain were planned and that "the highest ranking person only has to press a button to set it off." He and Hess—who is referred to throughout the Haushofer correspondences by the Japanese codename "Tomo"—had discussed the prospects of a negotiated peace, using Portuguese national celebrations as an occasion to meet on neutral ground with high-ranking British counterparts. The General reveals that he has heard from an old British friend, one Mrs. Violet Roberts, via the British war postage service in Lisbon, and that they should attempt to use her to communicate with the Duke of Hamilton. This letter is apparently in response to previous efforts by Albrecht, as his father is indicating to him to proceed to make contact, and gives him her address via the Lisbon address she had provided in her letter. [121]

Hess himself wrote General Haushofer on September 10, 1940. In the letter, Hess urges that the contact between Albrecht and his "old friend," i.e., the Duke of Hamilton, be initiated via Mrs. Roberts, and to inquire if he would be willing to meet on neutral territory, presumably Lisbon, which both the British and Germans could easily get to. Hess then writes something very peculiar:

---

[121] Harris and Wilbourn, op. cit., pp. 43-44.

The prerequisite naturally was that the inquiry in question and the reply *would not go through official channels, for you would not in any case want to cause your friends over there any trouble.*

It would be best to have the letter to the old lady with whom you are acquainted delivered through a confidential agent of the AO[122] to the address that is known to you. For this purpose Albrecht would have to speak either with Bohle or my brother. At the same time the lady would have to be given the address of this agent in L.[123] or if the latter does not live there permanently, to which the reply can in turn be delivered.

As for the neutral, I have in mind; I would like to speak to you face-to-face about it for some time. There is no hurry about this since, in any case, there would first have to be a reply received here from over there.[124]

What emerges from this letter is that Hess and the Haushofers had been engaged in these covert discussions for some time, but much more importantly, Hess is attempting to avoid "official channels," and his reason is that he wishes to avoid compromising the Haushofers' British contacts.

However, the question that has constantly hovered over the Hess Mess is how much—if anything—did Hitler know of the flight. Clearly, *someone* in the Nazi hierarchy knew about it, for we have already encountered the fact that Göring knew about it, ordered General Galland to shoot him down, and then, a day later in front of Hitler, claimed no knowledge at all! Consequently, the question arises, was Hess also trying to avoid *German* official channels as well, by recommending that Albrecht use not the German diplomatic service in the Foreign Ministry, but rather, the *party* apparatus of the *Auslands Organization? If so, why?*

My speculative thesis is that Hitler was kept in the loop *to a certain extent,* but not entirely, for reasons that we shall disclose momentarily, for there *is* something known to Göring, which he is

---

[122] AO, i.e., the *Auslands Organization*, the Nazi Party's own overseas intelligence service, which Hess, of course, commanded.

[123] "L.," i.e., presumably Lisbon.

[124] Harris and Wilbourn, op. cit., p. 45, emphasis added.

attempting to keep *from* Hitler, by feigning ignorance of Hess's flight. In all likelihood, whatever Göring knew, Hess knew.

In this respect, it is worth noting that Albrecht Haushofer suspected that there was something amiss with Hess's request not to use official channels, for on September 15 he writes a comprehensive memo in Berlin on the prospects of peace negotiations with the British. At the very beginning of this comprehensive memorandum, he states that it is a memorialization of the points he had discussed with Hess during a meeting in Bad Gotesberg that Hess had ordered him to attend. Albrecht Haushofer states that he "had the opportunity to speak in all frankness."[125] In this memorandum, which Albrecht had probably drawn up for his father, he makes it clear that:

> ...all Englishmen who mattered, regarded a treaty signed by the Führer as a worthless scrap of paper. To the question as to why this was so, I referred to the 10-year term of our Polish Treaty, to the Non-Aggression Pact with Denmark signed only a year ago, to the "final" frontier demarcation of Munich. What guarantee did England have that a new treaty would not be broken again at once if it suited us? It must be realized that, even in the Anglo-Saxon world, the Führer was regarded as Satan's representative on earth and had to be fought.
>
> If the worst came to the worst, the English would rather transfer their whole Empire bit by bit to the Americans than sign a peace that left to National Socialist Germany the mastery of Europe.[126]

Albrecht Haushofer continued to observe that the only genuine solution to European peace and security was a European federation, and a "fusion" between Germany and Britain with a joint navy and air force, with joint defense of all territories, a fusion that "the English are now about to conclude with the United States."[127]

Note firstly that Albrecht is *not* talking about an *alliance* of the UK and USA, but of *fusion*, the old goal of Cecil Rhodes.[128] If true,

---

[125] Harris and Wilbourn, op. cit., p. 46.
[126] Ibid.
[127] Ibid., p. 47.
[128] In this respect, see the celebrated book by Dr. Carroll Quigley, *The Anglo-American Establishment* (New York: Books in Focus, Inc., 1981), pp. 33-101.

then it provides yet another motivation for Hess's flight, for such a "fusion" had to be prevented at all costs, and in spite of any chances of the success of a "peace mission," the risks of *not* doing so were far higher. As we shall see, there *is* in fact evidence that something along these lines might indeed have been being discussed at the highest levels. Hess's mission, as we have seen previously, put the Churchill government into the dubious diplomatic position of looking like it was double dealing, and thus, *merely by landing in Great Britain, regardless of the success of the **other** parts of his mission, Hess may have forestalled and collapsed these plans.* The USA would not and could not negotiate such a fusion if there was the remotest *hint* of double dealing.

However, note secondly that according to his memorandum, Albrecht Haushofer was very frank and blunt with Hess, clearly implying to him that there was very *little* possibility of a negotiated peace with Hitler. He then nevertheless continues by recommending to Hess that approaches could possibly be made through the British ambassador to Hungary, O'Malley, or through Sir Samuel Hoare, the British ambassador in Madrid.[129] Then, toward the very end of the memorandum, Albrecht discloses something quite unusual, requiring rather close parsing of his words:

> For this extremely ticklish case and in the event that I might possibly have to make a trip alone—*I asked for very precise directives from the highest authority.*

Before proceeding to the very *next* sentence in the memorandum, pause and consider the possible implications of this statement, for Hess's request *not* to use "official channels" might have alerted Albrecht that something was amiss, and that, perhaps, the meeting he was attending with Hess was not with Hitler's, or perhaps, other high-ranking Nazis', knowledge. If one suspected this, then someone in Albrecht's position, being involved in such high-level and covert discussions, would then do what he did: he would seek to cover or guarantee his safety by having definite written orders "from the highest authority," namely, Hitler himself. *Why ask for*

---

[129] Harris and Wilbourn, op. cit., p. 48.

*such directives **unless** there was a suspicion that not everything was entirely "right" about the situation?*

But then, in the very next sentence, there is this statement:

> From the whole conversation I had the strong impression that it was not conducted *without the prior knowledge of the Führer,* and that I probably would not hear any more about the matter unless a new understanding had been reached between him and his Deputy.[130]

At first glance, these two statements appear somewhat contradictory, but there *is* a possible resolution to the situation, namely, that Hitler was *generally aware* of the meeting between his Deputy and Albrecht Haushofer, and of the purposes of that meeting, *but not the precise details.* In other words, Albrecht may have suspected that Hitler knew of the meeting, but he may also have suspected that Hess may not have informed him of the full details of the discussion and that Hess was holding something back, for whatever reason. Hence, he requests specific instructions.

Albrecht was taking no chances.

In any case, a return letter from Albrecht to Mrs. Roberts for forwarding to the Duke of Hamilton was apparently carefully composed and then sent. Why was Mrs. Roberts the involved? Because the Roberts and Haushofers met during visits to England by the Haushofers as part of Kaiser Wilhelm's entourage (1903), and during the Roberts' visits to the Haushofers in Germany (1925 and 1926).[131] This letter from Albrecht Haushofer, via Mrs. Roberts, to the Duke of Hamilton was duly intercepted by British intelligence, which was now alerted to the fact that covert discussions were being attempted.[132]

Albrecht Haushofer had good reasons for his skepticism about a peace settlement with Hitler in power, for the Hess initiative was *not* the only peace feelers being sent out. In fact, many levels of the Nazi regime were involved, all of them leading back to Hitler himself, who repeatedly indicated that Germany and Britain were

---

[130] Harris and Wilbourn, op. cit., p. 48
[131] Ibid., p. 56.
[132] Ibid., p. 61.

not natural enemies, an idea that he had, of course, absorbed from Karl Haushofer via his influence on his own Deputy, Hess, who had inserted Haushofer's ideas almost whole cloth into *Mein Kampf.* One such attempt was made via the Swiss diplomat Carl Burckhardt, the head of the International Red Cross. Buckhardt attempted to convey such peace feelers to Britain on July 9, 1940, via a telegram which was the subject of a meeting at Downing Street at which Churchill, Chamberlain, Clement Attlee, Lord Halifax and others were present.[133] The British legation in Switzerland stated that it had responded to Burckhardt's feelers by stating that "our distrust of Hitler, apart from anything else, was a fatal obstacle to any peace."[134] This pattern was repeated *again* when Burckhardt met with a Finnish art dealer, Lars Borenius, a businessman with connections both to the Royal Family and with MI-6.[135] Borenius apparently conveyed a message to Burckhardt that Germany would have to vacate Holland and Belgium, restore "some kind of Poland," and, most of all, that no peace was possible with Hitler.

Thus, the by-now familiar pattern is repeated again: no peace is possible with Hitler. Notably *absent*, however, is any reference to peace with *Germany*. In the ways of diplomacy, precision is required both in what is said, and what is *not* said, and by this point, the message was increasingly clear: "We'll talk, but not with Hitler." On the German side, the response to this was the exact opposite.

On May 4, 1941, Hitler and Hess had their last face to face meeting in Berlin, which lasted some time, before Hitler was scheduled to speak to the Reichstag. At some juncture, General Haushofer, who was also in Berlin at the same time, telephoned Hitler. It is likely that both Hess and Haushofer were in Berlin in connection with Hess's impending flight, for Hitler allegedly made substantial changes in the text of his speech. Harris and Wilbourn observe that the speech was a long, direct, and personal attack and harangue on Churchill. Because of this, they suggest that it was a

---

[133] Harris and Wilbourn, op. cit., p. 71.
[134] Ibid., p. 72, see also Harris' and Wilbourn's remarks on p. 73.
[135] Ibid., pp. 82-83, 84.

speech that was designed to send messages to the British peace faction to remove the Churchill government.[136]

For the German side, it was "get rid of Churchill," and for the British it was "get rid of Hitler."

The conclusion: *no peace was possible with **either** government,* and thus, if there was to *be* a negotiated peace, *both* governments would have to go. Consequently, yet another possibility arises in the Hess Mess, namely, that *his flight was not simply to "seal a peace deal" but that, in order to seal that deal, it was also a component in a wider scheme to overthrow both governments in internationally and bilaterally coordinated coups d'etat.* This, as we shall see subsequently, is not as crazy as it sounds.

(1) The 1938 Army Plot and the 1939 Göring-Dahlerus Peace Effort

Before we can look at that possibility in more detail, it is necessary to put the Hess peace mission into an even wider context, for *if* there was an element of a potential coup d'etat involved in the mix, then this could not occur without strong support; Hess could not undertake it on his own. In this respect it is worth recalling the "Generals' Plot" that was brewing in the German Army during the 1938 crisis over the Sudetenland. Hitler, as is now known, desperately wanted to launch a war against Czechoslovakia, a war that would inevitably not only have involved the powerful Czech military, but potentially France, Britain, and even Poland and the Soviet Union. Russia had in fact extended a guarantee to Czechoslovakia similar in nature to the guarantee that France and Britain would extend to Poland a year later. Faced with the prospects of a war which Hitler was determined to launch, the General Staff had determined to overthrow Hitler and place the military in control of the government, arresting other major Nazi leaders. The plot failed, of course, because of Neville Chamberlain's diplomacy, and the subsequent "Munich Agreement" of 1938 between Germany, France, and Britain, which surrendered the Sudetenland to Germany, effectively stripping Czechoslovakia of its frontier defenses and leaving it easy prey to its eventual complete occupation. With war averted, and Hitler's popularity at an all-time

---

[136] Ibid., p. 89.

high, the military did not dare to move against Hitler, and the Generals' Plot collapsed.

What is *not* well-known, however, was that Hermann Göring himself, the very next year, in August of 1939, as war was immanent with Poland and the West, sponsored a secret three-day conference on the small German island of Sylt in the North Sea with British businessmen. This conference came after initial feelers between Göring and Lord Halifax conducted by Göring's emissary, the Swedish businessman Birger Dahlerus.[137] At this secret island conference, the British made clear that the guarantee to Poland was firm, but they also proposed another Munich-style conference between the leaders of France, Germany, Italy, and Britain to resolve the Polish corridor-Danzig problems and avert war. Poland, like Czechoslovakia, was not, apparently, to be invited to its own dismemberment. One effect of these Göring-initiated contacts, however, was that the British businessmen—along with Lord Halifax himself—were persuaded of Göring's trustworthiness and straight talk. "From the British side," writes Peter Padfield, "it confirmed Göring as the acceptable face of the Nazi leadership. These impressions would persist."[138]

This is potentially highly significant, for it would place Göring himself in the "peace faction" inside of Germany, and with the means and contacts to pursue it. In other words, from 1939 to 1941, *the two highest ranking Nazis after Hitler himself were both involved in peace initiatives with the British, Göring, as Hitler's designated successor in the offices of state, and Hess, as Hitler's designated successor in the offices of the Nazi Party.* If indeed Hess's mission *was* a part of a wider international effort to coordinate coups d'etat against both Hitler's and Churchill's governments, then who better to guarantee the success of such a scheme—at least on the German side—than the two most powerful men in the Nazi state and Party?

With respect to the "coup" possibility it is worth noting that Padfield maintains that in July, 1940, after the Fall of France,

---

[137] Göring, it will be recalled, went to Sweden after World War One where he was, in effect, a barnstormer pilot, and then returned there after the failure of the Beer Hall Putsch, and married his first wife, a Swede from high Swedish society.

[138] Padfield, op. cit., pp. 52-53.

Reichsmarschall Göring[139] extended an extensive peace feeler to the British embassy in Stockholm via his nephew by marriage, Carl-Gustav von Rosen. While simultaneously other peace feelers were being sent via Dublin, Lisbon, Washington and Berne,[140] the one from Stockholm from Göring himself was apparently not committed to paper because of the *Reichmarschall's* reluctance to do so.[141] According to Padfield, the offer was standard fare: Germany was to be allowed a "free hand in Europe" in return for a cessation of hostilities, and a "helping hand" for Britain to defend itself against Japan.

However, this raises the question of why Göring should be reluctant to commit anything to paper. One explanation was, of course, that he was acting *ex officio* as a back-channel diplomatic effort, by-passing the Foreign Ministry. Hence, to protect Germany from possible embarrassment should anything be leaked, nothing was committed to paper. But another explanation would be that perhaps Göring had communicated *more* than just the "standard fare," namely, an acknowledgement of some sort that the British would not negotiate with Hitler.

4. The Aircraft: Messerschmitt Bf 110
a. The Fuel Tanks and Drop Tanks

Few analyses of the Hess Mess have dealt with the details of the actual flight itself, with most accounts stressing the basic outline of events: the Deputy Führer's take off from Augsburg Saturday evening, May 10, his flight northward over the Rhineland and thence out over the Frisian coast and into the North Sea, his subsequent turn westward, his "nose dive" to low altitude to confuse British radar, his full-throttle dash across the Scottish landscape, and finally, with fuel running low and darkness approaching and his failure to find his alleged landing place, his desperate parachuting into the nighttime Scottish landscape, where he was caught by a local farmer doing last-minute chores on his land. This is for all intents and purposes the "standard narrative,"

---

[139] Prior to the Fall of France Göring's *Luftwaffe* rank had been Field Marshal.
[140] Padfield, op. cit., p. 86.
[141] Ibid., p. 85.

and with it the other component of the standard narrative, that Hess acted more or less alone, with a minimum of help extending no further than his own personal adjutants.

It is this gap that the study of John Harris and Richard Wilbourn's book is meant to fill, for as they demonstrate, a technical analysis of the flight reveals that Hess could no more have attempted such a flight without significant amounts of high-level help and collusion both on the German and on the British sides, than the 9/11 hijackers could have successfully accomplished their airplane operations six decades later without significant "inside help." It most definitely could not have been, nor was it, a "solo effort," for the very simple reason that it was "extremely well planned, as it needed to be, and required considerable input from various German agencies if it was to succeed. This input alone raises obvious questions as to the level of German involvement."[142] Their argument focuses on the actual performance characteristics of Hess's Messerschmitt 110 twin-engine fighter, Hess's captured maps, and the details of the German air defense and air-guidance beacon system in 1941.

With respect to the aircraft, the Me 110 itself, the formula was quite simple: fuel consumption, plus average cruising speed, plus time, plus available fuel equals "what was possible."[143] In this respect, identification of the exact *type* of Me 110 became crucial, for the engines, speed, and fuel consumption differed among various types depending on the engines fitted. In the case of Hess's aircraft, through careful consideration of serial numbers of production runs and the serial number on Hess's crashed aircraft, Harris and Wilbourn were able to identify the production run as belonging to the 110E-2/N series.[144]

It is well-known that Hess had contacted Willi Messerschmitt himself to request specific modifications to his aircraft, among them the fitting of drop tanks beneath the wings for extra fuel, a common World War Two practice to extend the operational range of aircraft, as well as modifications to the radio equipment, which was placed in the rear cockpit of what normally was a two-seater

---

[142] Harris and Wilbourn, op. cit., p. 93.
[143] Ibid., p. 102.
[144] Ibid., pp. 95-97.

aircraft. With the largest possible drop tanks of 900 litres each, the 110's operational cruising range could support up to eight hours of flight at cruising speed, and since Hess himself described his flight as being of five hours and twenty-four minutes' duration to his British captors in 1942, the flight, with this modification, was possible.

A Messerschmitt Bf (Me) 110 Twin Engine Fighter

b. The Oil Tanks

Fuel and drop tanks were not the only technical factors to be evaluated, however. The Messerschmitt 110, as a high-performance high-speed fighter—indeed, at that time one of the fastest in the world—consumed massive amounts of oil to lubricate and cool its engines. While the aircraft could be fitted with auxiliary external oil tanks, the remains of Hess's aircraft in Britain had no such fittings. Relying only on the internal oil tank, Harris and Wilbourn, based on the Messerschmitt firm's own performance documents, conclude that Hess would only have had enough oil for a flight of approximately four and two-thirds hours' duration before the engines would have seized, sending Hess crashing into the North Sea.[145] This discovery is, as Harris and Wilbourn point out, "one of the most significant in respect of the Hess flight for the past

---

[145] Harris and Wilbourn, op. cit., pp. 114-115.

seventy years. Its implication is stark—Hess could *not have flown for as long as he claimed;* he may well have had enough fuel, but he did not have enough oil."[146] Accordingly, they conclude that Hess *had to have landed in Germany at some point during his flight to replenish the oil tank for the remainder of the flight.* That of course means that there had to be other people involved in his flight than just his personal adjutants at Augsberg.

By careful consideration of the flight plan maps, which we shall review more completely in the next section, Harris and Wilbourn come to a conclusion that this author finds enormously suggestive and pregnant with implications, and here it is best to cite their own stunning conclusion; they state that given the extraordinary secrecy surrounding the flight, and based on the maps, Göttingen emerged as a high probable contender for the place of Hess's stop to replenish his oil tanks. Why Göttingen? Because Göttingen "was then the research site for the Horten brothers, who were pursuing their revolutionary 'flying wing' designs. *We are aware that Hess was known to them and so this would seem to be a sensible choice.*"[147] The implications of this discovery are indeed profound, for it suggests that Hess made use of the Third Reich's existing *secret black projects research infrastructure* in order to accomplish this mission, in this case, the *Luftwaffe's* black projects infrastructure, with which as Deputy Führer he was doubtless aware. *It is this possibility that may also inform why, and how, Göring was aware of the mission and perhaps involved with it, since these projects would also clearly be known to him.*

c. The Maps, Flight Plans, and Their Implications

Harris and Wilbourn next turn to a detailed and thorough examination of the so-called Lennoxlove Map, which is part of an exhibit at Lennoxlove House in Scotland that commemorates the wartime career of the Duke of Hamilton. This map is actually two conjoined maps that appear to be based upon British Ordnance Survey maps, but of German manufacture. Harris and Wilbourn also note that this map contains various handwritten markings and

---

[146] Ibid., p. 119, emphasis added.
[147] Harris and Wilbourn, op cit., p. 195, emphasis added.

notes, with various points on the Scottish landscape clearly marked. Notably, Dungavel House, the residence of the Hamiltons and supposed goal of the Hess Flight in many investigations of the Hess Mess is *not* marked, while various RAF airfield maintenance units at Prestwick and Carlisle *are* marked.[148] While the lack of any markings for Dungavel House form part of Harris' and Wilbourn's argument that the Hamilton home and its small airfield were *not* Hess's goal, they do raise the important question of why the map was given to the Hamilton family after the war, if indeed the Hess flight had nothing whatsoever to do with them.[149]

The Lennoxlove map, as noted, was covered with careful handwritten notes and markings and was quite large, and they observe that the markings appear to have been carefully made so as not to reveal either his target, or any German military secrets, too readily.[150] Curiously, there were numbered markings all over the map, some in the North Sea, which meant that not all the markings were of geographical features. Because of this feature, they concluded that the map was actually Hess's meticulously crafted "radio navigational chart, interspersed with a host of visual recognition markers."[151] Thus the authors believe that the British Ordnance survey maps were chosen and marked in an attempt to disguise the fact that Hess charted his flight plan using the German radio beacon guidance systems.[152] One of these, the Kalundborg transmitter, was in Denmark and was the principle east-west guidance beacon for central England and southern Scotland.

This point becomes a crucial feature of their analysis, and to see how and why, we must now briefly review another component of the standard narrative: Hess, we are told, made landfall over Scotland at the wrong place, south of where he intended to be. In the failing sunlight and approaching darkness, he flew his aircraft over Scotland full throttle, at tree-top level, frantically looking for landmarks and his landing target. After flying across the entire peninsula and reaching the Irish Sea, he turned around again and

---

[148] Harris and Wilbourn, op. cit., p. 121.
[149] Ibid., p. 122.
[150] Ibid., p. 124.
[151] Harris and Wilbourn, op. cit., p. 127.
[152] Ibid., p. 139.

flew inland for a few more miles, apparently looking for his target. Being unable to find it, he took the aircraft up to 6000 feet, and bailed out.[153]

So, why did Hess arrive so late over the Scottish coast, in fading sunlight, when the rest of the mission had been so meticulously planned? Their answer is contained in the Lennoxlove map, for on it there is marked a point "C" approximately twelve minutes from the Scottish coast, with the handwritten notes indicating that at this point, the drop tanks were to be jettisoned, and the aircraft put into a full throttle power dive for twelve minutes. The purpose of this maneuver seems obvious, for Hess's aircraft would have been spotted by British radar, and most likely British air defenses might have assumed it was the pathfinding plane for a nighttime bombing raid on Glasgow or other Scottish targets. By diving into a power dive, he would slip under any scrambled British fighters sent to dispatch him, as well as slip under the radar itself.[154] Point "C" however, was apparently a beam intersection point, which Hess failed to detect on his initial approach. Hess later sketched his flight plan for his captors on August 8, 1941, detailing the mystifying "rectangle" of his flight plan, where, according to Hess, he "zig-zagged" to the east, then flew back to the north, and then once again to the west.

---

[153] Ibid., pp. 172, 174: Harris and Wilbourn point out that Britain had gone on "double summer time" in 1941, i.e., added two hours to Greenwich Mean Time, to avoid civilian traffic accidents during the blackouts due to the Blitz. Germany, which typically is one hour ahead of Greenwich time, had itself adopted "summer time" and added one hour to the time. Thus, in 1941, Germany and Britain were on the same time. This places Hess's landfall over Scotland at about 10 p.m., and his arrival near Dungavel Hourse at about 10:40 p.m.

[154] Harris and Wilbourn, op. cit., p. 200.

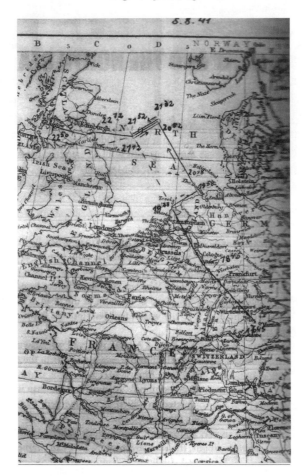

Hess's 1941 Sketch and Notes of his flight path for his British captors while at Mytchett palace; note the absurd rectangular "jog" or "zig-zag to the east."

But why would Hess have created such an absurd flight plan, one *increasing* the risk of his flight by consuming precious fuel and oil? Harris and Wilbourn hypothesize—I believe correctly—that Hess's *real* zigzag occurred much further north and later into the flight, when he was unable to locate the crucial point "C." He then did what all pilots would do: he attempted to retrace his steps and locate the crucial point again. The "Rectangle" zig-zag was thus most likely a story designed not to disclose any secrets about the German directional beam system.[155]

d. The Response of the British Air Defenses, and the Difficulty of Dungavel

British Fighter Command's response has always been suspect in the estimations of most Hess Mess researchers, for it is known that British radar *did* track Hess's flight,[156] but the response has always seemed lack-luster. Sergeant Maurice Pocock was scrambled in a Spitfire, and three Hawker Hurricanes of the nearby Polish squadron were also in the air. Four aircraft were now searching for Hess. The problem was, Pocock climbed to 15,000 feet, and Hess was already far below. Additionally, one RAF radio and radar operator, Cecil Bryant, maintained that he was given orders to relay to aircraft that the incoming German airplane was *not* to be attacked.[157] But as Harris and Wilbourn point out, whether or not one chooses to believe Bryant's story is, in effect, immaterial, because the grim reality of the statistical efficiency of British night fighters in May 1941 was only a little less than 3 percent, giving Hess a chance of survival of over 97 percent,[158] and looking for a lone Messerschmitt traveling full throttle over Scotland in darkening twilight would be like trying to find a needle in a haystack.

There is another suspicious factor, however.

Harris and Wilbourn observe that in February 1941, the eastern coastal wings of the Royal Air Force received a new group commander, Air Vice Marshal John Andrews. Andrews' appointment, they note, was a little unusual in that he lacked combat command experience, but he *was* proficient in intelligence matters, had spent time in Germany between the wars as part of aircraft compliance monitoring for the Treaty of Versailles, and hence spoke German. His appointment at that time might therefore have to do with the possibility that someone was expected.[159]

---

[155] Harris and Wilbourn, op. cit., pp. 200-202.
[156] Ibid., p. 157.
[157] Ibid., p. 158.
[158] Ibid.
[159] Ibid., pp. 159, 160.

The most damning bit of evidence that the RAF was "pulling its punches" on the late evening of May 10, 1941, is in the fact that Fighter Command was almost insistent that the German aircraft was targeting the RAF base at Dundonald on the *west* coast of Scotland, yet, only *one* aircraft was scrambled to deal with this possibility. This, they argue, is clear indication that at least *some* in the Royal Air Force command structure in Scotland were well aware of where Hess intended to land.[160] Most decidedly, it could *not* have been Dungavel house that Hess was targeting—as both the standard narrative, and most other revisionist histories, would have it—for Hess intended to *land* his aircraft, not bail out, *and the airstrip at Dungavel was, quite simply, not long enough to accommodate an aircraft of the Me 110's size.*[161]

Thus, if the target *was* an operational R.A.F. base, then this implies not only collusion, involvement and conspiracy at *some* level on the part of the R.A.F. in that region with the Hess flight, it also indicates the profile of who might have been dealing with Hess. In short, Hess needed (1) someone with R.A.F. command authority; and (2) he needed a peer, i.e., someone with access to the Monarch, and the Duke of Hamilton was both.[162]

It is important at this juncture that the reader understands that Harris and Wilbourn are *not* contesting the larger picture that other researchers have argued, namely, that the *personal* target of Hess's flight was the Duke of Hamilton and the "peace faction" that Hess thought he represented, but rather, that he intended—as other researchers also believe—to *land* his aircraft, rather than parachute into Scotland. A landing at a prearranged and agreed upon site would allow the mission to go forward, since Hess would be sure that he was dealing with whom he was intended to deal. *By parachuting, however, Hess was placing the entire mission at risk, for he might be apprehended by parties not privy to the whole scheme, which, of course, is exactly what happened.*

---

[160] Harris and Wilbourn, op. cit., pp. 216, 230.

[161] Ibid., pp. 180-182. This puts Harris and Wilbourn in sharp opposition to the scenario of Picknett, Prince, and Prior, who maintain that the airstrip at Dungavel *was* the target.

[162] Ibid., pp. 223, 227, 229-230, 241.

There is one final aspect of Harris' and Wilbourn's version of the Hess Mess that must also be mentioned, for it bears directly upon our review of the research in the next two sections: they do *not* subscribe to the hypothesis of Picknett, Prince, and Prior, that the Hess flight is connected to the death of the King's younger brother, the Duke of Kent, in an air crash in August, 1942.[163]

But as we shall now discover, Picknett's, Prince's, and Prior's hypothesis of a connection between the Hess flight and the Duke of Kent's death in an air crash a little over a year later, may be one of the most brilliant and tightly argued cases in the whole Hess Mess.

D. The Difficulties with the Dukes
1. The British Peace Faction

I stated previously that the research of Picknett, Prince, and Prior in their book *Double Standards, the Rudolf Hess Cover-up*, represented the most thorough one-volume book covering all aspects of the Hess Mess; if there is one book to own on the matter, this is it, for while they do not discuss *all* the details nor all the hypotheses, theirs is still the most sweeping synthesis of the case. They cast a very wide net.

One of the central aspects of the standard narrative which they review and analyze in some detail is the view that Hess's flight was the flight of a "lone madman," the narrative that both British *and* German propaganda curiously agreed upon *after* the flight had taken place. According to the standard narrative, then, Hess, in his delusions, assumed there was a peace faction in Britain large enough to afford his mission at least some chance of success, even if only a minimal one. According to the standard narrative however, there was no such faction. If anything, "lure" hypothesis advocates maintain that this was a carefully crafted psychological operation to "lure" an unstable high ranking Nazi leader to Great Britain. Picknett, Prince, and Prior ask the pertinent question, "But what if there *was* such a powerful British cabal?"[164] One of the high merits of their work is that they devote considerable time and detail in an attempt to answer this question. Accordingly, while it is impossible,

---

[163] Harris and Wilbourn, op. cit., p. 235.
[164] Picknett, Prince, and Prior, op. cit., p. 76, emphasis in the orginal.

obviously to capture all of their data and all of the subtle nuances of their argument, a review of their case is necessary if one is to see why the idea of a joint British-German coup plot might not be so far-fetched.

They point out that there were, indeed, several powerful "pro-peace" elements in Britain, and that indeed, "substantial elements" of what we would now call Britain's "deep state" were behind a push to an early negotiated peace in Germany.[165] Among these groups, there was the "Right Club," easily the most rabidly pro-Nazi, and yet whose membership included "prominent peers of the realm" including the Duke of Wellington, and William Joyce, the notorious "British version" of Tokyo Rose, infamous for his English language broadcasts from Berlin that earned him the nickname "Lord Haw Haw," and a hangman's noose for treason after the war.

Yet another of these groups was "the Link" a group fostering closer ties between Nazi Germany and Great Britain, whose rolls swelled to a membership of 4300 people, many of these peers or military officers themselves, including the Duke of Westminster and Admiral Sir Barry Domville, "director of naval intelligence, and a firm believer in the existence of a Jewish-Masonic conspiracy."[166] The Duke of Westminster is intriguing for another reason, for he provides a linkage between the anti-war peerage and the "City," Britain's financial district which was in Picknett, Prince, and Prior's words, "almost to a man" opposed to a war with Germany and which "desired Britain to extricate itself as soon as possible."[167] For these high-ranking elements of the British establishment, the financial district and the anti-war peers, the fundamental problem was that they feared Britain would further indebt itself to the United States, leading to an eventual breakup of the Empire. At the same time, these individuals also—rightly—saw the Soviet Union as the other major threat to Britain's Empire and hence, caught between the "bi-polar" world that would actually emerge after the

---

[165] Picknett, Prince, and Prior, op cit., p. 83. At this juncture, Picknett, Prince, and Prior are referencing an academic study of these groups conducted by Dr Scott Newton of the University of Cardiff's history faculty, and his 1996 study *Profits of Peace*.

[166] Ibid., pp. 82-82. The authors also note that Domville, not surprisingly, was detained as a threat to British security.

[167] Ibid., pp. 83-84.

war, these men argued for a "third position" of an *entente* or understanding with Germany, and perhaps, an eventual alliance, for Germany alone in Europe possessed enough weight to challenge the Soviet Union and offered the only counter-balancing weight to growing American power.

One of the more important pro-peace factions or groups was the Anglo-German Fellowship, a group which, like the Link, attempted to foster contacts and cooperation between the two nations. In the case of this group, however, its British membership reached very high indeed, and included the Duke of Hamilton and two of his brothers on its membership rolls; when peace feelers were advanced through neutral Sweden from Germany to Britain, it was very often the Duke of Hamilton's brothers, Nigel and David, members of the Anglo-German Fellowship, that were the targets.[168]

Picknett, Prince, and Prior also note something else of great significance with respect to the Hamiltons, for in 1938, the Duke (at that time, the Marques of Clydesdale) had received a personal invitation from Adolf Hitler himself to attend the 1938 Nuremberg Party rally. For these researchers, the significance of this invitation is that Hitler himself recognized the importance of the Hamiltons and their contacts within the British establishment and peerage, but also because the invitation was *not* delivered via the German Foreign Ministry, but rather through the "unofficial channels" of the Anglo-German Fellowship. This leads them to wonder if, in fact, the Anglo-German Fellowship had any ties with the Nazi Party's own party intelligence service, the *Auslands Organization*, which Hess controlled.[169] Given that both General Haushofer and his son, plus many others, were connected with the Fellowship, I strongly suspect that this is, in fact, the case.

Why would Hitler himself single out the future Duke of Hamilton for a personal invitation to the 1938 Nuremberg rally? One very significant answer is that the future Duke had been invited "to join a German study group set up by the then Prince of Wales (later King Edward VIII and then the Duke of Windsor), proof at least that his interest in such matters *was well known in*

---

[168] Picknett, Prince, and Prior, op. cit., pp. 145, 148. They also note that Kim Philby was ordered to join this group to report to Moscow. (p. 259)

[169] Ibid., p. 146.

royal circles."[170] . Many Hess Mess researchers also believe that the real reasons for parliamentary pressure on Edward VIII to abdicate was precisely his pro-German stance, rather than his stated intentions to marry the American divorcee, Wallis Simpson. In the case of Edward VIII, later Duke of Windsor, after his abdication and marriage, he and his wife *did* dine with the Hesses at their home in Munich. This important point must be appreciated for what it is, for it is yet another indicator that not only did the Deputy Führer's contacts reach directly into the Royal Family itself, but also because it shows that at least some elements of the Royal Family were indeed favorable to the "peace faction."

There were other prominent members of the various peace groups, and three of them require mention. The first of these is Sir Samuel Hoare, the British ambassador to the sensitive embassy post in Madrid, a post requiring considerable finesse and diplomatic skill since Britain had been a supporter of the Republicans during the Spanish Civil War. Hoare had to overcome this difficulty and keep the fascist, Nationalist Spain of Franco out of the war. A Spanish entry into the war on the side of the Axis would open the country to German and Italian Axis forces, and therefore endanger Gibraltar. The loss of that key British base would unhinge its entire position in the Mediterranean and endanger its lifeline trade to its far eastern Empire, for it would no longer be able to travel through the Mediterranean, but would have to go around Africa, and then *still* be subject to heavy interdiction from Iberia. Additionally, the loss of Gibraltar would allow elements of the powerful Italian fleet to have direct access to the Atlantic. It would have been a loss that would be difficult for Britain to recover from, and perhaps a fatal loss.

In such a circumstance Hoare was the perfect man for the post, for he had no sympathies for Bolshevism, having seen its effects first hand during a posting in Russia during World War One and hence could play to Franco's anti-Bolshevik passions and fears. Hoare had also cultivated personal contacts with Mussolini after World War One, "encouraging him in his anti-Communist activities."[171]

---

[170] Picknett, Prince, and Prior, op. cit., p. 146, emphasis added.
[171] Ibid, p. 87.

Another prominent figure in the "peace faction" was Hoare's friend, Lord Beaverbrook, a Canadian industrialist who had emigrated to Britain.[172] Then there is the head of British foreign intelligence, MI-6, Sir Stewart Menzies, who was also a part of this "pro-peace faction," and who viewed British friendship with Germany as an essential component for that nation to be strong enough to challenge the Soviet Union openly and directly. Menzies' view was entirely cynical, for he knew that both countries would fight themselves to exhaustion (as actually happened) and that whoever emerged as the victor in such a conflict would be in a weakened state, and easier for the British Empire to deal with.[173] Additionally, Menzies had a vast network of contacts and friends in the City.[174] And finally, the former World War One Prime Minister Lloyd George was also a member of this pro-peace faction.

We have previously made reference to the Duke of Westminster, and it is crucial to note his key role in the coordination of these various "pro-peace" factions and groups, for he actually organized the anti-war peers into a powerful lobbying group within the House of Lords. One of these was the Duke of Buccleuch a key figure in the British establishment of that day. His sister was married to King George VI's younger brother, the Duke of Gloucester, More importantly, Picknett, Prince and Prior point out that he was also appointed to be the Keeper of His Majesty's Household in 1937, an appointment that automatically enrolled him as a Privy Councillor. Effectively, the Duke of Buccleuch was George VI's personal liaison to and from the House of Lords. Buccleuch was also part of the pro-German peace faction within the peerage, and obviously, a very powerful one. Buccleuch's views were well-known and it is thus significant that the King would appoint him to that liaising position; the sensitivity of that appointment was acknowledged when Churchill, having come to power by appointment from the same King, removed Buccleuch from his liaison position.[175]

---

[172] Picknett, Prince, and Prior, op. cit., p. 89.
[173] Ibid., p. 91.
[174] Ibid.
[175] Ibid., p. 85.

Consequently, the pro-peace group was hardly non-existent, as some versions of the standard narrative would have it, nor was it a small affair from any perspective, unable to effect any change in British policy or bring down the Churchill government. On the contrary, these various groups and their many networks and connections, leading all the way to the peerage and Royal Family itself, constituted

> ...an enormously powerful upswelling (sic) of opinion that was by no means as unpopular in its day as some historians would have us believe. We have the King, the Queen, the mother of the King, a former Prime Minister and two potential Premiers, a large part of the aristocracy and many of the country's leading industrialists and financiers all sharing the same desire to make peace with Germany. However, although all these different parties wanted to negotiate with the enemy, it was not to be peace at any price. Although they firmly believed that it was either in Britain's or their own best interests not to become embroiled in a war, they were not advocating surrender. Then terms would have to be acceptable, but what could they have been? Obviously they would have varied from group to group. Halifax ... for example, wanted Hitler to be removed from power, whereas other insisted that the safety of German Jews was part of the deal. Others still would probably simply have been happy for Britain to get out of the war in one piece, without giving anything up to Germany. Yet although they had their different variants on the same theme, together they formed one great organic whole, a large and powerful body of opinion highly receptive to offers of negotiations.
>
> Their power can be illustrated by Churchill's riposte, when on 8 June 1940—his premiership just a month old—there were calls for an inquiry into the 'appeasement party' with a view to prosecuting members. He replied that this would be 'foolish' as 'There are too many in it."[176]

Note once again that one of the primary "sticking points" for the British was Hitler himself; it is as if we are looking at a replay of the European Allies after Napoleon Bonaparte's return from Elbe and the "ninety days" of his short-lived "return reign" prior to Waterloo,

---

[176] Picknett, Prince, and Prior, op. cit., pp. 93-94.

when the governments of Austria, Prussia, France, and Russia declared war, not on France, but on Bonaparte himself.

2. Anglo-American Union, Altered Speeches, and Strange Messages

As was seen previously, Albrecht Haushofer made allusion to his fears that an act of union, or a "fusion" as he called it, of the USA and the UK would soon be enacted, and that this meant that any peace mission from Germany had little chance of success. Nonetheless, because of the strategic implications of such a fusion, the mission had to be attempted.[177] Such a fusion was, as I noted previously, always the stated goal of Cecil Rhodes, and his Rhodes scholarships were established as one of the mechanisms to effect this goal.

But Picknett, Prince, and Prior uncover a sliver of evidence to suggest that Albrecht Haushofer's intelligence may have been well-informed:

> Astonishingly, there is evidence that such a union was being seriously contemplated at that time—and that its timing was directly related to Hess's flight. According to White House spokesmen, President Roosevelt was to make a speech to the Pan-American Conference on 14 May 1941 of a 'historic' nature. The White House leaks left the media buzzing with speculation, mostly about the possibility that the President was going to announce the union of Britain and the USA. The respected Washington-based journalist Leonard Engel, wrote:
>
> "I have strong reason to believe Roosevelt will come out in favour of a union of the United States and Britain. He will probably specify the end of the war as the occasion for such a merger of the two great English-speaking nations, but I believe he will suggest an earlier date.
> "I am making a guess, but that guess is supported by a considerable amount of evidence."
>
> Because virtually no one seems to know about this proposal, it is tempting to deny that such a thing was even a possibility. But after the fall of France and before its armistice with Germany, the

---

[177] Picknett, Prince, and Prior, op. cit., p. 136

British government seriously proposed an Act of Union between Britain and France. Not surprisingly, this peculiarly unrealistic notion was rejected out of hand by the French cabinet.

In the event, two days before Roosevelt was scheduled to give his momentous speech—and two days after Hess's arrival—he cancelled it.[178]

Let us pause briefly to speculate a bit further than Picknett, Prince, and Prior have done, based on our earlier reference to the work of Georgetown professor, Dr. Carroll Quigley, and his celebrated underground "conspiracy theory" classic, *The Anglo-American Establishment*.

In that work, Quigley details the "pro Atlanticist-unionists" within the United States and the United Kingdom who did, indeed, seek an actual union of the two countries. In the hands of Cecil Rhodes and his secret society, this was to be based on a *reincorporation of the United States into the British Commonwealth*, i.e., by integrating it back into the British empire system. There was thus, within British aristocracy at that time, not only a widespread "pro-Germany" peace movement, there was also another movement ideologically at loggerheads with this goal, represented by Rhodes and his own deep contacts within the aristocracy that wished for Britain, not to cast its lot with Germany, but with the USA. Churchill was a half-American himself and his ancestral homes included residences near Oxford, where the heart and hub of Rhodes' society and plans, were located. In other words, one may speculate that the tug-of-war within Britain was between a "treasonous" pro-Germany peace group represented by the Dukes of Hamilton, Westminster, Gloucester, Windsor and(as we shall see, Kent) and thus implicating significant swaths of the Royal Family, and a "treasonous" pro-America-unionist or Atlanticist group represented by Churchill and his associations to Rhodes.

In any case, the "peace group," as Picknett, Prince and Prior point out, was actively engaged in sending messages *back* to Hess and the Haushofers, and whoever else that was part of their group.[179] On the 6th of October, 1939, a month after the beginning of

---

[178] Picknett, Prince, and Prior, op. cit., pp. 136-137.

[179] Göring? Army generals? One might include even the possibility of Grand Admiral Räder, since he was opposed to beginning the war any earlier than 1944-

the Second World War, and after Poland was crushed beneath the German invasion, the future Duke of Hamilton wrote a letter to the London *Times*. Initially, the letter had been intended as a *group* effort, since it was to have been signed by various members of Parliament who supported its contents. It was also shown to Prime Minister Chamberlain, who in effect approved of its contents, but who did not wish it to be a group letter for fear it would undermine the efforts of the armed forces. In this original "group letter" version, the future Duke of Hamilton's letter to the *Times* began with the following paragraph:

> We are Members of Parliament, representing all parties and at the same time serving officers in the Royal Navy, Army and Royal Air Force. We believe that we speak for the young men and women of the Empire in saying that Britain has no choice but to accept the challenge of Hitler's aggression.[180]

When the letter was actually published in the *Times*, per Chamberlain's "request," this opening paragraph was removed.

The letter itself, however, coming as it did from Scotland's highest ranking peer, was nevertheless stunning in its implications, and Picknett, Prince, and Prior reprint it in full. As it is a large component not only of their argument, but of mine, I do so again here:

> Sir,
> Many, like yourself, have had the opportunity of hearing a great deal of what the men and women of my generation are thinking. There is no doubt in any quarter, irrespective of any party, that this country had no choice but to *accept the challenge of Hitler's aggression* against one country in Europe after another. If Hitler is right when he claims that the whole of the German nation is with him in his cruelties and treacheries, both within Germany and without, then this war must be fought to the bitter end. It may

---

45, when his planned expansion of the German Navy would have been complete. There is no evidence of Räder ever having been a component of the early anti-Hitler coup groups, but certainly the generals were always wary of the Hitler government, and Göring, as has been seen, hovers uneasily over the Hess Mess in some as yet unknown and undiscovered role.

[180] Picknett, Prince, and Prior, op. cit., p. 148f.

well last for many years, but the people of the British Empire will not falter in their determination to see it through.

But I believe that *the moment the menace of aggression and bad faith has been removed, war against Germany becomes wrong and meaningless. This generation is conscious that injustices were done to the German people in the era after the last war. There must be no repetition of that.* To seek anything but a just and comprehensive peace to lay at rest the fears and discords in Europe would be a betrayal of our fallen.

I look forward to the day when a trusted Germany will again come into her own and believe that there is such a Germany, which would be loath to inflict wrongs on other nations such as she would not like to suffer herself. That day may be far off, but when it comes, then hostilities could and should cease, and all efforts be concentrated on righting the wrongs in Europe by free negotiations between the disputing parties, all parties binding themselves to submit their disputes to an impartial equity tribunal in case they cannot reach agreement.

We do not grudge Germany *Lebensraum*, provided that *Lebensraum* is not made the grave of other nations. *We should be ready to search for and find a colonial settlement, just to all peoples concerned, as soon as there exist effective guarantees that no race will be exposed to being treated as Hitler treated the Jews on 9 November last year (Kristallnacht). We shall, I trust, live to see the day when such a healing peace is negotiated between honourable men* and the bitter memories of twenty-five years of unhappy tension between Germany and the Western democracies are wiped away in the responsible co-operation for building a better Europe.

Yours truly,
Clydesdale[181]

It is important to note the following things:

1) The letter refers to *Hitler's* aggression, not to *Germany's*;
2) The letter recognizes the principle of *Lebensraum*, and further mentions the post-World War One injustices, an implicit way of evoking the "injustices" of the Versailles treaty: when these statements are read together, what it

---

[181] Picknett, Prince, and Prior, op. cit., pp. 143-144, citing the Marques of Clydesdale's Oct 6 1939 letter to the *Times* of London, emphases added.

appears to be saying is that German territorial claims in central Europe would be acceptable to the British *if* it did *not* result in secondary status for non-Germans in those territories of the Reich;[182]

3) Then a curious statement appears regarding "colonial settlements," a strange phrase, especially when following so closely on the reference to *Lebensraum*. The British peace faction could hardly have been ignorant of General Haushofer's understanding of the term, since it had been in open contact with him and his son Albrecht before the outbreak of the war. As we have seen, Haushofer's concept was elaborated in part as a rejection of the imperial policies of the German Empire prior to the First World War, namely, the acquisition of overseas colonies and a large— and to Britain therefore a very threatening—navy. For Haushofer, the *Lebensraum* concept meant eastward expansion of the borders of the Reich to incorporate the resource-rich regions of Eastern Europe and European Russia, not the acquisition of overseas colonies. Thus, while Hitler from time to time had made reacquisition of Germany's lost African and Pacific colonies and bases a matter of public discussion, it was not high on his list of priorities. *Why, then, does a reference to colonies appear in Clydesdale's letter?* As will be seen, this is not an "overly-nuanced" point. It may be one of the most important points in the whole Hess Mess, raising often overlooked questions;

4) Finally, note the reference to the *Reichskristallnacht*, the infamous night when Jewish shops and synagogues were vandalized and burned throughout Germany, and the immediately following sentence referring to "a healing peace negotiated between honourable men." Again, a clear though not explicitly stated signal is being sent: we *are* willing to negotiate with anyone we consider honorable, but that cannot be Hitler. *This means that Hess was willing to negotiate on the "Jewish Question," and implies that **the***

---

[182] Indeed, in the German Empire prior to World War One, Poles were one large minority in the eastern territories of Silesia, Pommerania, and Prussia, and were regarded as full citizens of the Reich.

failure of his mission sealed their fate. This will become a very crucial point, when we finally consider the "Holocaust hypothesis."

Interestingly enough, Hess, while a co-signatory to the Nuremberg Race laws and, as most Nazis were, a thorough-going anti-Semite and believer in international Jewish-Zionist plots, nevertheless protected the Haushofers since Frau Haushofer was one-half Jewish. More importantly, however, it appears that Hess had been appalled by the *Kristallnacht,* and sought to mitigate its harsher measures as leader of the Party; Padfield records that Hess's friends had observed him in despair because of the pogrom, urging Hitler to "stop the outrages, without success."[183] The Marques of Clydesdale's appeal may thus have been a *direct* appeal to parties in Germany that it knew to be quite uncomfortable with the direction Hitler's Reich was taking, namely, the Haushofers, and through them, the connections to the Germany Army, and to Hess himself, whose discomfort with the *Kristallnacht* was probably known to British intelligence, and whose despair over it might have driven him to contemplate an overthrow of Hitler.

3. Was the Peace Plan also a Coup d'Etat Plan?

The future Duke of Hamilton's "peace message" letter in the *Times* was *not*, however, the only channel through which the British "peace faction" attempted to send the message, for the BBC German service *broadcast* the letter the same day.[184] But the message was much more subtle, and here, Picknett's, Prince's and Prior's assessment of this maneuver must be looked at carefully, for it carries huge implications:

> There is another important subtext, however. They were looking forward to a time when they could make peace with 'honourable men'—in which category the peace lobby did not include Hitler. *The implication is that they were only willing to discuss peace if he was replaced as leader.* The letter also makes clear that a

---

[183] Padfield, op. cit., p. 48.
[184] Picknett, Prince, and Prior, op. cit., p. 149.

settlement must take account of the plight of Germany's Jews, but the most important message being sent *is that Clydesdale is to be the contact within the peace group. Should anyone in Germany be willing to discuss these terms they should talk to him. It is therefore clearly aimed at those in Germany who opposed Hitler, into which camp both Haushofers fell.*[185]

This may be one of the most important conclusions any researchers have come to in the Hess Mess, for it implies vis-à-vis an interpretation of Hess's motives and Hess himself, that he either undertook his mission with the intention of dissembling to the British, concluding a peace, and keeping Hitler in power; or he undertook his mission with the intention of participating in the overthrow of Hitler's government, in order to procure a peace with Britain.

While this may seem to be utterly out of character for Hess, whose loyalty to Hitler almost approached adoration and even infatuation, these considerations *do* rationalize another strange occurrence in the Hess Mess: *Reichsmarschall* Göring's apparent foreknowledge of the scheme, his strange telephone call to General Galland, made far too late to shoot down Hess but just in time to cover his own possible role should it ever be discovered. In this respect, it is worth recalling once again that Göring, who had *already* conducted peace negotiations with the British, and who was also viewed as "acceptable," was Hitler's designated successor in offices of *state*, while Hess was his designated representative and successor in the *party*. In other words, there never was a potential "colonels' coup" with more powerful colonels, for between them, Hess and Göring had the power and connections to pull it off.[186]

---

[185] Picknett, Prince, and Prior, op. cit., p. 149, emphasis added.

[186] Picknett, Prince, and Prior also note that General Walther von Reichenau, one of the few "ardent Nazis" within the General Staff, and a very capable tactician, was a close collaborator with Hess in the latter's many political intelligence networks. This gave Hess *entré* and influence in the General Staff that *few* if any other Nazis with the exception of Göring, had. (See Picknett, Prince, and Prior, op. cit., p. 150). It may be that the so-called rivalry between Hess and Göring, while real, has been greatly exaggerated, and perhaps deliberately so, for it would disguise the much deeper ties and agendas that possibly united these two very powerful men.

In any case, recall now that a reply to British inquiries had been sent back to the Duke of Hamilton, via his and the Haushofers' mutual contact, Mrs. Roberts. Here, as Picknett, Prince, and Prior argue, a strange circumstance occurs. The letter reached the Duke of Hamilton in early 1941, and arrangements were process of being made for a meeting between Hamilton and Hess *on neutral territory, namely Lisbon*, as the initial British and German plans suggested. To this end, the Duke had shown the letter to Lord Halifax, who was of the peace party that wanted to see Hitler removed. Halifax, in turn, did *not* share the letter with Churchill(whom, it will be recalled, had been chosen prime minister over Halifax just a few months previously!) However, the Haushofer response letter was also copied and forwarded not only to the Duke of Hamilton, but also, because Hamilton was also an RAF officer, the Haushofer reply was also forwarded to counter-intelligence, that is, to MI-5, which unlike MI-6, was *not* infested with pro-peace party advocates, but, on the contrary, with pro-war "Atlanticist" and "Churchill" elements. When confronted by MI-5 with this letter, the Duke and his powerful backers had to shelve the Lisbon meeting until actual authorization came from Churchill's war cabinet.[187]

In the meantime on the German side, preparations for a meeting continued, and notably, these preparations *utterly invalidate* the notion that Hess decided—on some "crazy lark"—to seize the initiative and like the Mountain going to Mohammed, fly to the Duke of Hamilton and drop in on him unannounced. Quite the contrary: the Nazi Party *Ausland Organization* was busily translating various documents into English, which Hess would eventually take with him on the flight, *and this indicates planning.*[188] Additionally, in early February of 1941, Albrecht Haushofer made a trip to Sweden, and while the purpose of this visit is not known, it is likely it had something to do with the planned negotiations, since his visit coincided with a period when the Duke of Hamilton was on leave from the Royal Air Force.[189]

---

[187] Picknett, Prince, and Prior, op. cit., p. 160. See also pp. 139-141, 142.
[188] Ibid., p. 161.
[189] Ibid., pp. 161-162.

Most importantly and *"at Hess's express bidding"*[190] Albrecht Haushofer had opened negotiating channels to the British ambassador in Madrid, Sir Samuel Hoare. As a result of these preliminary negotiations, *Haushofer and Hoare agreed on the principle that a negotiated peace could not be reached without the removal from power both of Hitler and of Churchill.*[191]

Note what has happened:

1) Albrecht Haushofer was dispatched to Madrid to confer with Sir Samuel Hoare, a man many considered as eligible for the British premiership, on the express orders of Rudolf Hess, Deputy Führer;

2) As a result, Haushofer and Hoare agree on the principle that a negotiated peace—*per Clydesdale/Hamilton's October 1939 letter to the London Times*—cannot take place except between "honourable men," and that this translated into the removal from power of Churchill and Hitler!

In other words, like it or not, Hoare and the men and factions behind him, and Hess and the men and factions behind *him*, are now both involved in *de facto and de jure treason*; the peace plot is now, *by agreed principle*, also an international bilateral *coup d'etat* plot.[192]

There is yet another fact uncovered by Picknett, Prince, and Prior, that indicates just how high-level this meeting between Albrecht Haushofer and Sir Samuel Hoare really was, for in 1959, Albrecht Haushofer's Spanish representative, Heinrich Stahmer, claimed that Albrecht, Hess himself, Sir Samuel Hoare and Lord Halifax himself had planned a secret meeting somewhere in Portugal or Spain in early 1941.[193] If this meeting really did take

---

[190] Ibid., p. 162.

[191] Picknett, prince, and Prior, op. cit., p. 162.

[192] See in this connection the remarks of Harris and Wilbourn, op. cit. p. 252: "As far as the Germans are concerned, this course of action would get over the stumbling block of the Churchill government not negotiating with Hitler; firstly the Churchill government would be replaced, and secondly the replacement would be negotiating with Rudolf Hess—not Hitler."

[193] Ibid., p. 165.

place, then the alleged meeting between Haushofer and Hess on the one hand, and Hoare and Halifax on the other, was most likely a follow-up meeting to iron out more details. The problem is, there is no evidence for it as Stahmer never stated whether or not the four men actually met.

However, citing again the research of Cardiff University history professor Scott Newton, Picknett, Prince, and Prior point out that the Vichy French press did indeed report that Hess *was* in Spain in early 1941. Not only that, but the German press even went so far as to issue a denial of the French story![194] But there's more:

> The British Foreign Office contacted King Carol of Romania— then exiled in Seville—for details. He confirmed that Hess had visited Madrid. Puzzled by Hoare's silence on the presence of such a high-ranking Nazi, the Foreign Office demanded to know if this was true: Sir Samuel's reply is a masterpiece of diplomatic—but curiously transparent—evasion. He said that if Hess were in Spain 'his arrival has been kept remarkably secret and his presence in town is not even rumoured yet.' Most telling of all is that, although the files of correspondence between the Madrid Embassy and the Foreign Office were routinely released to the Public Record Office after fifty years, all the documents relating to the weekend of 20-2 April 1941 have been held back until...

(You guessed it!)

...2017.[195]

Of course, as we've already discovered, by that 2017—this year and the year this book is being written—there will have been plenty of time to remove the occasional embarrassing file, to doctor file equally embarrassing indices of files, and, if necessary, to plant new files and false information.

What might have been discussed at a Madrid meeting of Hoare, Halifax, Hess, and Albrecht Haushofer? Oddly enough, three of these men—Hess, Haushofer, and Halifax—had something in common: they all were deeply disturbed by the policies of the Nazi

---

[194] Picknett, Prince, and Prior, op. cit., p. 165.
[195] Ibid., p. 165.

regime toward the Jews. Haushofer was, of course, himself part Jewish, and because of this, he and his family were under the personal protection of Hess himself. Hess, as we have seen, was in despair over the nation-wide pogrom of the *Reichkistallnacht* in 1938, and Lord Halifax had attempted to initiate discussions in the War Cabinet about providing a Jewish homeland in Western Australia or British Guiana.[196]

4. The Coup Hypothesis, and Hess's University Essay

There is an additional bit of debris that researchers of the Hess Mess usually mention in connection with the "coup" hypothesis, and this is an essay that Hess composed shortly after enrolling in the University of Munch after World War One. As previously observed, the idea that Hess, the Deputy Führer himself, would be involved in a peace negotiation that was also a coup d'etat plot seems, on first glance, to be absurd. But we have also seen that the Hoare-Haushofer meeting, which occurred under Hess's express orders, had made the removal of Churchill and Hitler a *sine qua non* of any further negotiations, and, as Picknett, Prince, and Prior conclude, "it is inconceivable that Hess, as the most high-ranking go-between, was not aware of this."[197]

However, in this university essay on leadership, Hess—already under the spell of Hitler's oratory—outlined what characteristics the future German leader should have. He would have to be severe and ruthless, but notably, once he had succeeded in restoring Germany's power and standing in the world, he would have to stand aside, and allow a more moderate government to assume power. As Picknett, Prince, and Prior point out, in his initial contacts with the British after his capture in Scotland, he indicated that he was *not* speaking for Hitler, but for *Germany*,[198] an obvious and calculated reference, perhaps, to the London *Times* letter of Clydesdale/Hamilton, and perhaps as a reinforcement of the principles of the meeting in Madrid. "As Hitler's secretary in 1925 Hess had also written that he would not always be beholden to his

---

[196] Padfield, op. cit., pp. 47-48.
[197] Picknett, Prince, and Prior, op. cit., p. 500.
[198] Ibid.

Führer. Just as he deemed it necessary for Germany that Hitler should become leader, he might just as easily have advocated his standing down if he believed it to be in Germany's best interests."[199] In this respect they go on to note that the German press, in the weeks and even days immediately prior to Hess's now infamous flight, the Deputy Führer was being given even more attention than usual by the Nazi-controlled German media, stressing his importance to the regime and to Germany.[200] The implication is clear: Hess not only was capable of being involved in such a scheme, but there may have been a quiet, concerted propaganda campaign to prepare the German people for his assumption of power with a more moderate coalition government, perhaps one, as we have seen, including Göring.

With all the careful preparations for a meeting on neutral ground, however, why did Hess finally decide on the far riskier expedient of an actual flight to Great Britain itself, and to Scotland in particular, a flight that as Harris and Wilbourn superbly demonstrated, was fraught with risk, demanding a high degree of planning and technical competence?

Picknett's, Prince's, and Prior's answer to this question is simple, and in terms of their reconstruction of the Hess Mess, quite brilliant: Hess *had* to go to Britain, because his British counterpart, for whatever reason, was unable to meet Hess on "neutral territory."[201]

With this, we now need to deal with yet more debris in the Hess Mess, namely, the bizarre set of anomalies surrounding his *arrival in,* and his planned, but never successfully concluded, *departure from* Britain, and the equally bizarre behavior that he exhibited during his four years in British captivity prior to being brought back to Germany to stand trial at Nuremberg for war crimes, after having missed most of the war!

---

[199] Ibid.
[200] Picknett, Prince, and Prior, op. cit., p. 500.
[201] Ibid., p. 166.

5

"HESS" IN BRITAIN, 1941-1945:
MORE MIND MANIPULATION, DUCAL DILEMMAS, AND DOUBLES DIFFICULTIES

"Though a good deal is too strange to be believed,
nothing is too strange to have happened."
Thomas Hardy, *Personal Notebooks*

RUDOLF HESS PARACHUTED INTO HISTORY over Scotland in the closing twilight minutes of Saturday, May 10, 1941, his mission from that point forward becoming the subject of analysis, speculation, and of course, a baffling secrecy that continues to this day. It should therefore come as no surprise, even though there are a number of publicly-known and available details about his four year stay in Britain, that those details and facts raise more questions than they answer. Quite simply put, the mystery deepens during this period because according to some, it would appear that at some point Hess became "Hess," and a double entered the picture.

It was, of course, W. Hugh Thomas that first proposed the double theory after discovering the discrepancies between Prisoner Number Seven's *lack* of wounds where he thought the real Hess had suffered them. In Thomas' view, the double was substituted during Hess's flight itself; a theory which we have previously discounted. If that is the case, however, exactly *when* was the substitution made, and, more importantly, why?

It is this question that lies at the center of Picknett, Prince, and Prior's meticulous combing and sifting of the known data and facts of Hess's stay in Great Britain. Whether or not one *agrees* with their analyses and conclusions, one **must** contend with them for the simple reason that the interpretation of the total Hess Mess depends upon this point, and changes dramatically depending on whether or not "Spandau Hess" was the Rudolf Hess that took off from Germany. Mere "academic dismissal" of their case and arguments is simply dodging an uncomfortable issue. One must confront it head on.

Their qualification of this period is an apt one, for people "slip in and out of the action"[1] at the oddest points. Or to use a different simile, it is like a Mozart opera, with all the main characters not only slipping in and out of the action, but wearing several masks to boot, constantly in disguise and never appearing as themselves. Indeed, the title of this chapter—"'Hess in Britain"—could easily be the title of an opera or even a part of some Wagnerian operatic cycle: "The Ring of the H's" (the Haushofers, Hess, Hitler, Hoare, and Halifax), with Siegfried being played by a stocky Scotch-and-whiskey-loving, cigar-smoking man who wore bowler hats.

A. Capture and Immediate Aftermath
1. The "Manifestation" of Morris and McBride

No composer or librettist, however, could possibly have put together the story which Picknett, Prince, and Prior uncovered nor made of such a messy plot a plausible structure and argument. They begin their lengthy review of Hess's time in Britain by recounting the standard narrative of the night of Hess's apprehension by the British, and the first days of his captivity. In that narrative, Hess's parachute landed him in a farmer's field, which farmer promptly took Hess captive and held him in his cottage. From there, Hess—who called himself Captain (*Hauptman*) Alfred Horn—was taken into official custody by the Home Guard, and he was moved about from various points until he finally ended up in the Maryhill Barracks in Glasgow. Throughout this entire episode, Hess/Horn insisted he had flown to Scotland to meet the Duke of Hamilton, and constantly requested that he be taken to him. During this episode, the standard narrative also maintains that no one recognized "*Hauptmann* Horn's" peculiar resemblance to Rudolf Hess. Supposedly, his real identity remained completely unknown.[2]

Hess had landed on a farm outside of Eaglesham owned by Basil Baird, just a few hundred yards from the cottage of David McLean

---

[1] Picknett, Prince, and Prior, op. cit., p. 193.
[2] Ibid., p. 194.

and his wife, a farmer and ploughman who took care of the land. The reader will recall that by this point of his flight, Hess was flying his Messerschmitt 110 twin-engine aircraft at full throttle, and very low over the countryside, the engines producing a deafening roar. McLean, hearing the low aircraft and then the subsequent crash, ran outside to see the burning aircraft some distance away, and Hess descending slowly on his parachute. McLean, finding only a pitchfork for a weapon, took the man prisoner.

From here on out everything is a muddle.

Once he was taken prisoner, according to McLean's account, Hess's first words were "Am I on the estate of the Duke of Hamilton?"[3] An early *American* account indicated that Hess later stated to the police and Home Guard that he was on a mission to see the Duke, his original intention having been to land at Dungavel, the Duke's residence which had a small landing strip.[4]

How does one interpret this?

The *real* Hess would have known that the airstrip at Dungavel was simply inadequate to land a Messerschmitt 110. An imposter Hess may not have known this, but as we have seen previously, it was indeed the real Hess who parachuted into Scotland; the difficulties of substituting a double and a plane *ala* the Thomas scenario being too difficult. So why would the real Hess dissemble on this point? The answer has to be that he was protecting someone, or something, or both.

In any case, whatever Hess's first words to the police and Home Guard were, he was taken to the McLean's cottage where Mrs. McLean offered to make him some tea, which Hess declined in good English, albeit with his heavy German accent. At this point, the two soldiers in the McLean cottage who had heard the crash, responded that beer was what they drank in Britain, to which Hess replied that they drank it in Munich, where he came from.[5]

The reader may well ask, "Wait a minute, where did these guys come from and when did *they* get there?" And that is the problem: this is an opera, after all, and McLean never gave any explanation of when the soldiers had arrived. They are just suddenly "there,"

---

[3] Picknett, Prince and Prior, op. cit., p. 194.
[4] Ibid., p. 195.
[5] Ibid., p. 195f.

onstage, participating in the action.[6] Even more interestingly, these two soldiers, Emyr Morris and Daniel McBride, were from a nearby top secret anti-aircraft signals unit.[7]

a. The McBride Anomalies

Soldiers that "suddenly manifest themselves" into the action are not the only anomaly in the early minutes of Hess's stay in Britain, for two years after the end of World War Two, McBride gave his version of the story to the *Hongkong Telegraph*, in which he stated that "high-ranking Government officials were aware of his coming," giving as his reason for this assertion the fact that no air-raid warnings were sounded, nor were the anti-aircraft gunnery control rooms plotting the course of Hess's plane alerted. Then, in a telling statement, McBride states that it was *he*, not Daniel McLean, who first apprehended Hess.[8]

At this juncture, Picknett, Prince and Prior ask the obvious question: if McBride's story about being the first to find and apprehend Hess is true, then why was this information suppressed from the Scottish news reports and only revealed two years after the war, and in Hong Kong at that?[8] McBride then gives *his* version of the "beer remarks" exchanged between them,[9] and then the article continues by stating that his companion from the secret anti-aircraft signals station began to notice that the man looked "familiar." Asking his name, the German pilot gave it as "Alfred Horn," and then, according to the article, he removed from one of his pockets a picture of his wife and son, and reiterated in his German-accented English that he had not come to bomb Scotland, but to see the Duke of Hamilton, emphasizing that his aircraft was not outfitted to carry bombs.[10]

Then follows what can only be said to be a remarkable exchange and event; according to McBride's *Hongkong Telegraph* article:

---

[6] Ibid., p. 196.

[7] Picknett, Prince, and Prior, op. cit., p. 197.

[8] Ibid., pp. 199-200. While space considerations prevent us from posting McBride's *Hongkong Times* article, Picknett, Prince, and Prior reproduce the article, with a much more in-depth analysis, on pp. 199-201.

[9] Ibid., p. 201.

[10] Ibid., p. 203.

(Horn/Hess) asked me to take him to the Duke's home, which, he said, was not far away. *To this I could only reply that I had no power to do so but my superiors would probably do so later on.*

Shortly afterwards there was a commotion outside. The door was flung open and a Home Guard officer rushed in, followed by a number of his men.

The pilot said to the officer: 'I wish to see the Duke of Hamilton. Will you take me to him?'

'You can save all that for the people concerned,' said the officer. 'At present you are coming with me.'

I resented this attitude and protested to the officer that the prisoner was in my charge awaiting an escort from my HQ.

'Are you questioning my authority?' demanded the officer truculently.

'I cannot leave my prisoner, sir,' I said. 'If you take him I must go with you.'[11]

Why the "commotion" and the apparent hostility between the various groups of Hess's captors?

Again, time and space do not allow us the luxury of a complete review of all the subtle details and nuances of Picknett, Prince, and Prior's analysis and argument; suffice it to say that it appears *two factions* were looking for Hess in western Scotland that night: the pro-peace party, which was, of course, expecting him, and another faction representing Prime Minister Churchill and his government which had got wind of the plot (possibly through MI-5's copy of the Haushofer response to Violet Roberts).[12] If so, then at this moment, neither faction has complete or secure control over Hess.

There is one more strange fact about McBride that suggests that even his *Hongkong Telegraph* article was not entirely forthcoming, for after his death, in his papers, a letter from his former commander, W.B. Howieson, dated 8 May 1974, was discovered. It advised McBride in no uncertain terms to "drop this Hess business" lest continued exposure of something to which they had both subscribed to the British Official Secrets Act "stir up a hornets'

---

[11] Picknett, Prince, and Prior, op. cit., p. 203, emphasis added.
[12] See their discussions on pp. 222, 261.

nest."[13] Once again, this draws us nearer to that One Nagging Question that hovers over the entire Hess Mess from beginning to end:

> How could this story 'stir up a hornets' nest' in 1974? Howieson's letter implies that if the seemingly minor point of who captured Hess is admitted, other—much more damaging—information will somehow naturally flow from it, which is presumably why McBride's official report is still withheld. It seems that Howieson knew that something passed between McBride and Hess that night that is not even mentioned in the signaller's papers, which he seems to have been about to make public. Presumably Howieson's words of caution persuaded McBride not to do so. But something significant must have passed between the two, *because Rudolf Hess gave McBride his Iron Cross that night.*[14]

Whatever it was that threatened to "stir up a hornets' nest" that night certainly had the phone lines in Scotland buzzing late that Saturday evening, for shortly after the "commotion" caused by the arrival of the Home Guard in the McLean cottage, and after some transfers from one small local hut to another, its commander attempted to place a call to the local army headquarters to ask for a prisoner's escort. "All the lines were busy," according to Picknett, Prince, and Prior, and this is "another sign that there was a major flap on in the area that night."[15]

One is tempted to offer a reason for the busy phone lines, for if Hess *was* expected, as McBride's *Honkkong Telegraph* article stated, then when he did *not* show up on schedule, this must have provoked a flurry of phone call-conveyed "BOLO" (Be On the Look Out for") alerts, as the peace plan plotters realized the gravity of their situation if Hess should be apprehended by units *not* privy to their plans.

b. The Inventory of What Hess Brought with him: A Strange, and Old, Irish Manuscript?

---

[13] Picknett, Prince, and Prior, op. cit., p. 206.
[14] Ibid., their emphasis.
[15] Ibid., p. 208.

By this time, Hess/Horn was at Giffnock scout hall, where he was finally searched, with an inventory made of his belongings, which included a variety of homeopathic medicines, a syringe, his wife's Leica camera, the calling cards of Karl and Albrecht Haushofer and most likely a letter to the Duke of Hamilton and, presumably, several papers prepared by the *Ausland Organization*. One does not know exactly what this inventory consisted of, for the simple reason that it has never been disclosed,[16] though most accounts do mention the homeopathic medicine.

However, we have seen in our review of Harris and Wilbourn's research that Hess took with him at least one large map, meticulously covered with his own hand-written notes, the so-called Lennoxlove map. Additionally, we have also noted that the *Auslands Organization* also undertook extensive translations of documents into English, presumably for the meeting in neutral country that never materialized. One may assume, therefore, that whatever these documents were—drafts of a treaty based on previous discussions, perhaps?—that Hess brought them with him in his aircraft, and perhaps on his person, to Scotland.

There is also an interesting though unsubstantiated allegation that appeared recently on the Internet, and therefore, *after* Picknett, Prince, and Prior published their research in their book. According to this short article, the ancient Celtic text, the Lebor Feasa Runda, had come to the attention of the *Reichsführer SS*, Heinrich Himmler. The text was part of a larger document, an old Irish text called the Black Book of Laoughcrew.

> The Nazi's [sic] interest in the Lebor Feasa Runa stemmed from the fact that the text mentions a mysterious island called Tir nan'Og that once existed in the Atlantic Ocean and was considered to be the equivalent of Thule, an island they considered to be the original homeland of the Aryan race.
>
> The Lebor Feasa Runda also mentions four great treasures possessed by the Celtic gods which were believed to weild [sic] amazing powers. Convinced that these mystical objects were the equivalents of such legendary artifacts as the Holy Grail, the Spear of Destiny, the Stone of Scone and the Sword Excalibur, Reichsführer Heinrich Himmler sent the Ahnenerbe across the

---

[16] Picknett, Prince, and Prior, op. cit., p. 208.

continent of Europe on a scavenger hunt to acquire these renowned treasures.[17]

The article also notes that the manuscript had been brought to Prague by Queen Elizabeth I's occult advisor and spy, Dr. John Dee during his visit to the court of German Holy Roman Emperor Rudolf II. By the 1930s, however, the article states that it had come into the hands of the Thule Society, whence Himmler's SS confiscated it, presumably after the Nazi assumption of power. From there, it made its way into the archives of the SS *Ahnenerbedienst*, the SS's secret "archeology and occult research bureau," whence the manuscript disappeared, supposedly on the day of May 10, 1941, the day of Hess's flight. The article also states that an "old book" had been seen by "a young man by the name of John Peterson" among the items inventoried with Hess, who said he intended to present it to the Duke of Hamilton as a gift.[18] An English translation of the text, which allegedly also deals with the ancient practices and belief system of the Druids, was made by Heinrich Thorensen, a German army officer and linguist on assignment to the *Ahnenerbe*.

While there is no substantiation within the article for these allegations, it is worth noting that it is diplomatic custom, especially during negotiation or during state visits to present one's host, or negotiating party, with a gift, and an ancient Celtic manuscript, especially one brought from England to Prague by John Dee, would be a highly appropriate gift to bring. More importantly, it is to be remembered that Himmler himself, later in the war, would also attempt to conduct his *own* peace overtures to the Western Powers, using many of the same intermediaries and channels. It is thus not necessary to assume that Hess, himself a general in the SS, stole the manuscript from under Himmler's nose. If the allegations in the article are at all true, it is much more probable that Himmler was a party to the peace-and-coup d'etat

---

[17] "The History of the Lebor Feasa Runda," http: leborfeasarunda. weebly.com/history/html. I would like to deeply thank my friend and colleague Walter Bosley for bringing this important bit of information to my attention.

[18] "The History of the Lebor Feasa Runda," http: leborfeasarunda. weebly.com/history/html.

plot, since it is well known that Himmler entertained notions of replacing Hitler, and his own later peace initiatives were conducted with that in mind. It is thus also probable, if this speculation be true, that Himmler's *later* peace proposals grew out of his possible and very covert participation in the Hess Mess, where, as we have seen, the *sine qua non* of any negotiated peace in the West was the removal of Hitler from power.

c. Major Graham Donald Identifies Hess by means of Another Absurd Conversation about Beer

Returning to Picknett, Prince, and Prior's analysis, they next concentrate on Major Graham Donald's role. Donald was an officer in the Royal Observer Corps, and sat on the board of directors of the Glasgow-based company, Graham & Donald Ltd., a machine-tool company. Donald's version of meeting Hess on the night of May 10, 1941, appeared in the Observer Corps' journal in October 1942, almost a year and a half later. Major Donald claimed to have been alerted to the crash of Hess's aircraft and set off to find the scene. He arrived at the farm and the McLean's cottage prior to Hess having been moved, and followed the entourage to Giffnock where he questioned Hess. There, Donald also records that there was a tension in the air because of the presence of a Polish officer.[19]

According to Donald, Hess then repeated what he had told others, namely, that he was on a mission to Britain, that his destination had been Dungavel and the Duke of Hamilton. At this point, Hess allegedly produced his flight map and showed Major Donald a red circle around Dungavel, clearly marking the Hamilton residence. Donald then turned the conversation to Munich and its good beer, the second time—they note—that the conversation has turned to the absurd, for Donald then goes on to assert that Hess reacted very disapprovingly at the mention of beer. Donald concluded that he was a teetotaler, and since there were only two teetotalers in the upper echelons of the Reich—Hitler and Hess—and since the man in front of him obviously was not Hitler, he had to be Hess![20]

---

[19] Picknett, Prince, and Prior, op. cit., p. 209.
[20] Picknett, Prince, and Prior, op. cit., p. 210.

This is, of course, a long way to go—around Harvey's Barn once again—to explain an obvious thing by unobvious and completely absurd deductive processes, for Hess was a familiar face in newsreels of the period; one had only to look at him and see that it was Hess, or at least, a close facsimile thereof. One did not need absurd explanations about "teetotalers in the Nazi regime."

2. Anomalies:
Glaring Absences, and a Polish Officer Talks to Hess

There are other odd anomalies that occur in the very first hours and days, in the "first act" of "'Hess' in Britain," anomalies that point consistently to the idea that Hess, or at least, *someone* high ranking in the Nazi hierarchy, was arriving. One of the most glaring examples is the Hess Mess version of the Sherlock Holmes "dog that didn't bark in the night." One of those glaringly non-barking dogs in the night was the fact that *the Messerschmitt 110 was a two-man aircraft, and that there was no search on the night of May 10-11 for a second crew member.*[21]

There is yet another glaring absence that night. We have already seen that Hess dressed in the *Luftwaffe* uniform of a captain, and hence, for all his initial captors knew, Hess *was* a *Luftwaffe* pilot. Yet, on that night and contrary to *all* standard procedure, the Royal Air Force was kept carefully excluded from the initial encounters with the "officer."[22]

The most peculiar "non-barking-dog" that night, however, is that there are two very divergent accounts of where the Duke of Hamilton himself was. The Duke, after all, was the very individual whom Hess and his backers had hoped to contact. However, according to the standard narrative that was eventually to evolve, Hamilton received a call about the mysterious visitor in the middle of the night in his capacity as an R.A.F. operational commander, and promptly went back to sleep. But not so, according to a story from the Glasgow *Herald* of May 16, 1941, a story that appeared *prior* to the finalizing of the standard narrative, for according to it, the Duke of Hamilton did meet Hess, along with members of the

---

[21] Ibid., p. 214.
[22] Ibid., p. 215.

Foreign Office and unspecified intelligence services while the latter was being transferred to a hospital to treat the sprain in his ankle that he had sustained after parachuting into Scotland. Nor was this story merely unsubstantiated rumor, for Hamilton's wife confirmed that after receiving the phone call, the Duke departed, and did not return home until the afternoon of Sunday.[23]

Another strange event that night was the mysterious appearance of a Polish officer, Roman Battaglia, at Glasgow Police Headquarters to interrogate Hess. Battaglia was an intelligence officer to General Sikorski's Polish government-in-exile, and proceeded to interrogate Hess for two hours, unsupervised, and in German, which, again, is highly unusual, since no one else present during this session spoke German![24] This suspicious incident, as will be seen, is a crucial component to Picknett's, Prince's, and Prior's scenario of what was happening that night, and why.

In any case, the reactions of the R.A.F. in breaking its standard protocols for the interrogation of German pilots, the strange two hour session with Battaglia, the Glasgow *Herald* article, all point to the conclusion the Hess—or *someone*—was expected that night. Indeed, the daughter of one observer corps officer, Nancy Moore, was told by her father that though he was breaching his security procedures, the pilot was none other than the Deputy Führer himself.[25]

We have seen that Harris and Wilbourn, through careful analysis of the technical features of the Messerschmitt 110, concluded that the small airstrip at the Duke of Hamilton's residence at Dungavel could *not* have been Hess's landing target that night. For many, this ends the speculative scenario that Picknett, Prince, and Prior have carefully pieced together and argued. They opined, instead, that one of the local R.A.F. airfields alone had landing strips adequate to handle the landing (and takeoff!) lengths required for a Me 110.

However, I do not believe that Harris and Wilbourn's reconstruction does any damage to Picknett's, Prince's, and Prior's larger scenario at all. To see why, one must review their conclusions

---

[23] Picknett, Prince, and Prior, p. 215.

[24] Ibid., p. 213.

[25] Ibid., p. 219.

and reconstructions very carefully and closely, for they realize that such an elaborate plot would have factored in the need for contingencies from the very beginning:

> From start to finish the story of Hess's arrival and capture looks like one of the most serious indictments of British military—and intelligence—incompetence ever recorded. It is littered with bungling, indifference and blatant dereliction of duty, often by top men, and in a crisis—a matter of national security. If that is a fair summary, then perhaps it is understandable why the authorities should try to bury the whole thing and forget it ever happened. But if it isn't a case of wide-ranging ineptitude, *we can only understand all the anomalies in terms of quite another scenario.*[26]

This, of course, is true, for the standard narrative asks us to believe that the British military and intelligence services, among the most competent in the world, suddenly took leave of their senses and reason on the night of May 10, 1941, and only in Scotland!

In their scenario, the Duke of Hamilton represented that peace faction that was in a position to assist on the British end, both with the particulars of Hess's flight and landing, but also on the particulars of the scheme itself. This would explain, in part, the obfuscation of when the Duke of Hamilton actually met with Hess. But because the flight had gone wrong and Hess had to bail out, not being able to find his targeted landing area—Dungavel in Picknett's, Prince's and Prior's scenario, and nearby airbases of the R.A.F. that could accommodate his Messerschmitt 110 In Harris's and Wilbourn's—the plan had gone wrong at a crucial juncture.[27] That juncture, as we saw, was the point at which Hess failed to make contact with the beacon signal at point "C," and had to retrace his steps, using both critical *fuel* and critical *sunlight* he needed to identify landmarks once over Scotland. As we also saw, Hess made landfall a few miles *south* of his intended landfall target, according to the reconstructions of Harris and Wilbourn. *Note, however, that the change of landing target* does not really collapse the larger scenario of Picknett, Prince, and Prior.

---

[26] Picknett, Prince, and Prior, op. cit., p. 220, emphasis added.
[27] Ibid., p. 220.

What went wrong was that Hess, in making landfall at the wrong point and behind schedule, set into motion a cascading series of errors that meant that he was apprehended *by the Home Guard*, in other words, by "outsiders" who were *not* part of the plot having become aware of the arrival of the Deputy Führer. In this respect, they point out that Hess himself attempted to correct the situation by repeatedly insisting that he wanted to see the Duke of Hamilton.[28] At this juncture the necessity of a contingency plan, in case something went wrong, becomes active; they argue that on the British side, there would be a contingency if in fact Hess was unable *to land at his designated site, which,* in Picknett's, Prince's and Prior's scenario, is Dungavel, the Duke's residence. However, *it is crucial to note that this would have been the case, on the British side, **regardless** of what the actual target landing site was.* Their overall scenario *does **not*** collapse simply because one detail may be off.

In fact, as they also convincingly argue, the idea of a contingency also rationalizes *Hess's* response to his initial situation in the United Kingdom, for he "would have been viewing each new arrival on the scene as a potential ally, but how was he to tell a friend from a foe? Presumably some form of password would have been pre-arranged, which would account for the surreal rerun of the conversation about German beer..."[29]

This scenario also rationalizes, in a way that other considerations of the Hess Mess do not, the manner in which the Duke of Hamilton responded, for the Deputy Führer was in the custody of those *not* part of the scheme. Hence their immediate problems were twofold: they had to gain custody of him, or somehow communicate to him. This consideration, in their opinion, explains the odd appearance of a *Polish* intelligence officer of the Polish government-in-exile, Roman Battaglia, conversing with Hess in German for two hours, while no one else present at the time understood German or was present with Battaglia and Hess when the conversation was held (or, at least, so we are told!).

Finally, there is the problem of the Duke of Hamilton himself: peer of the realm and an officer in the Royal Air Force. At any juncture after his involvement in the proceedings, he could have

---

[28] Picknett, Prince, and Prior, op. cit., p.. 220.
[29] Ibid.

"pulled rank enough to take charge of Hess,"[30] so why didn't he? The answer is evident from the implications and outlines of the plot itself: the *British* component of the conspiracy was not acting under orders or sanctions of the government; it was *Churchill's* government after all, and as has been seen, one of the previously agreed-upon principles of both parties was that Churchill and Hitler both had to go. But Hess had already fallen into the hands of those *not* involved in the scheme. Hence, Picknett, Prince, and Prior conclude that the British side of the plot was now "engaged in a damage-limitation exercise: too many people were now aware of the mystery airman who kept asking for the Duke of Hamilton. Sooner or later questions would be asked, and Churchill would get to hear of it."[31] At the very minimum, the British component of the plot had to *assume* this, whether or not it had actually happened, lest not doing so, it would misstep.

Another consideration has raised questions about their scenario, and it is worth briefly mentioning it, for again, this author does not believe it damages Picknett's, Prince's, and Prior's overall scenario.

In some versions of the Hess Mess, there is a "reception party" supposedly waiting at Dungavel for Hess's arrival. Some argue that a reception party at Dungavel makes no sense simply because (once again) Hess's Messerschmitt 110 could never have safely landed on its small airstrip, and the implication that might be drawn from this is that no such party existed. I contend, however, that the existence of such a party at Dungavel does *not* invalidate their scenario, but rather, strengthens it, for such a reception party makes sense simply from the protocols of the situation itself. But why wait at Dungavel? The answer is that it would be the logical place to gather, whether or not Hess's intended landing site was there, for from there they could proceed with the Duke—an RAF officer—to Hess's intended RAF landing site, or arrangements may have been made to bring Hess from his landing site to them. This reception committee was composed of Red Cross officials, which in effect made their environment neutral territory, plus representatives of General Sikorski's Polish government-in-exile. The significance of

---

[30] Ibid., p. 221.
[31] Picknett, Prince, and Prior, op. cit., p. 221.

this point will be explained in due course, but it does rationalize why a Polish officer was able to converse with Hess in German unsupervised.[32]

3. *Telegrams, Coville's Strange Statement, and the Marx Brothers*

According to the "standard narrative," the Duke of Hamilton did *not* see Hess until *ordered* to do so on the morning of May 11, 1941, at 10 A.M. at the Maryhill Barracks, and was not supposed to have known his actual identity, the implication of which is that the Deputy Führer's arrival was already being discussed.[33] As we have seen, however, the Glasgow *Herald* gave indication that there might have been a prior meeting between the Duke and Hess.

In any case, the standard narrative has it that after the Sunday morning meeting, the Duke then contacted London to apprise Prime Minister Churchill of his arrival, and then immediately flew south to meet Churchill personally at Ditchley Hall—Churchill's secret wartime country residence—and apprise him of the development. This was supposedly done after dinner that night, May 11, 1941. The next day, Churchill ordered Ivone Kirkpatrick to Scotland in order to identity the prisoner. Kirkpatrick served in the Foreign Office, had been in the British Embassy before the war, and personally knew Hess.[34]

While all of this is going on, something very important was *not* happening in Germany. As has been seen, in a plot such as this, contingency plans, passwords, and so on, would have been worked out in case something went wrong (which it very much did). Equally, however, it would have been necessary to work out a contingency for the *German* side of this conspiracy, to indicate a safe arrival of Hess in Britain. It is worth noting that in his contact with Hamilton, Hess *did* make the unusual request that a telegram be sent to an aunt in Zurich (one Emma Rothacker), an obvious "signal that he had arrived safely."[35] This message, more

---

[32] Picknett, Prince and Prior, op. cit., p. 286.
[33] Ibid., p. 224.
[34] Ibid., p. 223.
[35] Ibid., p. 226.

importantly, was to have been delivered via the Red Cross, which again invokes the presence of Dr. Burkhart. The telegram, of course, did not arrive.

It is worth pausing to consider this point in more detail, and I am not aware that anyone else investigating the Hess Mess has advanced the following extremely speculative scenario concerning the telegram's "non-arrival." The non-arrival itself was also, of course, a predetermined signal, indicating that something had gone wrong, and that the "plan" was "off." But assume, for a moment, that the telegram *had* been sent, and assume also that (1) Hitler had some knowledge, but not *full* knowledge, of the scheme, and (2) that the component of the scheme he did *not* know about was a putative plot to overthrow *him* and install a government more acceptable to the British. One may argue that for Hess to participate in such a plot and yet to conceal its true purpose, that Hitler had to have been made aware of the intended flight, and its ostensible purpose to conclude a peace with Great Britain, which Hitler certainly favored. *Including Hitler in the plot to partial knowledge was, in essence, essential to its success.*

However, the telegram—which Wolf Rüdiger Hess maintained that his mother insisted was intended for her, which she would have then conveyed to Hitler(!)[36]—was actually, on the view that the scheme was a plot to overthrow *both* Churchill's *and* Hitler's governments, a *double* signal, which Hitler, *unknowingly, would then have revealed to his senior hierarchy, Göring among them, signaling that the moment had come for his overthrow.*

When the telegram *did not* arrive, Hitler flew into his tirade— an act, if one is of the view that Hitler knew of the flight beforehand—and Göring, as we have seen, put on another act and pretended to know nothing about the whole thing, even though he also "covered his tracks" by ordering General Galland to shoot Hess down, long after it was even possible to do so!

While this (possible) circus was taking place in Germany, things would have been no less messy on the British side, for the Duke of Hamilton, on *his* account of the events, made no attempt to contact London until the afternoon of May 11th, *after* he had seen Hess and after he had visited the crash site of his Me 110. When he did

---

[36] Picknett, Prince, and Prior, op. cit., p. 226.

contact London, he phoned the Permanent Under-Secretary at the Foreign Office, Alexander Cadogan. Cadogan, however, was away, and a heated exchange occurred between the Duke and another official who refused to put a call through to Cadogan without knowing the reason. Fortunately, perhaps, for the blood pressure of both men, Churchill's private secretary, John Colville suddenly showed up, and the call was given to him![37]

If one suspects that Colville's arrival at this precise juncture is a little too much like a badly written libretto, just wait, for Colville and Hamilton both wrote accounts of this incident, which "make somewhat odd reading, not least because of the extraordinary discrepancies between them."[38] In the Duke's account, Coville is alleged to have stated that the Prime Minister ordered him to the Foreign Office because the Duke had "some interesting information" to convey.[39]

Coville's account, however, is pure Mozart.

According to *his* version published in 1985, his very first words to the Duke of Hamilton were "Has somebody arrived?," a statement that suggests that "he, at least, was expecting a certain 'somebody.'"[40] But his explanation for *why* he expected a "certain 'somebody'" is pure farce, for he claimed to have been thinking "unaccountably" of a novel by Peter Fleming—and yes, that's the brother of Ian Fleming, the author of the James Bond novels—titled *Flying Visit*, published in 1940. In the novel, Hitler *himself* parachutes into Great Britain, whereupon he has some "adventures" which include "winning first prize in a village fête fancy-dress competition"![41] More importantly, in his version, the conversation between him and Hamilton took place in the morning and not, as Hamilton maintained in *his* account, in the afternoon. Why concoct such a silly tale? In Picknett's, Prince's, and Prior's opinion, it was because his first question "gave the game away."[42]

---

[37] Picknett, Prince, and Prior, op. cit., p. 226.
[38] Ibid., p. 227.
[39] Ibid.
[40] Ibid.
[41] Ibid.
[42] Ibid.

In any case, phone calls *were* made, and the Duke of Hamilton *did* fly to have dinner with Churchill at Ditchley Hall. It was after dinner that Hamilton briefed Churchill, when

> Churchill uttered words that have become the stuff of legend: 'Well, Hess or no Hess, I'm going to see the Marx Brothers.' This insouciance is usually taken to show the true bulldog spirit at its best. Deputy Führers may fall out of planes, but old Winnie is so unimpressed that he calmly watches Groucho and the gang as planned. However, as with much else in this story, Churchill's words might not have meant quite what they seemed.[43]

Who were the "Marx brothers"? This was not a reference to a film, but rather, a code that Churchill used with the Duke of Hamilton to refer to the Royal Family, and in particular, the brother-princes of King George VI.[44]

B. From the Tower to Maindiff

Much of Picknett's, Prince's, and Prior's work is concerned with a very careful reconstruction and analysis of Hess's stay in Great Britain, based on the work of David Irving and others, and a careful analysis and well-argued speculation on what the various moves meant. Accordingly, it is simply too lengthy to be reviewed here. There are, however, certain features of these moves that must be mentioned. As has already been seen, Hess was eventually brought to the Tower of London under conditions of extreme secrecy, where he remained briefly, during which period he was drugged, and measured for a duplicate of his *Luftwaffe* uniform. From there until June 25, 1942, Hess was held at Mytchett Place under very tight security. Here, all accounts agree: Hess's mental and emotional behavior appeared to deteriorate dramatically, with Hess claiming he was suffering from amnesia, unable to recall the circumstances of how he had come to be captive, and even at times unable to recall prominent features of his life and family.

On June 25, 1942Hess was moved to Maindiff Court in Wales. This move, however, occurred with *no military escort*. Hess was

---

[43] Picknett, prince, and Prior, op. cit., p. 229.
[44] Ibid., p. 285.

simply driven to Maindiff minus any of the normal security one would assume a prisoner of his stature merited. The reason for the move appears in part to have been because the British learned of a plot by the Polish government-in-exile to try to kidnap Hess.[45] Oddly, however, in spite of this apparent threat, news of Hess's transfer and location was carefully leaked to the *Daily Mail*, a national tabloid published a further article on his life in captivity in September 1943.[46]

Yet in early May, 1942, SS *Obergruppenführer* Reinhard Heydrich circulated a report to Foreign Minister von Ribberntrop stating that his agents had placed Hess in *Scotland* at the same time that according to the standard narrative he was supposed to be in Mytchett, soon to be transferred to Maindiff.[47] According to Peter Padfield, this report was generated by contacts between one of his agents and a Briton who had contact with an influential circles in Great Britain, which one may reasonably assume to be the "peace group" Hess came to see. According to the report,

> The Englishman stated that in December last year he had spent four days in London with Hess at his (Hess's) express with with the approval of Churchill. Hess was housed in a villa in Scotland, had his personal servants and wanted for nothing. Churchill had expressly decreed that Hess, on account of his rank as *SS Gruppenfürer*, should be accommodated as a general. On the agent asking whether the Englishman had the impression that Hess was, perhaps, somewhat mentally confused, he received the answer that the Englishman had not gained this impression.[48]

The rest of this report has an incredible element, for far from being imprisoned in the Tower of London, Heydrich's report states that the Englishman had Hess driving around London under escort. These features lead Padfield to conclude that the report may have been part of an intelligence deception campaign.[49]

---

[45] Picknett, prince, and Prior, op. cit., pp. 353-354.

[46] Ibid., p. 355.

[47] Ibid., p. 356.

[48] Padfield, op. cit., p. 28of, citing R. Heyrdrich to *Reichsaussenminister*, 4 May 1942, F & CO 434005, Annex, pp. 1-2, 434006-7.

[49] Padfield, op. cit., p. 288.

But like everything else in the Hess Mess, the report is capable of more than one interpretation depending on the scenario one is arguing. For Picknett, Prince, and Prior, the Heydrich report poses a much more significant problem, for if one assumed that its basic premise that Hess was in Scotland was true, then "what was going on at Maindiff Court? If he was not there in the period between June 1942 and October 1945, what about the carefully stage-managed 'public appearances': the drives in the country, the picnics and the walks?"[50]

Their answer, simply, is that the fact that the "Hess" who returned to Nuremberg in 1945 *lacked* the proper scaring from World War One war wounds means that at some point during his stay in Britain, a double was substituted for the real Hess, who remained, in their view, in Scotland.

Thus, on their view, the drugging sessions "Hess" underwent, particularly after his arrival at Maindiff in Wales, were mind-control sessions, to create the necessary "memories" in the double and to test their resiliency under drugged interrogation.[51] Recall, in this respect, not only "Hess's" own strange statements in this regard, but his peculiar behavior at Nuremberg, and American intelligence mandarin Allen Dulles own suspicions. One may add an additional speculation here: why did the British build an entire "Hess suite" at their military hospital in Berlin? One answer might be that an elaborate, and secure, facility was needed to conduct any memory "reinforcement" mind control sessions that a double may have required. In this respect, the strange visit of Wolf Rüdiger to Spandau, and his father's equally strange behavior that caused the visit, should be borne in mind.

This hypothesis has its difficulties, not the least of which, as Picknett, Prince and Prior admit, is persuading a double to accept the real Hess's fate,[52] yet, this difficulty disappears if, indeed, sophisticated mind-control techniques were employed on the double. In any case, a double *does* appear to have been planted, and very early on at that. This rationalizes a number of things, including the strict prohibition of taking pictures of "Hess" while he was in

---

[50] Picknett, Prince, and Prior, op. cit., p. 356f.
[51] Ibid., p. 364.
[52] Ibid., p. 368.

captivity, plus the duplicate uniform. Indeed, Fraser-Smith, the man whom we saw was tasked to create this uniform, entertained doubts about the identity of "Hess."[53]

There is other anecdotal evidence to support this hypothesis, for Picknett, Prince, and Prior indicate that a Scots Guards member, who was a member of Hess's guard detail, asserted Hess was in the Tower of London, and had been taken to secret meetings with Churchill in late June 1941. This story of secret meetings between Hess and Churchill were corroborated by RAF military police. The problem is, these meetings took place while "Hess," according to official accounts, was at Mytchett Place.[54]

Politically, there could be any number of reasons for the creation and substitution of a double, from the need to protect the real Hess from assassination, kidnapping, or rescue attempts,[55] to the need of the Churchill government to present a façade that "Hess was cooperating" with the sitting British government and not trying to topple it.[56]

C. Ducal Difficulties, Royal Protection and Reception Committees

The various versions of the double hypothesis—from Thomas' to Picknett's, Prince's, and Prior's—also raise a very different question: If a double was indeed inserted into the opera in Britain, then what happened to the *real* Hess?

In my estimation it is here that Picknett, Prince, and Prior have offered the most complete scenario, one that makes the most sense of the most data points in the whole Hess Mess, and which, in turn, raises in even starker relief that as yet One Unstated Question. The key to this scenario is one very significant fact: when Hess realized

---

[53] Picknett, Prince, and Prior., p. 370.

[54] Ibid., p. 371.

[55] Ibid. They note that the rumored Polish kidnapping or assassination plot, one of the ostensible causes of Hess's move from Mytchett Place to Maindiff Court, may actually have been a *rescue* attempt. This fits with the composition of the "reception" committee that was in Scotland to meet Hess, some of which was comprised of representatives of the Polish government in exile. As we shall discover, the likelihood of such an attempt grows once one knows the full scope of their scenario.

[56] Ibid.

his situation and that he had fallen into the hands of people who were *not* part of the scheme, he repeatedly stated that he had come, and was under, "the King's personal protection," and repeatedly insisted that messages be taken directly to George VI.[57]

In other words, the Crown itself may have been one component of the British "peace faction" with which Hess had been indirectly negotiating.

In this respect, Picknett, Prince, and Prior make mention of a bit of information that came from a "confidential source" in Britain's Ministry of Defence, who had high-level contacts with the Foreign Office. Like all information from anonymous contacts, it should be evaluated accordingly. However, this bit of information is so significant that it must be mentioned. Their contact, whom they codenamed "Alexander," was asked about Hess's claim to be under Royal Protection. His answer concerned a British colonel named Pilcher, whom the Royal family had ordered to be held incommunicado at Balmoral Palace from 1941 to his death in 1970. Why had Pilcher been subject to such a "palatial prison"? Because according to "Alexander," *Colonel Pilcher had signed "a letter of safe conduct in the King's name."*[58] This, as they point out, would explain a great deal about the apparent confusion on the night of Hess's capture, for if he indeed had on his person a letter of safe conduct, what were the apprehending authorities to do? Was the letter fake? Was it real? As we shall see in a moment, the possibility of such a letter *does* rationalize the mysterious presence of the Polish officer Battaglia that night.

For the moment, however, one must inquire whether or not there is any corroborating fact of royal involvement in the scheme at such a high level; was the Crown itself possibly involved.

There does appear to be one intriguing fact that would indicate Royal family interest in such a negotiated peace with Germany, beyond Edward VIII, the Duke of Windsor's, own personal friendliness toward the Nazis. This is the fact that the Queen Mother's brother, David Bowes Lyon, was a member of the Anglo-

---

[57] Picknett, Prince, and Prior, op. cit., p. 263.
[58] Ibid., p. 266f., emphasis added.

German Fellowship,[59] an organization also heavily suffused with peers and other members of British high society.

All of this brings us finally to Picknett's, Prince's, and Prior's masterstroke: the relationship of the Hess Flight to the death of the Duke of Kent, King George VI's younger brother, in a tragic air crash in Scotland in August 1942. The Duke of Kent was urbane, sophisticated, multi-lingual, and most importantly, functioned as a kind of *personal* intelligence officer to his brother the King, and had personally met and dined with Hess, Rosenberg, and Ribbentrop before the war.[60]

He was also allegedly a member of the "reception committee" waiting at Dungavel for Hess's arrival, along with representatives of the Polish government in exile and the international Red Cross. With the mention of the Poles, we arrive at one crucial element of their scenario, for they point out that the head of the Polish government in exile had *offered the throne of Poland—long vacant—to the Duke of Kent.*[61] The presence of the Poles in the reception committee thus is logical from two points of view: (1) the Poles would *have* to have been involved in any general peace settlement between Britain and Germany, because of the former's guarantee and the latter's military occupation of the country, and (2) in this author's opinion, because the offer of the Polish throne to the Duke of Kent may have been a *component* of the peace plan previously negotiated between Hess and his British counterparts; for the Germans, the Duke would have represented an acceptable head of state for any reestablished Polish rump state. This now rationalizes why a *Polish* officer was allowed to speak to Hess for two hours in German without supervision. One may even speculate that, perhaps, he was a personal liaison from the Duke of Kent.[62]

All of these things suggest additionally that the "peace plan's" details were already worked out in considerable depth; Hess, in other words, had come not to *continue* negotiations, but rather, to "finalize" the deal. This also explains another fact previously

---

[59] Picknett, Prince, and Prior, op. cit., p. 264.

[60] Ibid., pp. 276, 277.

[61] Ibid., p. 286.

[62] Ibid., p. 284f.: They also point out that in the records that speak of meetings between Hess and "the Duke" that in some cases this may *not* be the Duke of Hamilton, but the King's younger brother, the Duke of Kent.

mentioned: the strange and sudden decline in the intensity of the two countries' bombing campaigns against each other.[63] It had become a "second phony war."[64] *This near cessation of intense bombing suggests once again that not only was there coordination between the British and German sides surrounding Hess's peace mission, but that Hess and Göring were both involved in the plot. This idea was confirmed by Hess himself in his statements to Churchill's representative, Ivone Kirkpatrick, for he stated that "he and Göring were working to the same agenda."*[65]

We have seen that at some point, a "double" is created and makes his appearance in the opera. But this does not resolve yet another problem, for as we have seen, the *real* Hess was in the hands, not of the "peace party" but of Churchill's government.

Enter the Duke of Kent.

Picknett, Prince, and Prior recount the story of Evelyn Criddle, whose father was related to the Earl of Pembroke, a relationship whose significance will be evident in a moment. According to her story, when she was a little girl she spent time near Maindiff Court in Wales, and saw a "very tall man" whom her father told her was Rudolf Hess. The only problem was, Hess was not in Maindiff Court itself, but in a small house nearby owned by the Herbert family, i.e., by the Earl of Pembroke![66] The real problem, however, is not the apparently "bi-locating" Hess, but that Hess was in the home of the Earl of Pembroke. Why is this significant? Because the Earl was "the *equerry to the Duke of Kent,*"[67] a point that indicates that the "peace party" *had regained control of the real Hess.*

---

[63] Picknett, Prince, and Prior, op. cit., p. 323.

[64] Ibid., pp. 324-325. It should be noted, however, that there was another problem as far as the British, and later, the American bombing campaigns were concerned, and this was the extensive network of radars, anti-aircraft guns, and fighter air defense coordination that Germany had constructed in Western Europe that was making bomber losses too high even for nighttime raids. This system had to be degraded sufficiently for the bomber offensive to have any real hope of success, and this degradation did not really begin to show its signs until 1943. This system was so effective that the British staged a commando raid on the coast of France in 1942 to literally *steal* one of the German radar equipments in order to learn its secrets and to aid in the air defense system degradation campaign.

[65] Ibid., p. 315, emphasis added.

[66] Picknett, Prince, and Prior, op. cit., pp. 373-374.

[67] Ibid., p. 374, emphasis in the original.

The real Hess was apparently returned to Scotland, where he was seen in 1942 by Robin Sinclair, the Lord Thurso, in 1942, while "Hess" stayed in Maindiff Court.[68] According to Thurso, Hess was quartered in Braemore Lodge. At this juncture, the Duke of Kent and his tragic flight enter the picture.[69]

On the 25th of August, 1942, the Duke of Kent took off in a Short-Sunderland flying boat, allegedly on a good-will flight to visit British troops stationed in Iceland. Tragically, his aircraft crashed on a rocky crag in Scotland known as Eagle's Rock. The Duke was killed, becoming the first member of the Royal Family to die in military service in five centuries.

However, it appears that the Duke may *not* have been flying to Iceland, but rather, that this was a cover story. For one thing, the Duke's flying boat, curiously, was painted *white*, the color for aircraft flying to and from neutral *Sweden*,[70] suggesting that Sweden, not Iceland, was the destination. After all, a flight from Scotland to *Iceland* would be unlikely to encounter hostile *Luftwaffe* aircraft. A flight to *Sweden*, however, easily could.

There is another anomaly, however, and that is by careful consultation and comparison of various records, there appears to have been an unaccounted-for body on the Duke of Kent's aircraft, a body, moreover, that it appears that King George VI himself personally made inquiries about when he visited his younger brother's crash site.[71] Additionally, the flight plan itself has disappeared, and the weather service personnel on the east coast of Scotland were sworn to secrecy and forced to sign Britain's Official Secrets Act. Why the weather personnel on the east coast of Scotland? Because the Duke of Kent's aircraft had taken off from the east coast and not, as one would expect for a flight to Iceland, the west coast.[72]

---

[68] Ibid.

[69] Again, space simply does not permit a thorough review of the Duke of Kent's flight. This is one of the most fascinating and meticulously researched and detailed components of Picknett's, Prince's and Prior's reconstructions, and they subject the Duke of Kent's final flight to a very thorough and intense analysis from pp. 377-408.

[70] Ibid., p. 423.

[71] Picknett, Prince, and Prior, op. cit., pp. 406-408.

[72] Ibid., p. 423.

It seems reasonable to conclude along with Picknett, Prince and Prior that the Duke of Kent perished in a flight that was designed to return the *real* Hess to Germany via Sweden, a country through which Göring had conducted his own peace discussions. Whether the Duke was acting out of the protocols of war and returning an envoy who had come under a flag of truce, or was flying on to Germany to complete final arrangements in the deal, or was simply removing Hess from imminent danger from Churchill's government, is unknown.[73] I suspect that the Duke's flight was about more than mere chivalry, but in any case, they are correct to note all the *other* possibilities for his flight, because like everything else in the Hess Mess, it is open to interpretation.

There is one final and quite disturbing possibility about the Duke of Kent's flight. Noting that the memorial in Scotland erected to him and his companions on the flight reads that they were "on a special mission,"[74] they also produce a cable from the German Ambassador in Portugal to his boss, von Ribbentrop, in the German Foreign Ministry. The subject of the cable was the Duke of Kent's death in the crash of his flying boat:

> As the Embassy has learned, confidentially, the death of the Duke of Kent has been discussed recently in the innermost circles of the British Club here. The gist of the talk being that an act of sabotage was involved. It is said that the Duke, like the Duke of Windsor, was sympathetic towards an understanding with Germany and so gradually had become a problem for the government clique. The people who were accompanying him were supposed to have expressed themselves along similar lines, so that getting them out of the way would also have been an advantage.[75]

Similarly, General Sikorski, head of the Polish government in exile and who had offered the Polish crown to the Duke of Kent, also died, mere months later, in July 1943, in an air crash off Gibraltar.[76]

In other words, two principal players had been eliminated, Hess himself and the Duke of Kent, and with them were removed key

---

[73] Ibid., p. 434.
[74] Ibid., p. 387.
[75] Picknett, Prince, and Prior, op. cit., p. 434f.
[76] Ibid., p. 417.

components of the possible peace plan—the Duke of Kent as proposed Polish monarch, and Hess as acceptable replacement for Hitler—had been removed from the equation. Additionally, a very serious message had been sent to the King and Royal family, one indicating that further interference would not be acceptable. And finally, of course, the head of the Polish government in exile might also have been "taken out." Everyone who could talk about the "details" of the plan—many of which have not *yet* been discussed, were eliminated.

D. A Short but Necessary Final Tangent: The Hess Flight and the Rise of Martin Bormann

There is a final aspect of Hess's flight, one that, unusually, is not considered by the main Hess Mess investigators, but which is normally only mentioned in books *not* concentrating on Hess's flight. That aspect is the relationship of Hess's flight to the rise of Martin Bormann, for Hess, of course, was replaced by Bormann as the head of the Nazi Party itself, when Hitler abolished the office of *Stellvertreter* (Deputy) and made Bormann Party *Reichsleiter.*

This has caused some, such as William Stevenson, to view Bormann as a hidden architect in the affair, not so much participating in the Hess-Göring scheme, as simply encouraging Hess to undertake the mission as a purely selfish political maneuver to remove Hess from power and allow Bormann to advance himself into the powerful position of commanding the party hierarchy.[77] In Stevenson's hands, Hess was the gullible fool, and Haushofer the "crackpot genius" that was used by the master manipulator Bormann to manipulate Hess.[78]

This, as we have seen, relies far too heavily on the *post-flight* "narrative" that Hess was a fool, insane, weak, and stupid. As we have seen, he was anything but. Additionally, one gets the measure of Hess the man because it was Hess who spotted Bormann's unique "talents" and promoted him to the post of being his personal secretary, the "deputy" of the Deputy Führer.

---

[77] William Stevenson, *The Bormann Brotherhood: A New Investigation of the Escape and Survival of Nazi War Criminals* (New York: Bantam Books, 1973), p. 52.
[78] Ibid., p. 53.

If anything, what emerges from this is that Bormann probably knew, along with Göring and Hitler, that his boss intended to fly to Britain to conclude secret peace negotiations. What Bormann and Göring also possibly knew that Hitler did *not*, was that those negotiations perhaps included a plan, not only for the removal of Churchill's government, but of Hitler himself. This turns the narrative of those who believe Bormann played Hess in order to advance his own personal power on its head, for had *Hess* become the head of state, or even retained his role as head of the party in a non-Hitler government, Bormann's power would in all likelihood increased beyond what it did under Hitler.[79]

It is in this context that I believe one must examine another fantastic allegation of Stevenson, namely, that Bormann may have had Heydrich assassinated. He notes that Heinrich "Gestapo" Müller and Walter Schellenberg both thought that Bormann was behind Heydrich's death.[80] If so, then I doubt this was simply a personal maneuver to get rid of a powerful rival, for as we have seen, Heydrich kept a close watch on the Hess affair and was attempting to track his movements in Britain, making his reports to Ribbentrop's Foreign Ministry, *and thus by-passing Bormann in the Party headquarters*. If Bormann *was* involved in a plot with Hess (his boss) and Göring to conclude a peace with Britain at the cost of overturning Hitler, sooner or later, Heydrich would have discovered it. Under such circumstances, Bormann had to act, and under such circumstances probably did so with Göring's full knowledge and consent.

As a final note in the Hess Mess, it should be observed that Bormann took over the Hess compound south of Munich in Pullach, which, of course, eventually became the actual head-quarters of the Gehlen Organization of German intelligence after the war.[81]

The reader will, of course, have been asking himself a significant question throughout this chapter and, indeed,

---

[79] Bormann's big rival was, of course, Göring, who hated him and who recognized his "talents" for removing and eliminating rivals in the Nazi hierarchy.

[80] Ibid., p. 59.

[81] Stevenson, op. cit., p. 113.

throughout the book thus far: does *any* of this *really* explain the vast amount of secrecy surrounding the Hess Mess?

Does a secret peace plan and coup-plot between elements of the British peerage and the Royal Family on the one hand, and powerful elements of the Nazi hierarchy like Hess and Göring, and possibly Bormann as well, *really* explain that secrecy to this day? In the contemporary cynical atmosphere toward political institutions and leaders, are we surprised that the Royal Family or elements thereof, or the British nobility, or Nazis, would be kept secret simply to save any of them or their memories potential embarrassment?

As has been outlined thus far, is such a plot *really* weighty enough to warrant secrecy to this day, Royals or no Royals?

I would contend that it simply is not, and that the biggest question in the whole Hess Mess of doubles, covert operations, planned coups-d'etat against Churchill or Hitler or both—*what is the Big Secret?*—remains unanswered, and that to appreciate the reason that London and Berlin both went into a tailspin of panic has yet to be answered. The trouble is, no one *can* answer it.

All we have is speculation, and a few clues in the statements and research of the principals, to which we shall add our own dataset. What emerges is something horrifyingly grandiose, and grandiosely horrifying.

Left to Right: Martin Bormann, Rudolf Hess, and Willi Ley

H.R.H. Prince George, Duke of Kent (1902-1940)

6

SACRIFICES, SURRENDERS, STATEMENTS, AND STATES

"... after one of the Berlin crises, the Western Powers should have immediately declared that now they also no longer felt bound by the agreements with the Soviet Union on joint responsibility for Spandau. But, as it is, they never made such a declaration. On the contrary, the Western Powers continued to emphasize the Four-Power agreement on Berlin of 1972... the Four Powers again reaffirmed their intention to maintain their joint responsibility for Germany and Berlin, i.e., including Spandau."
Wolf Rüdiger Hess[1]

"To deal with these peoples, thus regarded as only semi-human, Lanz recommended variously: ...deportation to Madagascar; enslavement, incineration as a sacrifice to God; and use as beasts of burden."
Joscelyn Godwin[2]

O NE OF THE MOST OBVIOUS BITS OF DEBRIS in the whole Hess Mess, and therefore, one of the most *overlooked* things about the Hess Mess because of that very obviousness, is the fact that for four decades and two years after the end of the Second World War, through all the vicissitudes of the Cold War including the Cuban Missile Crisis, the four powers, even as they were on the brink of nuclear war with each other, remained oddly united about the matter of Rudolf Hess; though the ICBMs might fly and hydrogen bombs might burn and fallout flake down in a deadly rain, Hess—or his double—had to remain imprisoned at Spandau.

To put that astonishing consideration in simpler terms: Prisoner Number Seven transcended the momentary Cold War confrontations and geopolitics, and this fact alone suggests the immensity of whatever secret lies buried in all the debris of the Hess Mess.

---

[1] Wolf Rüdiger Hess, *My Father Rudolf Hess* (1986), pp. 303-304.
[2] Joscelyn Godwin, *Arktos: The Polar Myth in Science, Symbolism, and Nazi Survival*, p. 49.

When put this way, the implication follows that whatever the secret is, all four powers knew it, or, knew at least a *part* of it, and were thus complicit in... "something."

It might be objected that at the time of the Cuban Missile Crisis that Hess, or his double, was not the sole remaining Nazi in Spandau Prison, and this is true. But this only highlights *another* glaring problem, namely, that Grand Admiral Karl Dönitz, the actual legal head of state and government at the end of World War Two, had been in Allied custody since its end. Yet, they had taken no steps to ensure that *he personally* signed any document of the surrender of the German state itself, nor any document outlawing the Nazi Party. After his death, this left only Speer—released the same day as Dönitz—and "Hess" as the last remaining individuals who could have any legal claim to any offices of the Reich, and between the two, "Hess," as we have seen, held far more official posts both within the state and, as Hitler's Deputy, the Nazi Party. Yet, no effort was undertaken to tidy up the legal niceties, and that indeed may have been the point: so long as "Hess" was alive, those niceties remained to connect the modern German state to the previous one in an unbroken chain of legal ties dating—if one wanted to assemble the mountain of documentation to sustain the argument—all the way back to the Holy Roman Empire. Perhaps, for whatever reason, the Four Allied Powers wished to break that link entirely.

The peculiarities of the surrender of the Nazi Party (or rather, the lack thereof) notwithstanding, the uneasy fact is that "Hess" remained a point of odd and anomalous unanimity among the Four Powers even at *other* moments of heightened tension during the Cold War, long after the other Spandau Nazis were dead.

The One Question, in other words, does not disappear with these considerations; they only serve to emphasize its immensity. In this connection, it will be recalled that "Hess" himself stated to his nurse, Abdallah Melaouhi, that if the Soviets reversed their veto on his release, then the British, at least, would murder him, and it is unlikely that the Soviets would not have known this. Their offer was thus quite cynical, given the fact that it was the *Soviets* had who had pressed for the death sentence for "Hess" at Nuremberg in the first place.

His death itself, and its timing, also forms part of the mystery, for it is as if "Hess's" death was the agreed-upon signal to flip a switch, for within half of a decade of his death, the leaders of three of the countries that had stood guard over him—Gorbachev, Reagan, and Thatcher—were gone; Reagan's vice president, George Herbert Walker Bush, whose father had his own odd connections to the Nazis, was President; Germany was reunified, and within months, Czechoslovakia and Yugoslavia were broken up; Margaret Thatcher was ousted from her premiership and from the Conservative Party leadership, fulminating against the growing signs of a European Union from the back benches, warning of the dangers of a common currency and the loss of British sovereignty.

Lest any connection between the Hess Mess and the sudden and dramatic fall of Mrs. Thatcher seem to be stretching a point, Picknett, Prince and Prior revealed that during their contacts with their anonymous whistleblower "Alexander," the latter had mentioned that the Prime Minister's personal secretary, Ian Gow "had told Hugh Thomas that in return for the latter's dropping of his allegations that Hess was murdered, the government would be prepared to admit that there was *doubt about the identity of the prisoner.* We were able to confirm this."[3] That corroboration came in the form of an appearance of Thomas on Dutch television in 1998, where he stated that a group of "Tory Dry"[4] members of Parliament had approached him, claiming to represent Mr. Gow and wanting to "clear the cupboard of skeletons" first.[5] Thomas, of course, refused to drop his murder allegations and the negotiations ended. Perhaps one should not be surprised that Mr. Gow was murdered by a car bomb a few months later, with the murder, which remains unsolved, said to be the work of the IRA.[6] While there might be many possible motivations for Mr. Gow's murder, the Hess Mess must remain as one of those possibilities.

Like all dark operas, however, the last analytical act is usually the most dramatic and foreboding.

---

[3] Picknett, Prince, and Prior, op. cit., p. 487, emphasis added.

[4] Tory "Dries" were the right wing of the Tory Party and more or less the wing of the party solidly backing Mrs. Thatcher.

[5] Picknett, Prince, and Prior, op. cit., p. 487.

[6] Ibid., p. 488.

A. Israel, Hess, and the Grand Dame of Conspiracy Theory
1. The Israelis and Hess

While Picknett, Prince, and Prior have done yeomen's work in filtering, examining, and analyzing a veritable mountain of details of the Hess Mess and constructing one of the most comprehensive scenarios, it is Peter Padfield who has analyzed details that suggest new twists to their own scenario of Royal involvement with Hess's peace plan, and their corollary scenario of a possible international and bi-lateral coup d'etat plot against Churchill and Hitler. Padfield's analysis, when integrated with theirs, and with additional information uncovered by this author in the 1980s and disclosed in a previous book, gives hitherto unknown—and horrific—depths to the Hess Mess, and begins to approach a real basis from which to rationalize all the secrecy, obfuscated data, and "removed files."

The core of Padfield's analysis integrates the other great tragedy of World War Two—the Holocaust and the so-called "Jewish Question"—into the parameters of Hess's peace plan. In this respect, it is worth pointing out a few details that that strongly suggest this factor not only is in play, but may be a principal element.

Other researchers, however, have uncovered indicators of a relationship to Hess's peace mission and the so-called "Jewish Question." For example, Picknett, Prince, and Prior point out that the government of Israel made numerous requests to Great Britain to be able to interview "Spandau Hess" about his peace proposals. These requests were always refused.[7] One may, of course, speculate as to why these refusals were made. If "Spandau Hess" was a double, there was a risk that the Israelis would discover this, and this discovery would in turn ignite inquiries about what had happened to the *real* Hess, and when, and why. If "Spandau Hess" was the real Hess then this might jeopardize a much larger secret, which I will advance in this chapter for the first time.

Wolf-Rüdiger Hess went further, stating that during the Camp David accord meetings in September, 1978 between President Jimmy Carter, Egyptian President Anwar Sadat, and Israeli Prime Minister Menachem Begin, that Begin allegedly privately and

---

[7] Picknett, Prince, and Prior, op. cit., p. 499.

secretly warned Carter that "Hess" must not leave Spandau alive. Wolf Hess records no source for this allegation, nor does he indicate whether or not Begin communicated the *reason* for this solemn warning to Carter or not.[8] As will be seen, the speculative scenario I will offer in this chapter might explain, in part, why such a warning might have been made, if indeed Wolf Hess's allegation is true.

It was Wolf Hess who was the first researcher who thought that there was a connection between "the Jewish Question" and his father's peace mission:

> As is known, my father presented Churchill with the plan for a world peace conference. Perhaps the European Jewish Question was to be solved at this meeting as well. For years, Germany had had an interest in the emigration of as many Jews as possible. Due to the Haavara Agreement, which enabled Jewish emigrants to transfer their entire fortune—albeit only to Palestine—emigration was no problem. In 1939, however, the British had imposed strict quotas on the immigration of Jews into Palestine—a country which did not even belong to the British—and restricted such immigration to wealthy Jews only. So the Haavara Agreement saw to it that Jews with insufficient wealth could get a loan large enough for them to meet the immigration criteria so that they could leave Germany nevertheless. And in fact, Jews left Germany for Palestine as late as 1941. (This is proven, for example, by Werner Feilchenfeld,*Haavara-Transfer nach Palästina*... Tübingen, 1972...) Despite that, the stubborn anti-Jewish attitude of the British hampered Germany's plans and incidentally does not shine a very positive light on British policies with respect to Jews. It is not impossible that my father was to negotiate with the British on this issue.[9]

Obviously, Wolf Hess's statements should be taken cautiously, for whatever British policies may have been towards its Jews, it certainly was not rounding them up, shipping them to camps, forcing them to work exhausting hard labor on a starvation diet, gassing them to death, and cremating them!

---

[8] Wolf-Rüdiger Hess, *Who Murdered My Father, Rudolf Hess?*, p. 156.
[9] Ibid., p. 158.

Or... did Wolf Hess perhaps *suspect* something, a deeper story? There *is* a deeper story, one outlined by Peter Padfield, but as we shall now discover, even that story has a much deeper root than anyone ever imagined.

2. Hess, Halifax, Hamilton, Chamberlain, Churchill, the Reichskristallnacht, The Balfour Declaration, and the "Jewish Question"

Padfield notes that Hess, as the "Conscience of the Party," lived up to his nickname. During the planning for the "Night of the Long Knives," Hitler's abrupt counter-coup and murder of Ernst Röhm and other top leaders of the SA, it was Hess who, according to witnesses, could be heard arguing with Hitler behind closed doors, insisting that this or that name on Hitler's death list be spared. After the Night of the Long Knives, Hitler's brutality had aged Hess by several years, and even changed his signature. Hess's stomach problems and insomnia date from this time.[10] It was, in Padfield's estimation, the first of two major "psychic shocks" to Hess's system.

The other was the nation-wide pogrom against Germany's Jews, the *Reichskristallnacht*, which had a similarly profound effect on Hess. Padfield states that "The oppositionist von Hassell recorded in his diary how Hess's old Munich friends, the Bruckmanns, had told him of Hess's despair at the nation-wide pogrom; he had been depressed 'as never before' and beseeched the Führer to stop the outrages, without success."[11] Interestingly enough, Lord Halifax, an alleged member of the British "peace faction" which Hess was trying to contact on the night of his infamous flight, was similarly disgusted by the pogrom. Halifax initiated a discussion in the cabinet to try to help Germany's Jews. The idea of a Jewish homeland inevitably occurred, and even though the British had a mandate in Palestine, this solution was rejected for fear of angering the region's Arabs. Western Australia and British Guiana "were considered briefly as possible Jewish homelands."[12]

---

[10] Padfield, *Night Flight to Dungavel*, pp. 32, 33.
[11] Ibid., p. 48.
[12] Ibid., pp. 47-48.

Later, with war looming, the Chamberlain government actually published a White Paper on the Jewish Question in May 1939. In the paper, the Chamberlain government outlined a proposal for Palestine to become an independent state in ten years[13] with the population ratio of Arabs to Jews to be carefully regulated at a ratio of two to one, with initial Jewish immigration to be limited to 75,000 people for the first five years, and after that, no further immigration without Arab consent. Churchill, appealing to the Balfour Declaration of 1917, "denounced this blatant propitiation of the Arabs as a repudiation of Balfour's pledge to the Zionists, which it was."[14] Nonetheless, Parliament approved the plan.

The Balfour Declaration itself may be one of the shortest yet most explosive political documents in history:

Foreign Office, November 2nd, 1917

Dear Lord Rothschild,

I have much pleasure in conveying to you on behalf of His Majesty's Government the following declaration of sympathy with Jewish Zionist aspirations, which has been submitted to and approved by the Cabinet:

"His Majesty's Government view with favour the establishment in Palestine of a national home for the Jewish people, and will use their best endeavours to facilitate the achievement of this object, it being clearly understood that nothing shall be done which may prejudice the civil and religious rights of existing non-Jewish communities in Palestine or the rights and political status enjoyed by Jews in any other country."

I should be grateful if you would bring this Declaration to the knowledge of the Zionist Federation.

Yours sincerely,
Arthur James Balfour[15]

---

[5] It is interesting to note that the timing was unusually accurate in one respect, for Israel was recognized as a nation in 1948.

[14] Padfield, op. cit., p. 49.

[15] Robert John, *Behind the Balfour Declaration: The Hidden Origins of Today's Mideast Crisis* (Costa Mesa, California: Institute for Historical Review, 1988), p. 28.

For our purposes, what is to be noted is that the British branch of the Rothschild family was functioning as the intermediary between the British government and Zionist organizations.

Foreign Office,
November 2nd, 1917.

Dear Lord Rothschild,

I have much pleasure in conveying to you, on behalf of His Majesty's Government, the following declaration of sympathy with Jewish Zionist aspirations which has been submitted to, and approved by, the Cabinet

His Majesty's Government view with favour the establishment in Palestine of a national home for the Jewish people, and will use their best endeavours to facilitate the achievement of this object, it being clearly understood that nothing shall be done which may prejudice the civil and religious rights of existing non-Jewish communities in Palestine, or the rights and political status enjoyed by Jews in any other country"

I should be grateful if you would bring this declaration to the knowledge of the Zionist Federation.

The Balfour Declaration

The Zionist movement cast a wide net of influence prior to and during World War One[16] and this network of influence continued up to World War Two, and included prominent Nazis in its network. Padfield, for example, points out that none other than Adolf Eichmann visited Palestine in November 1937, with the express purpose of visiting Zionist leaders there, four months after the Peel Commission had published its recommendations. This commission was yet another British government study on Palestine. It recommended dividing the region into two states, a Jewish one in the north, and a larger Arab state in the south. The Zionist leaders in Palestine "told Eichmann that if the English showed an inclination to postpone partition, the Jewish defence organisation would open hostilities against them. They further said they were delighted by the 'radical' German Jewish policy which would drive more Jews to emigrate to Palestine and give them a majority over

---

[16] Robert John, op. cit., pp. 50-51, 54. John notes that, peculiarly, the central executive of the Zionist organization was in Berlin, and that it had memberships throughout Eastern Europe, the bulk of its membership strength being in Austria-Hungary and Imperial Russia. This state of affairs moved Chaim Weizmann, who would later figure so prominently in the affairs of the state of Israel, to locate provisional executive offices in the USA. This was done, with prominent Jewish-Americans formally becoming a part of this committee, including US Supreme Court justice Louis Brandeis, Felix Frankfurter, and the famous Rabbi Stephen Wise, who would later organize the pre-World War Two Jewish boycott of Nazi Germany. Both the European and American branches of this movement viewed Tsarist Russia as their principal target during World War One, while continuing to lobby both the Western Allied Powers and the Central Powers for the creation of a Jewish homeland. Henry Morgenthau, for example, became a major contributor for President Wilson's campaign, and was rewarded by an ambassadorship to Turkey. (John, op. cit. p. 53). Later, of course, he became Franklin Roosevelt's Treasury Secretary, and a feature of the bearer bonds scandals, as well as authoring the notorious "Morgenthau" plan for the sterilization of Germans after World War Two, and the breakup of Germany into three smaller, agrarian states. While Zionists in Britain lobbied through Lord Rothschild for a Palestinian Jewish state, their counterparts in Berlin during World War One dangled the prospect of a puppet Turkish government in front of Berlin, a new market for German goods, in return (again) for a declaration in favor of a Jewish homeland in Palestine, and soliciting friendly declarations for this purpose from the German Foreign Ministry. Konstantin von Neurath drew up such a declaration, and it was signed by then Reich Chancellor Theobald von Bettmann-Hollweg in 1915. (John, p. 54) Von Neurath, of course, was one of "Hess's" fellow prisoners in Spandau Prison, and was the German Foreign Minister from 1932-1938, and Reich Protector of Bohemia from 1939-1943.

the Arabs within foreseeable time."[17] Eichmann's visit was not without fruits, for noted scholar Christopher Simpson records that an arrangement was made between the Zionist guerilla-terrorist organization Haganah and the SS, with the latter actually providing funds to the Zionist organization in return for intelligence on British activities in Palestine.[18] The Zionists, in other words, were prepared to deal with anyone, even the sworn enemies of their own people, if it served to advance their cause.

What emerges from this is a pattern, both on the Zionist side of the equation, and on the Great Powers side of the equation, of a concerted interest in having an established Zionist-Jewish state. In the interwar period, several versions of the "international Zionist-Socialist" conspiracy raged, not only on the continent of Europe, but in Great Britain as well, where the "grand Dame of conspiracy theory," the scholarly but erratic Nesta Webster, influenced the peace-circles which were connected to the Duke of Hamilton.[19]

3. Lord Victor Rothschild, MI-5, the Communists, and Colonel Pilcher Again

Unfortunately, these ideas of international Zionist-Socialist conspiracies were not entirely unfounded. Before World War Two, Lord Victor Rothschild became a member of a Cambridge secret society called the Apostles society, a group enamored of Communism ostensibly because of its "scientific Marxist" views. But Rothschild had unusual friends in this society: Anthony Blunt and Guy Burgess—two of the notorious "Cambridge Five," the five moles for Soviet intelligence in British society, government and intelligence.[20] One researcher actually believes that it was Victor Rothschild who was the unknown "fifth man" in the notorious spy ring, and who actually recruited Philby, Blunt, MacLean and Burgess. It was, for example, Rothschild who joined MI-5's counter-

---

[17] Padfield, op. cit., p. 50.

[18] Christopher Simpson, *Blowback: The First Full Account of America's Recuitment of Nazis and Its Disastrous Effect on our Domestic and Foreign Policy* (New York, Collier, 1988), p. 253.

[19] Padfield, op. cit., p. 45

[20] Padfield, op. cit., p. 271.

sabotage division in 1940, and then sponsored his friend, Blunt, into MI-5.[21]   Much more importantly, Victor Rothschild may have exercised influence via the Churchill government to have Colonel Pilcher neutralized and, effectively, internally exiled.[22] Pilcher, it will be recalled, was on the King's personal staff, and allegedly wrote the cover letter for Hess granting Royal protection.

It is with Colonel Pilcher that Padfield's scenario really begins, for the mysterious British colonel apparently communicated a note to another 1970s Hess Mess researcher, De Courcy, outlining what the Hess mission had really been all about. Here it is necessary to cite Padfield extensively, and his citations of De Courcy's note about Pilcher. According to Padfield, Pilcher's note to De Courcy

...suggested that Hess came over with the knowledge of the *Abwehr* chief, Admiral Canaris, and the real object was to topple Hitler. This runs counter to everything known about Hess's character and his blind loyalty to the Führer... The note continued:

"Hess had become alarmed about the war and coming Nazi excesses. He believed a total reversal of strategy and policy to be essential. He had heard stories that Queen Mary, the Duke of Windsor, the Dukes of Westminster and Bucclech, the Marquis of Londonderry, Lords Halifax and Rushcliffe, Basil Liddell Hart and R.A. Butler thought so too.

"His idea was the evacuation of France, Belgium, Holland, Norway and Denmark, peace with England and placement of the Jews to Palestine...

"War with Russia would however be prosecuted."

The *Special Office Brief* went on:

"It was that factor which aroused the profound anxieties of the pro-Russian Party in Britain which brought vast pressure upon Churchill to stifle the whole project.

Before continuing, note what is really being said here: the "pro-Russia" party is that faction that Picknett, Prince, and Prior, and

---

[21] Ibid., p. 272.
[22] Ibid., p. 273.

other Hess Mess researchers, have called variously the "Churchill party" or "Churchill clique." Indeed, this was its name among Hess and his German co-conspirators. But this party, we now note, is comprised of a certain circle within MI-5, with direct ties to Victor Rothschild, whose family was pro-Zionist, and who sponsored at least one later-known Soviet mole—Blunt—into MI-5, and who was certainly suspiciously associated with the rest of the Cambridge spy group of Burgess, MacLean, Blunt, and Philby. We continue with the citation of Padfield:

"One man threatened to leak the facts—Colonel W.S. Pilcher... commanding the Grenadier Guards at Windsor. He was dealt with, relieved of his command... and thereafter ordered to Scotland. He lived the rest of his life a virtual recluse until he died in 1970... His exit from a former social life was remarkable..."

In a confidential memo headed 'Colonel W.S. Pilcher, de Courcy expanded on the aim of toppling Hitler:

"When Hess arrived Pilcher learned something at (sic) his mission which, to a limited extent, fitted into his opinions—at least it was clear that Germany could be turned East, would reduce in the West to a substantial extent and that as Germany became weaker powerful elements within the armed forces and upper classes would turn against Hitler.[23]

This isn't even second-hand dead man's testimony, but fourth-hand dead man's testimony, with the ultimate and penultimate sources, Hess and Pilcher respectively, both long dead. We are thus dependent on a claim about the peace plan that runs from Hess to Pilcher to de Courcy and finally to Padfield.

Nevertheless, there are certain features to note here: Hess's peace plane was also

    1) A comprehensive peace plan that included all of Western Europe's German occupied territories in France, Belgium, Holland, Luxembourg, Denmark, and Norway; in return for

[23] Padfield, op. cit., p. 274f.

2) A British guarantee of a German free hand in Eastern Europe; and,
3) A *Jewish homeland* component.

In this, Hess's plan does not vary with other researchers' conclusions except in two details: the Jewish homeland component, and, here for the first time, the mention of *Norway*, which, as we shall see in part two, carries further deep implications.

Given what Padfield himself already noted about Hess's character, namely, that he appeared to suffer psychosomatically from Hitler's brutality toward his enemies during the Night of the Long Knives, and later, during the *Reichskristallnacht*, it is *not* in my opinion unlikely that Hess would have participated in a coup d'etat against Hitler. As was seen in previous chapters, the peace plan mission has all the hallmarks of being a simultaneous coup plot in London and Berlin.

But with the addition of Padfield's information, one may speculate *why* such desperate measures were being considered in Germany and Britain, for note that the coup plotters, both British and German, were attempting to *provide a Jewish-Zionist homeland, whereas the government they were trying to overthrow in London was opposed to this measure, and the government in Berlin that they were trying to overthrow was prepared to pursue extermination of Jews in the absence of a peace with Britain and a Jewish-Zionist homeland.* In this respect, it should be noted that Churchill himself believed that the influential American-Jewish lobby was highly successful in mobilizing support for America's entry into World War One,[24] and thus, from his point of view, could be influential in doing the same in World War Two. To pursue a peace with Germany at the expense of throwing the Soviet Union to the Nazi wolf would only activate those influential lobbies against his government and the British Empire, for those lobbies were, as noted previously, very pro-Soviet.

Padfield, let it be noted, believes that wholesale extermination of Jews was the intention of the Nazi leadership *ab initio*, and that the various "homeland" proposals, such as Eichmann's proposal for a Jewish-SS (!) state in Madagascar was simply a propaganda ploy to

---

[24] Padfield, op. cit., p. 68.

lull Europe's Jewish population into inaction. He cites the fact that long before there was a continent-wide organization of extermination and genocide machinery—the notorious "Final Solution" machinery decided upon at the notorious and infamous Wannsee conference in early 1942—that there were local exterminations and atrocities against Jews.[25] Indeed, it should also be remembered that Hitler conceived operation Barbarossa and the invasion of the Soviet Union as a genocidal war against what he viewed as the Great Power that was home, host, and shelter to the international "Bolshevist-Jewish conspiracy."[26]

However, the standard view that the Final Solution was only given the 'Green light" after 1942 may not be so easily dismissed, for it also cannot be denied that the machinery of a continent-wide genocide was not completely enacted or authorized until *after* it became clear that a negotiated peace settlement with Britain was no longer possible.

These two views—that (1) local extermination activity presaged the later organized continent-wide activity, and that the latter was *planned*, and (2) that the plan was activated when a homeland option was no longer feasible—need not be mutually exclusive. For the German peace party, including Hess, it was likely that they knew of the extermination plans, and knew that they would be

---

[25] Padfield, op. cit., p. 79.

[26] Nor should it be forgotten that Hitler apparently "changed his mind" between the publication of *Mein Kampf*, in which he advocates a Jewish homeland in Madagascar or other place, and the actual beginning of the war in the east. By that time, Hitler came to hold the opinion that a "Jewish homeland" would only become a kind of Jewish Vatican, a sovereign entity playing home and host to various conspiracies all around the world, and taking special advantage of the "dual status" this would confer. Under such circumstances, it is clear that the "extermination option" was favored by Hitler. But in this regard, it should also be recalled that *Hess* was largely responsible for those passages in *Mein Kampf*— which was also his title for Hitler's "memoirs"—that dealt with questions of geopolitics. The homeland solution was favored by his mentor, General Haushofer, whose wife, let it be recalled, was half Jewish. I therefore do not have difficulty believing that Hess's "homeland" views conflicted with Hitler's growing tendency to favor genocide, and that this would possibly have led Hess to the crisis of conscience and participation in a wider plot against Hitler, in order to stave off the genocide.

activated come what may, unless a peace could be concluded that would allow the anti-Hitler factions to topple his government.[27]

Lest this anti-Hitler faction be thought to be a fiction, recall that the brother to the famous author of the James Bond spy novels, Peter Fleming himself, authored a spy novel that was published in 1940 during the height of the German bombing of Britain. In this novel, it will be recalled, Hitler himself parachutes into Great Britain. There is some truth to this novel, for Padfield records that

> ...Air Intelligence was confronted with an extraordinary proposal said to have come from Hitler's personal pilot, General Hans Bauer. It originated in Sofia, Bulgaria, in late December 1940. A peasant farmer named Kiroff approached the British Military Attaché claiming his daughter was married to Baur. As proof he produced family photographs, Baur, he said, had lost two brothers in the war and had become 'fed up' with the continuous duty for Hitler. He was prepared to aid world peace by attempting a forced landing in England with the Führer and his entourage aboard his plane.
>
> The Military Attaché passed the matter to the Air Attaché, who reported it to the Air Ministry and the Foreign Office. No one could be found to identify the 'Baur family' photographs; nonetheless the contact was approved by Cadogan; Kiroff was handed instructions detailing signals Baur should fire when approaching the English coast, and special instructions for receiving him in Hitler's four-engined Focke-Wulf Kondor were sent to Lympne aerodrome in Kent.
>
> ...
>
> In the event Baur's Kondor did not arrive. The special arrangements for receiving him were nonetheless kept in force.

---

[27] Padfield, op. cit., pp. 85-86: Padfield here mentions yet another peace initiative that came from Sweden via personal representatives of *Reichsmarschall* Göring in July 1940, in which the offer was essentially that Britain had to recognize all German conquests in Europe, and allow Germany a "free hand" on the continent in return for German support and recognition of British imperial interests. In this proposal, Germany was apparently ready to throw off its pending alliance with Japan, and to contribute to British defense against the Japanese! This initiative is noteworthy because it resembles the components of Hess's plan insofar as the "free hand in Eastern Europe" is concerned, but omits the general peace plan parameters regarding Western Europe and "the Jewish Question." It *does*, however, show that Göring was also involved in these peace efforts. Padfield maintained that this effort was done with Hitler's knowledge.

They were about to be called off in May (1941), but Hess's arrival in Scotland caused the Air Ministry to continue them until the end of the month. Finally on 1 June they were annulled...

It is possible that this curious plot had some connection with Hess's mission.[28]

Again, Padfield dismisses the idea that Baur could be involved in such a plot on the basis of his loyalty to Hitler,[29] but it should *also* be noted that according to Padfield, *it was Baur who supplied Hess with the highly secret air defense maps of Germany that enabled the first leg of Hess's flight!*[30]

Like everything else in the Hess Mess, Padfield's reconstruction is certainly possible: certainly one can view the whole Baur plot as a strange footnote, and dismiss the whole idea that Baur would ever have flown Hitler and his entourage to Britain. But psychology and personal loyalty are a flimsy basis on which to argue a scenario in which mind control drugs and *doppelgängers* have already made a heavy appearance!

So let us consider the alternative, that the Baur story *is* true, and that Hitler's personal pilot *did* offer to fly Hitler himself, and his entourage, in their big Focke-Wulf Condor into Britain and hand the whole rotten ring of rogues over to the British. Does this make sense in the wider scenario of a peace plan that, moreover, was a possible *bi-lateral coup-d'etat* plot against both Hitler *and* Churchill? I contend it makes *eminent* sense, for a very important reason: the capture of Hitler and his staff would represent not only a coup d'etat successfully accomplished, it would be the seal of *bona fides* on whatever deal had already been concluded by Hess and his backers on the one hand, and Hamilton and his on the other. In this respect, let us recall that Baur was the one who gave Hess his flight map. Baur might thus, additionally, explain the curiously ambiguous presence and behavior of Göring himself in the Hess Mess, who is involved in one peace initiative *with Hitler* via Sweden, and yet feigning ignorance of *Hess's* initiative when summoned to the Berghof after Hess's flight, which he *fully* knew

---

[28] Padfield, op. cit., pp. 121-122.
[29] Ibid., p. 122.
[30] Ibid.

about, since he ordered General Galland to shoot Hess down, long after it was possible to do so! Göring is the clue that suggests that Hitler knew of the Hess mission, *but only to a limited extent;* he was obviously kept out of any knowledge that the "peace plan" was also a coup d'etat plan. With Hitler out of the way in Britain, the British faction could have moved against Churchill, while Hess returned to Germany to "take control."[31]

B. The Holocaust Hypothesis and the Hess Peace Plan

Whatever one makes of the previous speculations, or of the case that Hess's mission included proposals for dealing with the "Jewish question" in terms of a homeland, Padfield notes something else;

> It is probably significant that on 20 May, 1941, ten days after Hess had taken off on his flight for peace, and still nothing having been heard from the British, the Reich Central Office of Emigration issued instructions *on Göring's authority* banning further emigration of Jews from the Reich; the reason given was the 'doubtless approaching final solution (*Endlösung*)...
>
> If these orders are indeed linked to the apparent failure of Hess's mission they add credibility to de Courcy's claim that the peace proposals Hess brought included the resettlement of European Jews in Palestine.[32]

Indeed, Göring's role in the Hess Mess is once again under suspicion, for if he *was* involved in Hess's plans and more thoroughly briefed about them than was Hitler, he would have wanted to conceal his involvement in trying to thwart the "extermination option" favored by Hitler for the far more benign "homeland" options apparently negotiated by Hess and his British counterparts.

With this decree, he did so, and then some.

In this respect it should also be recalled that—in the view of Picknett, Prince, and Prior—Hess was not coming to Britain to *discuss* the peace plan, but rather, to *conclude* and *seal* a deal that had already *been* negotiated.

---

[31] Assuming of course, that Göring would have allowed him to do so!

[32] Padfield, op. cit., p. 277, emphasis added.

This implies that extreme pressure was placed on the deal's demise, and, as Picknett, Prince, and Prior have suggested, may have been a factor in the Duke of Kent's tragic demise in an airplane crash, along with, as they aver, the real Rudolf Hess himself. It was a *return* flight. If the features of Hess's peace plan, including those for a Jewish-Zionist homeland were known, this in turn implies something truly profound, and tragic, for it implies *that someone on the British side* **wanted** *the extermination and genocide to proceed:* "It is not difficult to see why these proposals had to be buried," Padfield writes,

> ...If they had leaked to the governments of the occupied western countries in exile in London, and to the dedicated advocates of compromise peace in Parliament and the City of London and among the country's great landowners, or to isolationists in the United States, then arming Britain to continue the struggle, Churchill would have been in dire trouble. The plan Hess brought with him showed diabolical ingenuity: the proposals could hardly be refused, yet they came from a man, Hitler, who had broken every treaty and solemn undertaking he had made, and could not be trusted.[33]

This was, indeed, as we have seen, a *sine qua non* of the British peace faction: Hitler had to go before a peace could be concluded. But if that is the case, then Hess's arrival to "seal a deal already negotiated" implies that on the German side, there was agreement to remove Hitler, and this implies that Hess was a part of it. Thus,

> There is another possible reason for the continuing secrecy over Hess's mission: that is, if he brought a warning about the impending fate of European Jewry.

This, of course, makes sense, for given Hess's position atop the Nazi Party hierarchy itself, plus all his other state, party, and intelligence appointments and connections, and as we have observed previously, there was little that happened in the Third Reich before 1941, including atomic bombs and "final solutions," that Hess was not privy to. Consequently:

---

[33] Padfield, op. cit., pp. 346-347.

Hess also knew of the preparations for the *Endlösung*, the 'final solution' to the Jewish problem in Europe. If he revealed that too, Churchill's failure either to denounce or act to stop the coming slaughter could so damage perceptions of his and Britain's wartime record as to justify hiding the fact for ever.

There was, of couse, nothing Churchill could have done. Had he accepted the peace plan it would only have made the assault on Russia more certain, and Hitler could not have been relied on to keep any promise to deport rather than physically annihilate the Jews.[34]

But as we have seen, Churchill had already acted contrary to the desires of the Chamberlain government and Peel Commission for a Jewish homeland, and in any case, Hess had not come to negotiate with *Churchill*, but with other parties altogether, and under Royal protection—as he claimed—to boot. He aim was to *replace* Churchill's government with one more amenable to peace, and ultimately to replace Hitler's government. With both new governments in favor of a Jewish-Zionist homeland, a peace could be concluded.

All of these considerations suggest that somewhere within the bowels of the deep states of Britain, the USA, and Nazi Germany itself, a decision either had been taken—or had been manipulated—for genocide. And that implies a transnational network to manipulate that decision, with an agenda of its own.

Is there any evidence to suggest something so monstrous and hideous?

Sadly, there is, and it is a little known but highly suggestive and explosive fact lurking in the center of the Hess Mess that, as far as I am aware, no other author has ever previously considered in relationship to it.

---

[34] Padfield, op. cit., pp. 347-348. See also Padfield's statement on p. 349: "...if Hess gave advance warning of German preparations for genocide in the east Churchill would certainly have communicated this explosive information to Roosevelt, and both would have borne equal responsibility for the subsequent silence and inaction." But "inaction" may have served someone *else's* goals perfectly.

C. The Nordau Quotation and Its Implications for the Hess Mess

To explain this explosive fact, I must first resort to some personal history. I first became aware of this sensational bit of information in 1983, after reading a trilogy of fictional novels by Gloria Vitanze Basile—a noted authoress of romance novels in the 1970s and 1980s—called the *Global 2000 Trilogy*. This trilogy was, however, a complete departure for Ms. Basile from her normal romance novel fare, for these were a thoroughly researched but fictionalized version of grand conspiracy theory novels.

In the second of the novels comprising this trilogy, *The Eye of the Eagle*, Ms. Basile began certain chapters or sections of the novel with carefully chosen epigraphs from various sources dating back to the French Revolution, and even including some statements by the famous 19th century British Prime Minister Benjamin Disraeli. Over the years, I was able to verify the veracity of these quotations, all except one, *this* one, by the prominent Zionist leader Max Nordau;

> How dare the smooth talker, the clever official babblers, open their mouths and boast of progress? Here they hold jubilant Peace Conferences, talk against war. But these same righteous governments who are so noble, industriously active to establish eternal peace are preparing, by their own confession, the complete annihilation of six million Jews and there is nobody, except the doomed themselves, to raise his voice in protest, although this is a worse crime than any war.[35]

The problem with the Nordau Quotation (as I and the few with whom I shared it began to call it) was that it was allegedly made *in 1911, fully three years before the beginning of World War* **One**, *and therefore, obviously fully* **thirty-one** *years prior to the 1942 Wannsee conference authorizing the Final Solution. In fact, this quotation, if true, was the* **first** *occurrence of the number "six million" in connection with the Holocaust,* **long before the Holocaust had even occurred!**

I cannot convey to the reader my stunned shock, and the nauseating, horrifying feeling, that overtook me when I read this.

---

[35] Gloria Vitanze Basile, *The Eye of the Eagle* (New York: Pinnacle Books, 1983), p. 127, citing Max Nordau, 1911.

And the disturbing problem was, *every **other*** epigraph Ms. Basile had cited was verifiable, which put this quotation in the disturbing context that it might be true.

Stop for a moment and ponder its implications, taking Mr. Nordau's statements at face value, for when one *does* so what emerges is the following set of assertions:

1) A mass human sacrifice of Jews was being pre-planned;
2) The European powers knew about and were to some extent involved in the plan; but,
3) His quotation also implies that the Zionist leaders *also* somehow knew about the plan, and this implies their own potential involvement in it at some level, if only that of knowing about it; and,
4) This is the first occurrence of the number of "six million" in connection with it; and finally,
5) All of the above implies some international network of vast proportions, capable of pulling all this off.

Needless to say, I spent several years quietly and cautiously trying to verify the existence of this quotation.

Verification of the quotation finally came almost a decade later, when a friend of mine and I made a trip to the Library of Congress in Washington, D.C., for the express purpose of doing so. We were looking for a specific book, edited by Rabbi Stephen Wise (!) called *Max Nordau to his People*. In that book, several of Nordau's speeches to pre-World War One Zionist congresses were translated, and there Nordau's quotation exists, *although in Wise's version, the phrase refers not to six million Jews but six million "creatures,"* although Wise, in a footnote, remarks that this was "said before World War One!"[36]

---

[36] While I'm telling a personal history, I might as well add that initially my friend and I used the computer system to find the book, and then filled out the call slip and presented it at the desk in the main reference room of the Library of Congress. Approximately a half an hour later, the clerk informed us that the book could not be found in the stacks! I refused to believe this, and, for a reason I can only write down to providence, decided to look on the shelves in the main reference room which included a number of books on Judaica, and sure enough, there on the shelves, *where it should **not** have been*, was Rabbi Wise's book! My

Subsequently, I was able to verify yet *another* form of the same quotation in the book by famous Jewish playwright and sometime contributor of teleplays to Rod Serling's *Twilight Zone*, Ben Hecht, in his book *Perfidy*, about the trial of a Zionist doctor, Rudolf Kastner, in Israel for his complicity with Adolf Eichmann in helping round up Jews for the Holocaust! It is worth quoting Hecht's own astonishment, and his version of the Quotation:

> In the Zionist Congress of 1911, 22 *years* before Hitler came to power, and three years before World War I, Nordau said, "How dare the smooth talkers, the clever official blabbers, open their mouths and boast of progress... Here they hold jubilant peace conferences in which they talk against war.... But the same righteous Governments, who are so nobly, industriously active to establish the eternal peace, are preparing, by their own confession, *complete annihilation for six million people*, and there is nobody, except the doomed themselves, to raise his voice in protest although this is a worse crime than any war..."[37]

What must be noted is the discrepancies between various versions of the Nordau Quotation:

1) Basile's version: six million *Jews;*
2) Wise's version: six million *creatures;*
3) Hecht's version: six million *people;*
4) Robert John's version: six million *people*[38]

Ultimately of course, the original German would resolve the issue, but all my attempts to locate this have proven to meet— uncannily—with a complete lack of success. The original German, *Stenographisches Protokollen der Zionisten Kongressen*, is available,

---

friend and I quickly photocopied the copyright deposit notice—which, incidentally, indicated the book had been accepted for copyright deposit in December, 1941, a few days after Pearl Harbor—and we photocopied the actual page on which the Nordau Quotation occurred, and then beat a *very* hasty retreat from Washington D.C.!

[37] Ben Hecht, *Perfidy* (New York: Julian Messner, Inc., 1961), p. 254, n.4, emphasis in the original.

[38] See Robert John, op. cit., p. 44, n., where the Quotation exists in the form of "six million people."

but curiously, in versions I have been able to find, the Nordau Quotation is curiously absent. The important point to note, however, is that the fact that these minutes of the Zionist congresses were in German means that Hess may have known of it.[39]

Nonetheless, the four secondary sources for it comprise an interesting mix, for Rabbi Wise was certainly pro-Zionist, while Robert John and Basile could certainly be called anti-Zionist, or at least in Basile's case, highly skeptical, with Ben Hecht, a Jew himself, occupying a curious middle ground of someone appalled, and one might say, surprised and mystified at the very idea of a Zionist (Dr. Kastner) collaborating with a notorious Nazi such as Eichmann.

D. Taking Stock

What emerges from this are a set of implications that, when considered together, *begin* to approach an answer to that One Question that has been hovering uneasily over the whole landscape of the Hess Mess: what was the big secret that had to be kept, and kept secret to this day? In this respect, we take note again that the Hess files—as various researchers have pointed out—have already been carefully *weeded*, and thus, even with the presumed declassification of some Hess files this year, one must regard this source as tainted, for we will simply not know the extent of this weeding, nor, indeed, the extent to which files have been falsified, planted, or obfuscated.

In any case, what has emerged thus far is a disturbing picture:

1) Hess undertook his peace mission with the knowledge of Hitler, but this knowledge on Hitler's part was limited, and probably designed to throw him off the scent of a plot that was ultimately designed to overthrow his government;

---

[39] Speculating further, it also means that some knowledge of the implications of the Nordau Quotation might be lurking in the background of Hitler's notorious and chilling speech to the *Reichstag* in January, 1939, which begins "*Ich will wieder ein Prophet sein...*" (I will today again be a prophet...).

2) Hess was also apparently involved in this plot with Hermann Göring, whose own role was suspiciously ambiguous, as has been pointed out in the previous chapters;

   a) Göring called General Adolf Galland and ordered him to scramble fighters to intercept Hess and shoot him down, but did so *after* any chance of success in this respect was doomed to failure. Göring thus demonstrated inside knowledge of Hess's mission *before it became more widely known throughout the rest of the Nazi hierarchy.*

   b) Göring then *subsequently* denied knowing anything about it at the conference at the Berghof following the flight, and then

   c) Göring promulgated an order that prohibited emigration of Jews from the Reich *after* no British response to Hess's flight had been forthcoming;

   d) Göring's role is further, though indirectly, implicated by the Baur Plot, since Baur allegedly had contacted the British via Bulgaria to fly Hitler and his staff into captivity. While this plot has never been verified, Baur did supply Hess with a very secret map of forbidden "no fly" zones in the Reich's air defense system, and this implies that authorization for supplying such a map to Hess would have come from the highest *Luftwaffe* authority, i.e., Göring.

3) Hess undertook his flight with the belief that he was under Royal protection, a belief he repeatedly signaled to his British captors, to seal a peace deal with elements of the British deep state, represented by the Duke of Hamilton and the Duke of Kent;

4) Once in Britain, however, due to miscalculations during the course of the flight, Hess had to bail out of his aircraft, while a reception committee comprising the Duke of Hamilton was waiting to be informed of his arrival at an RAF base.

5) Because of the bail-out, Hess was apprehended by elements *not* involved in the scheme, and it was some time before the

pro-peace faction—in the scenario of Picknett, Prince, and Prior—was able to re-establish control over the real Hess;

6) During his first days in captivity, Hess was drugged, and covertly measured for a duplicate *Luftwaffe* captain's uniform, which many involved at the time thought was to be for the use of a double;

7) Then, at some point—probably at Maindiff or shortly before his transfer to Maindiff—the real Hess, according to Picknett's, Prince's, and Prior's scenario, is transferred to Scotland, while a double is created and undergoes drugging and other tests to implant false memories;

8) The real Hess, in Picknett's, Prince's, and Prior's scenario, then crashes with the Duke of Kent, who appeared to be on a highly secret mission to fly him to Sweden;

9) The other "Hess" then takes the real Hess's place at Nuremberg, where "Hess" then exhibits very erratic behavior, claiming amnesia, and then, recovered memories, and at first does not recognize Göring. Allen Dulles, leader of the American OSS in Switzerland, suspects that "Hess" is really a double, and brings in Dr. Ewen Cameron of subsequent MK-Ultra fame, to examine the prisoner. The presence of Dr. Cameron suggests that Dulles might also have suspected some mind control was in evidence;

10) Dr. Ewen Cameron, as was pointed out in previous pages, has the same clan surname of the British forensic pathologist, Dr. James MacDonald Cameron, who performed the official autopsy on "Hess" after the latter was "suicide" in Spandau in Augsut 1987. As was pointed out, both Camerons did their medical studies *in the same medical school in Glasgow*;

11) Dr. W. Hugh Thomas subsequently alleges that Spandau Hess lacks the appropriate scarring from his World War One wounds, and claims that Spandau Hess is a double;

12) Adding fuel to the double theory is the fact that Spandau Hess, as the last surviving "Reich Minister," was never approached, nor did he ever sign, any official document outlawing the Nazi Party, which, presumably, he had at least *some* status in law to do, since he was Hitler's Deputy

to the Party! Of course, if he was a double, he had no legitimate authority to do so, nor, if he was *not* a double, would any such document have been legitimate since it was signed under duress. Adding to the legal complications, we also saw that, according to Hess's son Wolf Rüdiger, Stalin had offered to allow German reunification both to then Chancellor Adenauer, and to Spandau Hess, who refused whatever terms might have been communicated to him!

13) In the midst of all the other confusion, Hess appears to have offered, as part of his peace plan, to allow a Jewish-Zionist homeland in Palestine, and since his mission was less to *discuss* rather than to *seal* a deal, one must assume that the British factions with which he was in contact also agreed to this plan. The fact that the plan fell through suggests that in this respect someone *wanted* the genocide to proceed, a disturbing implication, given the pattern of examples of Nazi-Zionist complicity documented in this chapter.

14) A scenario thus emerges—though, like everything else in the Hess Mess, can remain only an argued speculation and hypothesis—that Hess was on a coup-d'etat and peace mission—to replace Hitler, negotiate a peace with elements in Britain that were to replace Churchill. If one adds the alleged "Baur airplane-kidnapping" plot to the mix, then the latter may be viewed as the establishing of *bona fides* on the German side, for the British peace faction had repeatedly insisted that no peace was possible with Hitler in power. What better way to establish the good faith of the German side, than to deliver Hitler to the British, in Hitler's own plane, to boot?

Yet, even with all of this, we have still not examined all the debris in the junkyard of the Hess Mess.

There's one more important thing to be examined...

... and that's The Penguin Problem.

PART TWO:
THE PENGUIN PROBLEM.
OR,
A FINAL BIT OF ICING ON THE HESS MESS

"By these various means we aim to expose the fallacy of reasoning of Szabo, Robert, Stevens, Farrell, Bernhart, Friedrich, Mattern and others, and to convince the reader that the supposed mysteries surrounding German, British and American activities in Antarctica in this period result from a combination of inadequate research, vivid imagination, pure fakery and wishful thinking."
Colin Summerhayes and Peter Beeching,
"Hitler's Antarctic Base: the myth and the reality,"
Polar Record 43(224)1-21, (2007)

Highjump was primarily a military operation, and not a scientific expedition. It was one of a series of military operations designed to train the navy in Polar operations."
Colin Summerhayes and Peter Beeching,
"Hitler's Antarctic Base: the myth and the reality,"
Polar Record 43(227)1-21, (2007)

7
PENGUINS AND THE PEACE PLAN

*"As commissioner for the Four-Year Plan, Göring knew the
importance for Germany of whaling in Antarctica, and how essential
it was to ensure this, and to open up new fishing grounds It seemed
high time for him to send a large expedition to Antarctica.
"On May 9, 1938, a plan for an Antarctic expedition, drawn up by the
staff of his ministry, which was to be carried out in the Antarctic
summer of 1938/39, was presented to him. He approved, and
commissioned Helmut Wohlthat as Minister-Director for special
projects, with the preparation of the expedition, and conferred upon
him all his powers of authority."*
Heinz Schön[1]

AND THEN THERE'S THE "PENGUIN PART" of the Hess Mess. Most
readers of my books, blogs, and regular listeners to my
interviews, will know that I have never subscribed to the
idea that there was a big German "secret base" in Antarctica,
whether for submarines or, as one version of the story has it, for
"secret research on flying saucers." I have pointed out any number
of commonplace and very ordinary problems with these ideas, chief
among them that (1) during World War Two, the German Navy
would simply not be up to the logistical challenge of building and
supplying such a base, and (2) one would have to have a source of
power for the base, and that would require a *power plant*, with
materials and construction and technical personnel having to be
lugged from Germany, and so on. From the standpoint of the
massive war effort Germany was to deploy in Europe, such a
massive undertaking would have taxed powers with even larger
industrial bases, such as the United States, or powerful navies, such
as Great Britain, let alone Germany.

All of this, of course, argues quite strongly against secret
Antarctic UFO basis, U-boat bases and so on. If anything, as I have
stated in numerous interviews, at best the Germans might have

---

[1] Heinz Schön, *Mythos Neu-Schwabenland: Für Hitler am Südpol: Die deutsche
Antarktis-expedition 1939/39* (Selent, Germany: BONUS-Verlag, 2004), p. 11, my
translation from the German.

been able to construct—and possibly maintain—a small automated weather station such as those that they deployed in the Arctic.

The implication of the epigraph beginning this chapter is that the Göring Antarctic expedition was largely a scientific expedition, as indeed it was. Germany needed lubricants, food, and the whaling and fishing resources, and the southern polar region fit the bill perfectly. Indeed, it is difficult to imagine Hermann Göring sponsoring anything—expeditions or otherwise—that did not have an immediate or long-term benefit to the German economy or armed forces. Antarctica represented a vast, untapped continent of *resources.*

However, I have consistently maintained through the years that Hess was involved in this expedition. Yet, there has been, until recently, little evidence to connect Hess to the expedition. Hess's involvement—if any—changes the complexion of the expedition. But what, if any, is the evidence for Hess's involvement in the matter?

A. Heinz Schön and Operation Highjump
1. A Brief Review of Antarctic Strangeness

The problem with the "resources" explanation, however, is that it does not seem to explain the strange history of the people associated with the southern continent. It might, for example, explain the interest of Hermann Göring, or after the war, of American polar explorer Admiral Byrd and the U.S. military. It might explain the interest of U.S. Secretary of State John Kerry, who visited the southern continent in late 2016 while on a diplomatic junket, and during one of the most hotly contested and important U.S. elections in decades. It might explain even the visit of King Juan Carlos of Spain.

But resources as the sole interest in Antarctica begin to break down when one contemplates the visit to Antarctica in 2016 of former Apollo 11 astronaut Buzz Aldrin, or the 2016 visit of the Patriarch of Moscow, Kiril III. Other stories, at this point, had to be contrived to explain the strange list of visitors. Secretary Kerry's visit was explained as having to do with global warming; there never was a cover story for Aldrin, but in Kiril III's case the official explanation was that he was there to bless the Orthodox chapel in the Russian mission. It was, in other words, it was a patriarchal photo op.

None of this, of course, mentioned or included Rudolf Hess. Even so, it is a strange list of people when looked at "whole":

1) *Reichsmarschall* Hermann Göring, creator of the *Luftwaffe* and the Gestapo;
2) Admiral Richard Byrd, famed American polar explorer;
3) Secretary of State John Kerry;
4) The Patriarch of Moscow Kiril III;
5) Apollo 11 astronaut Buzz Aldrin; and
6) King Juan Carlos of Spain and other royals.

The list could be added to, and made much stranger, but perhaps the point is made, for the list would appear to be too strange for the simple "resources" or even the global warming/climate change explanations. Add Rudolf Hess to this list, and it becomes downright bizarre.

2. Disturbing Questions about Highjump
a. The German Antarctic Expedition and State Councillor Wohlthat

Just how strange Antarctica is can be measured by a more detailed—though unfortunately, necessarily brief—glance at the post-war American Operation Highjump. On the face of it, neither the pre-war German expedition, nor the post-war American expedition appear all that strange. For example, Heinz Schön, who has written the only thorough survey of both expeditions, writes that the scientific tasks of the German expedition were well-thought-out and thoroughly practical; the German expedition was to:

1) Survey the coast and interior by photogrammetry and thus produce more accurate maps;
2) Obtain meteorological data of upper atmospheric conditions by means of weather balloons and radiosondes and aircraft mapping of prevailing winds, and so on;

3) Obtain a profile of the ocean ground by echo sounding, survey currents and temperature conditions;

4) Make careful observations on whales, birds, and wildlife conditions;

5) Test nautical equipment and current German maps, tables, and depth measurements.

In other words, the expedition was to make as thorough a survey, in as brief a time of the Antarctic summer as it could, in the areas of geography, oceanography, biology, and navigational science.[2]

Göring's interest, in other words, was entirely economic, and thus, in the long term, military. Here, however, one encounters a "strangeness" that will only be revealed when viewed in connection to the Hess Mess:

> As commissioner for the Four-Year Plan, Göring knew the importance for Germany of whaling in Antarctica, and how essential it was to ensure this, and to open up new fishing grounds. It seemed high time for him to send a large expedition to Antarctica.
>
> On May 9, 1938, a plan for an Antarctic expedition, drawn up by the staff of his ministry, which was to be carried out in the Antarctic summer of 1938/39, was presented to him. He approved, and commissioned Helmut Wohlthat as Minister-Director for special projects, with the preparation of the expedition, and conferred upon him all his powers of authority.[3]

State Councilor (Staatsrat) Helmut Wohlthat

---

[2] Heinz Schön, op. cit., p. 12.

[3] Ibid., p. 11, my translation from the German.

What is so unusual about Helmut Wohlthat, besides being Göring's "plenipotentiary" for the Antarctic expedition? Wohlthtat *also* became one of Göring's own "peace ambassadors" as the German representative to the International Whaling Commission in London in June 1939. There he attempted to make back-channel contacts with the Chamberlain Government via one of the Prime Minister's advisors on industrial affairs.[4]

What this implies is that in any comprehensive peace negotiation with Britain, Antarctica would inevitably be included. Wohlthat's role was crucial, for in effect it was he who planned the *details* of the Antarctic expedition, including the choice of its captain, Alfred Ritscher.[5] There is a hint that Antarctica figured in some greater long term design—at least as far as Göring was concerned—in his congratulatory telegram sent to Captain Ritscher on the expedition's return to Germany in early 1939. The telegram reads:

> To Captain Ritscher,
> Leader of the German Antarctic Expedition,
> 7 March, 1939:

> I congratulate you most cordially on the important success which you and your expedition have earned in the exploration of a large area of Antarctica. I am proud of the excellent commitment of the pilots, the successful work of the scientists and the exemplary attitude of the whole crew. You and your expedition have been able to build on the greatest tradition of German research and have *performed a service worthy of the position of Greater Germany in the world*. (signed) Göring, Reichsmarschall.[6]

The final phrase of this telegram implies that Göring viewed the German expedition as connected to "Greater Germany's" geopolitical position, and that the expedition was *not*, therefore, simply an exercise in detached, altruistic "science," and thus, the use of Wohlthat as a personal peace emissary and representative of Göring himself, whom it will be recalled from previous chapters

---

[4] Picknett, Prince, and Prior, op. cit., p. 98.
[5] Heinz Schön, op. cit., p. 17.
[6] My translation from the German, emphasis added.

was viewed by the British as a "reliable" German, is telling. Wohlthat's position as Göring's emissary suggests that Antarctica figured largely in Göring's views of a postwar world, and therefore, in whatever peace was to be negotiated.

An Kapitän Ritscher
Leiter der „Deutschen
antarktischen Expedition"
7. III. 1939

Zu dem bedeutenden Erfolg, den Sie und Ihre Expedition

mit der Erforschung eines großen Gebietes der Antarktis

errungen haben, beglückwünsche ich Sie auf das herzlichste.

Ich bin stolz auf den hervorragenden Einsatz der Flieger,

auf die erfolgreiche Arbeit der Wissenschaftler und auf

die vorbildliche Haltung der ganzen Besatzung. Sie und

Ihre Expedition haben an die große Tradition deutscher

Forschung anknüpfen können und eine Leistung vollbracht,

die der Stellung Großdeutschlands in der Welt würdig ist.

Reichsmarshall

Hermann Göring's Congratulatory Telegram to Captain Alfred Ritscher

This is not simply argued speculation, for it is clear that Germany was not simply engaged in "scientific research," *but was staking a claim in Antarctica,* for on his return to Germany, Captain Ritscher

> ...was astonished to learn, in conversation with the State Councilor Wohlthat, that on January 18 1939, before the Motorship *Schwabenland* had even arrived in the working region of the Antarctic Expedition, that the Reich Foreign Ministry in Berlin had received a Royal Resolution from Oslo, dated January 14 1939, which stated that the Queen Maud region of the Antarctic was claimed by Norway, and that the intention of the German Antarctic Expedition was therefore illegal. The Norwegian

injunction against the German activities was justified by the fact that this area had been taken over by Norway after several Norwegian expeditions.

The Ministry of Foreign Affairs reacted immediately. It informed the Norwegian ambassador in Berlin that the Government of the German Reich rejected the possession of this area by Norway.

The fact was that Norwegians had not researched and entered any part of Queen Maud Land, which received the name Neu-Schwabenland by the German research conducted there, and that at no time had this territory been explored until the Antarctic expedition of 1938/39.[7]

In effect, what the German Foreign Ministry was claiming was two-fold: (1) the Norwegian government had not mounted nor sustained any recent exploration of the region and therefore had forfeited claim to the territory;[8] and (2) it had no claim in any case to Neu-Schwabenland, because it had never explored that far inland.

The bottom line, however, was that Germany *was* staking a sovereign claim, and that Norway recognized that fact and was rejecting it. The matter, in so far as Norway and Germany were concerned, was settled with the German invasion and occupation of the country in 1940. But the matter was *not* settled, so far as the Norwegian government in exile, nor Great Britain were concerned.

At this point, of course, one is back to Hess and the Hess Mess, for it stands to reason that Antarctica would have been a component of his peace proposals. But is there any *evidence* to suggest this? Indeed there is, but this will have to wait. In the meantime, we must deal with the *other* curious expedition to Antarctica,

b. The Post-war American Expedition of Admiral Richard Byrd in 1946-47.

If there are suspicious smoke signals hovering over the German Antarctic expedition of 1938-39, this is even *more* the case with the American Expedition of 1946-47, codenamed "Operation

---

[7] Heinz Schön, op. cit., p. 107, my translation from the German.
[8] Ibid.

Highjump." Again, like the pre-war German expedition, its purpose was ostensibly scientific, for the expedition included civilian researchers, many of whom, however, as Heinz Schön notes, worked for the US Army or Navy. There were scientists from the American Geological Survey, The Fish and Wildlife Service, the Coast and Geodetic Survey.[9] There were also, however, over four thousand people involved, an aircraft carrier, a submarine, aircraft, helicopters, and a variety of special land transport equipment including tracked vehicles.

The explanation for all this military equipment? At that time, the *Arctic* was viewed as a potential theater of operations should war break out between the Soviet Bloc and the West, and therefore, it became essential to "test equipment" in the harsh polar environment... of *Antarctica*.[10] To this day, this explanation is employed by various people to debunk the idea that there was anything unusual going on, either in Antarctica, or with Operation Highjump. Admiral Byrd even published a one-hundred-page plus article in *National Geographic* to underscore this idea.[11]

It was just to test equipment, and demonstrate the necessity of the Navy and Arctic operational proficiency of men and equipment should war ever break out.

This explanation has never made sense to me, for it has always seemed to have more the feeling of "convenient explanation." After all, the USA possessed Alaska, which had equally rugged terrain in which to "test equipment" in Arctic conditions. Additionally, Alaska was closer to hand, easier to reach, and so one question immediately arises: Why haul all those men and all that equipment to *Antarctica*, and at great expense at that?

Even Heinz Schön, who, like this author, is not buying the idea of secret Nazi UFO and/or U-boat bases, and who for the most part sticks very closely to the documentation, seems uncomfortable with the public explanations: "Why this excitement so soon after the ending of the Second World War?" he asks. "What new war did the

---

[9] Heinz Schön, op. cit., p. 119.
[10] Ibid., p. 118.
[11] Ibid.

US have in mind when Byrd spoke of himself and the navy 'between the wars?'"[12]

The oddities of Operation Highjump do not end simply with its *size* nor with the public narratives advanced to explain it. Much more strange were the people involved in its *planning*, which began in 1946. Schön observes that the importance of Highjump to the USA is revealed by who was involved in its detailed planning, for the operational planning commission involved not just Admiral Byrd, but Rear Admirals Good and Cruzen, Vice-Admiral Forrest Sherman, the naval Chief of Staff, Fleet Admiral Chester Nimitz himself, and, perhaps most importantly, the Secretary of the Navy, James V. Forrestal.[13]

With the mention of Forrestal, we are once again in strange territory, for Forrestal would, of course, go on to become Secretary of Defense under President Truman, only to die a mysterious death when he allegedly committed suicide during a stay in Bethesda Naval Hospital, by tying a crude rope of towels and such, and leaping from his window. It is the same James Forrestal who appears as a member of the alleged Majic-12 or Majestic-12 UFO research committee in the Majic-12 documents, a fact which many Ufologists suspect is related to his alleged suicide, or perhaps, murder. His presence in the extraordinarily high level of planning for Operation Highjump would thus seem to suggest *other* possible motivations for his suicide or murder.

Before continuing with this brief review of Highjump, it is worth pausing to consider the strange parallels between the German-Göring Expedition of 1938-39, and the American Byrd-Forrestal expedition of 1946-47:

1) Both expeditions were planned at an extraordinarily high level, in effect, at *sub-cabinet* level, in the American case, and at *cabinet* level in the German case, since Forrestal as Secretary of the Navy is one step removed from the Federal Cabinet (which he would subsequently occupy as Secretary of Defense), and Göring as *Reichsmarschall*, Four-Year Commissioner, Hitler's designated successor in offices of

---

[12] Ibid., p. 122, my translation from the German.
[13] Heinz Schön, op. cit., p. 119.

state, and as Reichsminister, occupies a cabinet-level position;

2) Both expeditions are planned at an extraordinarily high level of *military* participation, with Fleet Admiral Chester Nimitz and *Reichsmarschall* Göring both being the commanders-in-chief of their respective service branches;

3) Both expeditions have similar missions and equipment: both are charged with making extensive *aerial photogrammetric surveys* of vast regions, for cartographic purposes. Both expeditions to this end employ aircraft carriers. The chief *difference* between the two expeditions is one of *scale*: the German expedition is a one-ship, seaplane-tender expedition with a small personnel commitment, and only two seaplanes to conduct its survey. The American expedition is much more substantial in terms of its financial and material commitments, with an actual aircraft carrier supplemented by a much larger land-based personnel contingent.

3. The Operational Plan of Highjump

While these parallels are quite remarkable, there are other oddities about Highjump. When Admiral Byrd made his report of the expedition, he strangely omitted all reference to the 1938-39 German Neu-Schwabenland expedition,[14] a fact made even more strange by the additional fact that Byrd himself was brought to Nazi Germany prior to the German expedition in order to brief its captain and crew on conditions!

More importantly, the operational plan for Highjump involved three special groups, making landfall at three separate points on the continent, and then moving inland with aerial reconnaissance and photogrammetric efforts. Notably, none of the landing points were in Queen Maud-Neu-Schwabenland. These points might induce some to conclude, not unreasonably, that Operation Highjump had nothing whatsoever to do with the German Antarctic Expedition, or, to put it into cruder but starker relief, that Forrestal had nothing to do with Göring.

---

[14] Heinz Schön, op. cit., p. 122.

Unfortunately, however, Admiral Byrd himself made statements that could be taken to undermine such an interpretation, and to place Highjump into a clear relationship with the earlier German expedition, for in the operational plan, two of the groups landing on the continent were to move toward the null longitude, that is to say, eastward, for the null longitude *laid within the claimed area of Queen Maud Land/Neu-Schwabenland.* As Byrd himself expressed it, it was an "encirclement of conquest" and an "attack from three fronts."[15]

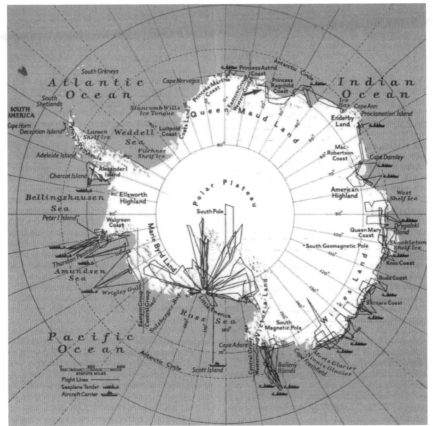

The Operation Highjump Landfalls and Coastal Expeditions. Notice the relative absence of coastal exploration in the Queen Maud Land/Neu-Schwabenland area.

---

[15] Heinz Schön, op. cit., p. 122.

Or to put it country simple: even though Highjump's three main operational groups made landfall away from Neu-Schwabenland, the purpose of doing so was to create a continental-scaled *"Kesselschlacht"* or "encirclement battle" condition. Whatever one may make of this, Byrd's very *non*-scientific but very precisely *military* terms are suggestive that something else, besides mere scientific and cartographical or equipment-testing exercises were being conducted.

While there is absolutely nothing in the documentary evidence to suggest this, I have long suspected that both the German and American expeditions were *looking* for something with all the aerial photogrammetry and cartography that they were doing. Such a photogrammetry purpose would be the perfect public explanation for a much more covert and secret purpose of looking for something. That the American expedition seemed to be following an operational plan deliberately avoiding any *initial* venture into Neu-Schwabenland-Queen Maud Land suggests both the "advance on three fronts" of Admiral Byrd, but also that the American expedition was deliberately exploring areas left *unexplored* by its German antecedent. If the American expedition was an "advance on three fronts," then the question inevitably occurs: an advance against whom?

As already indicated, I do not adhere to the notion of a German base in Antarctica, at least, not of the large size suggested by all the "Last Battalion" mythologies. Highjump itself is testimony to the difficulties of sustaining large-scale military operations on that continent, even when backed by an economy and navy larger than anything the Third Reich was capable of during World War Two. So, if it was not Germans, then against whom were the Americans "advancing on three fronts"? Or were Admiral Byrd's remarks to be taken in a merely rhetorical and metaphorical sense, as implying an advance and conquest of the continent itself?

The heavy military presence in Highjump is underscored by its almost complete absence in the prewar German expedition, and suggests that Byrd was *not* speaking merely metaphorically; which leaves the question of "who was he advancing against?" hovering uncomfortably in the air.

4. The Strange Death of Admiral Richard Byrd's Son

Every now and then when writing these books, I encounter the oddest synchronicity: someone will send me information or material which I was not aware of, whose relevance to whatever project I am writing about is astonishing.

Such is the case here, for three days prior to writing this very chapter, I received from not one but no less than four individuals—none of whom, I am certain, know each other—the following story by Peter Kerr, which appeared in the *New York Times* on October 9, 1988: "Body of Adm. Byrd's Son, 68, Found in Empty Warehouse." The initial paragraphs of the article make for intriguing reading, to say the least:

> Richard E. Byrd Jr., who lived his life in the shadow of his father, the admiral and Arctic explorer, was found dead last week in the darkness of an abandoned warehouse in Baltimore, his emaciated body clad in dirt-blackened clothes and one scuffed shoe, the police there said yesterday.
>
> The 68-yeard-old Mr. Byrd, a graduate of Harvard University *who as a young naval officer escorted his father on a journey to Antarctica in 1947*, apparently died of malnutrition and dehydration, the police said.
>
> The body was discovered Monday by a custodian who said he had chased Mr. Byrd and another man from the area on Sept. 28, according to Detective Charles Gilbert of the Baltimore police homicide squad. It was unclear, the police said, how the elderly member of a prominent Massachusetts family had come to wander and sleep in an area of warehouses and factories in the city's Hampden section.
>
> "He was just wearing a shirt and pants and one shoe, and they all looked dirty," Detective Gilbert said, adding that the custodian who had chased Mr. Byrd and the other man recalled that "they had booze with them in a paper bag at the time."
>
> Mr. Byrd's family described him as a resident of the affluent Beacon Hill section of Boston.
>
> His son, Leverett Byrd of Needham, Mass., was quoted in The Baltimore Sun yesterday as saying that Mr. Byrd left Boston on Sept. 13 *to attend a ceremony at the Washington headquarters of the National Geographic Society*. The ceremony honored his father, Adm. Richard E. Byrd, the pioneer aviator and polar explorer, who achieved fame with his long-distance flights over the Arctic and expeditions to Antarctica from 1924 to 1956.

"I put him on a train, and my wife was supposed to meet him," Leverett Byrd said. "What happened in between, I don't know. It's very strange, this whole thing. We're trying to come to grips with it."

...

Admiral Byrd died in 1957. Richard Jr. was born in Boston, attended the Milton Academy and Harvard, joined the Navy and served as an officer in the Pacific during World War II. In 1948, he married Emily Saltonstall, the daughter of Senator Levertt Saltonstall of Massachusetts.[16]

While Richard Byrd Jr.'s death might be viewed as entirely unrelated to the strange goings-on in Antarctica, or to the wider "Hess Mess," it is worth noting that the entire purpose of his visit to Washington DC was to attend an honorarium for his father at the *National Geographic* headquarters, the very magazine that ran his father's lengthy article about Operation Highjump in 1947, an expedition he himself accompanied his father on. He might thus have "known something" that others feared might have come out. In any case, his well-to-do background belies his end as a starving and dehydrated tramp and hobo in an empty Baltimore warehouse, being seen in the company of another man. This strange episode raises the prospect that the other unknown man—who to my knowledge was never found or questioned—might have been a "handler," someone whose job was to ensure that Byrd Jr. never made his appointment. The fact that the whole episode was handled by a Baltimore homicide detective raises this possibility even more.

B. Penguins, the Peace Plan, and the Hess Mess: What About Norway?

So how does all this relate to the Hess Mess? One may argue, and persuasively at that, that the sheer number of positions that Hess filled and occupied both in the Nazi Party as its leader and Hitler's Deputy, and in the Reich government itself, and the vast number of intelligence agencies to which he was thereby linked and networked, made Hess privy to whatever discoveries the German

---

[16] Peter Kerr, "Body of Adm. Byrd's Son, 68, Found in Empty Warehouse," *New York Times*, October 9, 1988, emphasis added.

Antarctic Expedition of 1938-39 uncovered, whether disclosed or classified.

However, Picknett, Prince, and Prior uncovered information in their dogged researches that make such awareness on Hess's part almost certain. On May 20, 1941, a mere ten days after Hess's arrival in Great Britain, the Foreign Secretary, Anthony Eden, wrote the following letter to Prime Minister Winston Churchill:

> I saw (Sir John) Simon and I think he will be willing to undertake the task of which we spoke. He has asked for 24 hours to consider the matter. We are agreed that he should make it plain that the Government know of the interview but that it would be unwise for him to indicate close collaboration with you and me—rather the reverse. Simon will be fully briefed before he goes to the interview and I propose to write him a letter saying that you and I would be glad if he would undertake this take.
>
> All this will be kept most secret and only Cadogan and I in the office are aware of the project.[17]

What was this "project"? The project was a meeting with Hess.

During the meeting, however, Simon asked Hess explicitly if he had come with Hitler's knowledge. Hess's reply was that he had come *without* the Führer's knowledge, to which he then added "*Absolut!*"[18] He then laughed and informed Simon that the terms that he, Hess, had written down for the British were the terms he had heard Hitler make on numerous occasions. Picknett, Prince, and Prior state that all of this slightly "spoiled" the effect of his reply that he had come *without* Hitler's knowledge.

But perhaps one needs to parse Hess's "*Absolut!*" response and subsequent laughter a bit more closely. As was argued in previous chapters, it would have been quite risky to keep any peace feelers entirely secret from Hitler. Rather, what I believe happened was that Hitler was apprised of those negotiations *but only to a limited extent*, since those negotiations had communicated both to Göring and to Hess and the Haushofers that no peace was negotiable so long as Hitler remained in power. Thus, the peace negotiations

---

[17] Picknett, Prince, and Prior, *Double Standards: The Rudolf Hess Cover-up*, pp. 301-302.
[18] Ibid., p. 303-304.

were also a complex bi-lateral coup d-etat process that included the overthrow of the Hitler and Churchill governments. Hess's *"Absolut!"* comment may thus be understood as a statement that Hitler was not informed of the full "absolute" extent of the peace being discussed.

But whatever one makes of this very speculative possibility, Simon's next inquiry is quite the crucial point, for he continued by asking Hess "about how the proposal *would affect other countries such as Norway* and Greece, to which Hess replied stiffly, 'The Führer had not pronounced.'"[19] This is highly significant, for as has been seen, Norway rejected the German claim in Antarctica, and Germany rejected Norway's rejection, laying claim to Neu-Schwabenland on the basis that the German explorations of the interior extended beyond the region explored by Norway.

In short, I believe that the real context of Lord Simon's question about "Norway" should be understood to be an inquiry about Norway and all its claimed territories. The question, in other words, was about Antarctica. In this respect, it is worth mentioning that Hess brought with him a written peace proposal, both in German and English translation.[20] In other words, Hess brought with him an *actual treaty*, which makes eminent sense in view of what has been argued in previous chapters, that Hess came not to *continue* negotiations but rather *to conclude them*.

In any case, this document, which has not surfaced to this day, was taken to the BBC where various translation teams worked on their own translations of the German of various sections of the document.[21] This treaty document

> ... was taken very seriously. It was no vague list of demands or threats, but a detailed set of proposals intended tom form the basis of a treaty between the two countries. It set our Germany's plans for eastward expansion and conflict with Russia and defined the respective spheres of influence of Germany and Britain. Although many of the proposals are by now familiar, there were others concerning areas other than the British Empire, such as the Suez Canal. Apparently, *the document recognized that there were*

---

[19] Picknett, Prince, and Prior, op. cit., p. 304, emphasis added.
[20] Ibid., p. 306.
[21] Ibid.

parts of the world where their respective interests could come into conflict, and made it clear that Hitler regarded the USSR as being within Germany's sphere of influence.[22]

In other words, the document was *comprehensive* in its scope, and Lord Simon's query about "Norway" should be seen and interpreted from that context and the previous disputes between Germany and Norway, the real implication being the large unclaimed areas of Antarctica, and what was to be done with spheres of interest on the strategically located and mineral-rich continent. Indeed, as we saw previously, the Polish government-in-exile figured into the negotiations between Hess and the British peace faction, and thus it would stand to reason that the Norway-Antarctica question figured into the mix as well.

The penguins were very *much* a part of the Hess Mess.

As for the document itself, the Hess Mess takes yet more strange turns and twists. Picknett, Prince, and Prior note that given its comprehensive scope and its dual translations, it was probably a bulky document, and therefore probably not capable of being carried on Hess's person, but in a briefcase which he had taken with him on his flight. The document may have burned with the briefcase along with Hess's Messerschmitt 110 when it crashed. In any case, it is not mentioned in any inventory of Hess's belongings.[23] They note, however, that it is also possible that the document was sent *ahead* of Hess, perhaps via Burkhart and the International Red Cross,[24] or that it may have been sent *after* Hess arrived, a circumstance which, they argue, also makes sense of "a cluster of three mysterious incidents that followed in the wake of Hess's arrival."[25]

The first of these incidents occurred on May 20, 1941, the very day that Anthony Eden was writing to Churchill about Lord Simon's upcoming visit with Hess, and ten days after the latter's arrival in Great Britain! On this occasion, a Dornier 217 flew from the German airbase at Alborg, Denmark, to an RAF airbase in Lincoln without

---

[22] Picknett, Prince, and Prior, op. cit., p. 307, emphasis added.
[23] Ibid.
[24] Ibid.
[25] Ibid., p. 308.

any interference from the Royal Air Force, landed, and handed over a package to a waiting RAF officer, before taking off and returning to Alborg! All of this is in the record because the German pilot, Heinrich Scmitt, told of the episode in a 1970s interview. Additionally, Schmitt stated that the RAF undertook similar highly secret missions to Germany, with RAF planes and pilots landing at German airbases without any interference from the *Luftwaffe*,[26] a point which, again, implicates Göring in whatever ongoing processes were occurring.

The final incident was revealed in 1979 by John McCowen, who in 1941 was a major with the 11th Fighter Group. According to McCowen, he was summoned by the group commander, Air Vice-Marshal Trafford Mallory, who informed him the group had received "a message from Germany" alerting them to an immanent raid by SS commandos, who would land at or near Luton, Bedfordshire during an air raid. McGowen was ordered to move an anti-aircraft gun unit to the area to intercept the raid, as its intended mission was to assassinate Hess! Picknett, Prince, and Prior state that the would-be SS assassins were apprehended by the British, with maps to Dungavel, and promptly executed without trial, the only two spies allegedly executed without any surviving record of a trial or of their execution![27] This raises, once again, the prospect that someone in Germany did *not* want the mission to succeed, just as elements in Britain did not, and that, similarly, there were elements in Germany that *did* want it to succeed, just as there were in Britain. In this case, the German element is betraying an assassination plot to the British, with the clear intent of asking the British to intervene and prevent it, which the latter obligingly do!

C. A Brief Review

So where have we ended up?

I believe that the main theses of the various researchers into the Hess Mess are correct in their general conceptual outlines, but that specific details need adjustment. For example:

---

[26] Picknett, Prince, and Prior, op. cit., p. 308.
[27] Ibid., p. 309.

1) W. Hugh Thomas and other advocates of the doubles hypothesis are correct: a *double* was replaced for Hess. Unlike Thomas, this replacement was not made by the Germans during the flight itself, but subsequently in Great Britain, where, according to the scenario outlined by Picknett, Prince, and Prior, Hess briefly fell out of the control of the Peace Faction, which ultimately regained control of him, and hid him in Scotland, awaiting a return flight with the Duke of Kent;

2) During his stay in Britain, both Hess and his double underwent sessions of drugging, the full extent and purpose of which we do not know. However, we *do* know that the original and real Hess was measured for a duplicate *Luftwaffe* captain's uniform, while the double "Hess" underwent what was most probably extensive drugging and psychological "programming" to become Hess. In this respect, we saw that there were unusual and possible connections between Ewen Cameron, the psychologist who would become such a central component of the postwar CIA's MK-Ultra mind control program, and who was the very doctor brought in by Allen Dulles to examine "Hess" at Nuremberg because of the latter's suspicion that "Hess" was a double, and Dr. James Macdonald Cameron, the British forensic pathologist who performed the official autopsy on "Hess" after his suspicious "suicide" in Spandau Prison in August 1987. In short, *Hess, and/or his double, became the first, and most infamous, example of mind-control on record.* In this respect, it should also be recalled that "Hess" maintained consistently that he—and others—were victims of some such technology, and attempted to rationalize and justify the Nazis' murderous and genocidal acts on this basis.

3) Hess and Göring both appeared to have been involved in peace negotiations with the British, both immediately prior to, and after, the outbreak of war. As noted in previous pages, Göring most certainly knew of Hess's plans, because he telephoned General Adolf Galland to shoot Hess's plane

down long after it was operationally possible to do so. Hess could not have undertaken a flight over Germany secretly without knowledge of the Luftwaffe's air defense grid, which was allegedly supplied to him in a map provided, in some accounts, by Hitler's personal pilot, Hans Baur himself! Baur, it will be recalled, was also implicated in a plot to fly Hitler and his personal entourage to Great Britain. While this may sound unfeasible, the basic outlines of the scenario as Picknett, Prince, and Prior have reconstructed it, is that both the German and the British ends of the peace negotiations were also involved in plans to remove their respective governments, Churchill in Great Britain, and Hitler in Germany. The reason for *this* aspect of the scenario was because, during the course of negotiations, both sides made it clear to the other that the current governments of both countries were unacceptable to the negotiators. On the British side, this included offers by the Polish government-in-exile of General Sikorski for the Duke of Kent to assume the long-vacant Polish throne.

4) Included in the peace plan, as Padfield revealed, was an attempt to settle "the Jewish question" without a genocide, but rather, with the establishment of a Jewish-Zionist state. In this respect, the Nordau Quotation enters the equation, for it implied the existence of a genocidal plan *before World War One*, in which the great powers, and the Zionist movement itself, are implicated. While such an assertion seems on the surface to be completely impossible, there is a pattern of unusual Zionist-Nazi collaboration during the war, as exemplified by the case of Dr. Rudolf Kastner, a Zionist doctor implicated, and tried, in Israel after the war, as covered by the famous Jewish American playwright Ben Hecht in his book *Perfidy,* in which Hecht makes explicit reference to Nordau's mysterious, supremely important, and highly troubling, statement. This is not only a crucial point but a horrifying one, for it implies that the failure of the Hess Mission, or a decision taken by either the German or British side of the equation to ensure that his mission was a failure, was also a decision taken to exercise and complete

whatever plot existed for such, and to which the Zionist leader Max Nordau referred in his unbelievable statement made prior to World War One. That there may be some such scheme in the background, whose exact lineaments are unknown to this day, would seem to be corroborated by the attempts of Israel to interview "Hess" while he was imprisoned at Spandau, attempts which the British government consistently rebuffed. Additionally, there is the strange allegation of Wolf Hess that Menachim Begin informed President Jimmy Carter during the Camp David peace summit with Egyptian President Anwar Sadat, that "Hess" must never leave Spandau alive. Israel did apparently follow the Hess Mess closely, because there were also the allegations made to Wolf Hess's wife, via a South African source, that Israel knew that "Hess" had been murdered by operatives of the SAS.

5) And to top off this explosive fuel tank, in the strangest bit of debris in the entire Hess Mess, it would appear that Antarctica was very much a subject of the covert and very secret negotiations made between Britain and Germany, with the inquiry of Lord Simon about Norway. In this final context, it is to be noted, that not only does Hess receive specific inquiry from Simon about Norway, but that one of Göring's own go-betweens for peace feelers with Great Britain was the very same State Councilor whom he appointed to oversee and manage the details of the German Antarctic Expedition of 1938-39, *Staatsrat* Helmut Wohlthat.

6) And finally, to round out this bizarre dataset, Admiral Richard Byrd described his Antarctic expedition as an "assault on three fronts," a kind of continental-scaled *Kesselschlacht* (battle of encirclement), against either a metaphorical enemy—the continent itself—or possibly against a much more literal, but unnamed one. Putting the biggest question mark of them all over this affair, Byrd's own son, who accompanied him on the expedition, dies under suspicious an unusual circumstances, emaciated, and dehydrated, in a Baltimore warehouse, when he was to be a

guest of honor at a *National Geographic* event celebrating and honoring his father.

As promised, the Hess Mess is indeed a colossal, gigantic, inexplicable mess. There are no easy answers here; there are only uncomfortable synchronicities and questions bordering on the absurd and bizarre, and speculative scenarios whose sweep and scope or truly immense, bizarre, and horrifying.

But there is yet *one more* uncomfortable and bizarre synchronicity with which we must deal...

8

EPILOGUE: SPANDAU BALLET
(AND YES, THIS TIME WE *DO* MEAN THE 1980S MUSIC GROUP)

"So true
Funny how it seems,
Always in time, but never in line for dreams,
Head over heels when toe to toe
This is the sound of my soul
This is the sound."
"True" lyrics, Spandau Ballet

WE BEGAN THIS ADVENTURE into the strange landscape of the Hess Mess by pointing out that the phrase "Spandau Ballet," which became the name of a successful 1980s rock group, was actually a German colloquialism or slang for the spasms of nerves in prisoners executed in the prison by hanging. As noted in the first chapter, I took this slang and colloquialism to refer also to the absurd dance of the four Allied powers once Prisoner Number Seven's death had been announced, and the equally absurd problems that emerged and then were rather weakly explained away. I noted in chapter one that the 1980s music group did appear to take their name from the slang expression, at least, that's the way *Wikipedia* put it, and of course, one must take anything at that source with several bags of salt.

As I wrote this book, however, it began to dawn on me that there may be more than just a synchronous connection of the group's name to the Hess Mess. One article, "Band Name Explained: Spandau Ballet—Almost Inescapable Artifacts," explained the name of the group—and the slang expression behind it—this way; Spandau Ballet designated

Performers of a number of genres conveniently categorized under the common denominator 'new romance'. The band is from Islington, London.
It is an almost inescapable fact that the band name was linked to the group in an indirect war. Journalist and disc jockey Robert Elms is said to have seen the words 'Spandau Ballet' on the wall of

257

a Berlin loo, as part of a few lines jotted down there that, translated from German, come down to: *'Rudolf Hess dances his Spandau ballet all alone.'*

Hess, was, as practically anyone over forty will know, the last Hitler-era prisoner, detained in Spandau Prison in the Berlin district of the same name.

Yet the term 'Spandau Ballet' does not originate from this Berlin clink.

Occasionally movies demonstrate how people have a tendency to dance a hasty little dance when bullets zing by their shins.

Allied soldiers who were taken under fire by the German Spandau machine gun, spitting out 1,200 bullets per minute, were no different in that respect.[1]

Needless to say, the story of the band name's origin in a bit of graffiti scrawled in a Berlin men's toilet, whether true or not, caught my eye, as did the specific mention of Rudolf Hess.

Then the lyrics of two of that group's major hits—"Gold" and "True"—began to run through my mind, and both revealed cryptic, perhaps unintentional, perhaps intentional, or perhaps merely synchronous, references to Hess. Consider the italicized lines from "Gold":

> *Thank you for coming home*
> *I'm sorry that the chairs are all worn'*
> *I left them here I could have sworn*
>
> These are my salad days
> Slowly being eaten away
> Just another play for today
> Oh but I'm proud of you, I'm proud of you
>
> Nothing left to make me feel small
> Luck has left me standing to tall
> Gold
> Always believe in your soul
> You've got the power to know
> You're indestructible

---

[1] "Band Name Explained: Spandau Ballet—Almost Inescapable artifacts," www.bandnameexplained.com.2013/08/spandau-ballet.

Hess and the Penguins

Always believe in, because you are
Gold
Glad that you're bound to return
There's something I could have learned
You're indestructible, always believing

After the rush has gone
I hope you find a little more time
Remember we were partners in crime

It's only two years ago
The man with the suit and the face
You knew that he was there on the case
Now he's in love with you, he's in love with you
My love is like a high prison wall
But you could leave me standing so tall

Gold
Always believe in your soul
You've got the power to know
You're indestructible
Always believe in, because you are
Gold
I'm glad that you're bound to return
Something I could have learned
You're indestructible, always believing

My love is like a high prison wall
But you could leave me standing so tall
Gold
Always believe in your soul
You've got the power to know
You're indestructible
Always believe in, because you are
Gold
I'm glad that you're bound to return
Something I could have learned
You're indestructible, always believing. [2]

---

[2] www.azlyrics.com/lyrics/spandauballet/gold.html

Worn chairs, an individual coming home, swearing that he left them in a certain place, a reference, perhaps, to "Hess's" claimed memory losses, love like a high prison wall... all words evocative in a way of Rudolf Hess, his state of mind, and his actual physical circumstances, and of the Hess Mess. There was a weird synchronicity, too, with the timing of the emergence of the group into fame and popularity: the early 1980s, in the last years of Spandau Hess's life.

Coincidence? Perhaps... *probably*.

But then there were the lyrics of Spandau Ballet's greatest, and most well-known hit, "True":

> *True*
>
> (ha-ha-ha, ha-ah-hi)
> (ha-ha-ha, ha-ah-hi)
>
> So true
> Funny how it seems,
> *Always in time, but never in line for dreams*
> *Head over heels when toe to toe*
> This is the sound of my soul
> This is the sound
>
> *I bought a ticket to the world*
> *But now I've come back again*
> *Why do I find it hard to write the next line?*
> *Oh, I want the truth to be said.*
>
> (ha-ha-ha, ha-ah-hi)
> I know this much is true
> (ha-ha-ha, ha-ah-hi)
> On know this much is true.
>
> *With a thrill in my head and a pill on my tongue*
> Dissolve the nerves that have just begun
> Listening to Marvin (All night long)
> This is the sound of my soul
> This is the sound
>
> Always slipping from my hands

Hess and the Penguins

Sand's a time of its own
Take your seaside arms and write the next line
Oh, I want the truth to be known

(ha-ha-ha, ha-ah-hi)
I know this much is true
(ha-ha-ha, ha-ah-hi)
I know this much is true.

I bought a ticket to the world
But now I've come back again
Why do I find it hard to write the next line?
Oh, I want the truth to be said.

(ha-ha-ha, ha-ah-hi)
I know this much is true
(ha-ha-ha, ha-ah-hi)
I know this much is true

(This much is a-true-oo)
(This much is a-true-oo-oo)

I know, I know, I know this much is true
(This much is a-true-oo)
(This much is a-true-oo-oo)

(This much is a-true-oo_
(Ha-ha-ha, ha-ah-hi)
(This much is a-true-oo)
I know this much is true
(This much is a-true-oo)
(Ha-ha-ha, ha-ah-hi)
(This much is a-true-oo-oo)
Know this much is true
(This mush is a-true-oo)
(ha-ha-ha, ha-ah-hi)
(This much is a-true-oo-oo_
(Know this much is true)
I know, I know, I know this much is true.[3]

---

[3] www.azlyrics.com/lyrics/spandauballet/true.html

A calm, dreamy harmony and melody, laughter, drugs, buying "a ticket to the world," was this a reference to the flight of Hess? "Now I've come back again?" a reference to his return to Germany, and imprisonment?

Maybe.

But then there's the reference to being "in time, but never in line for dreams." This began to hit closer to home, for as we have seen in the previous pages, Hess was certainly "on time" and expected in Britain, but he was in "the wrong line," the wrong place. And then, he's "head over heels when toe to toe," was this an odd poetical way to express his bailout from the Messerschmitt 110, tumbling head over heels until his parachute opens?

More strange was the lyrical reference to confusion of mind, "Why do I find it hard to write the next line? Oh I want the truth to be said." As we have seen, "Hess" certainly exhibited confusion of mind, whether acted, or genuine. Certainly such confusion could be explained "with a thrill in my head and a pill on my tongue," as the effects of a drug-induced state of mind. Here, again, was an unusual synchronicity, for "Hess" and Hess *both* were drugged.

Then, from out of nowhere, another image is invoked in the lyrics: "take your seaside arms and write the next line, oh I want the truth to be known." Seaside? A reference, perhaps, to Hess bailing out near the west coast of Scotland?

Once again, perhaps.

Maybe, perhaps, possibly...

Unintended synchronicities.

Nothing more.

On their own, with no context, the lyrics of one of the most popular songs of the 1980s are dreamy, flitting from one image to another, without context, without much meaning.

But...

... **within** *the context of the Hess Mess, they begin, at last, to make sense...*

BIBLIOGRAPHY:
WORKS CITED OR CONSULTED IN WRITING THIS BOOK

No author. "Operation Highjump 1946-47: A Tragedy on the Ice." www.south-pole.com/williams/htm

No author. "The Antarctica Enigma." Book IV. https://www.bibliotecapleyades.net/tierra_hueca/esp_tierra_hu eca_6c.htm

No author. "The Lebor Feasa Runda." http:// leborfeasarunda.weebly.com/history.html.

Allen, Martin. *The Hitler/Hess Deception. British Intelligence's Best-Kept Secret of the Second World War.* London. Harper Collins Publishers. 2003. ISBN 0-00-714118-1.

Bird, Eugene K. (Lt. Col., U.S. Army). *Prisoner #7" Rudolf Hess: The Thirty Years in Jail of Hitler's Deputy Führer.* New York. Viking Press. 1974. SBN (670-57831-2).

Buechner, Howard A. (Col., US Army, Ret.), and Bernhart, Wilhelm (Capt., *Deutsche Kriegsmarine*). *Adolf Hitler and the Secrets of the Holy Lance.* Metairie, Louisiana. Thunderbird Press, Inc. 1988. ISBN 0-1913159-05-0.

Buechner, Howard (Col. US Army, Ret.) *Emerald Cup – Ark of Gold: the Quest of SS Lt. Otto Rahn of the Third Reich.* Metairie, Louisiana. Thunderbird Press, Inc. 1994. ISBN 0-913159-07-7.

Buechner, Howard A. (Col. US Army, Ret.), and Bernhart, Wilhelm (Capt., *Deutsche Kriegsmarine*). *Hitler's Ashes: Seeds of a new Reich!* Metairie, Louisiana. Thunderbird Press, Inc. 1989. ISBN 0-913159-06-09.

Farago, Ladislas. *Aftermath: Martin Bormann and the Fourth Reich.* New York. Simon and Schuster. 1974. No ISBN.

Farrell, Joseph P., and deHart, Scott D. *Yahweh the Two-Faced God: Theology, Terrorism and Topology.* Lulu self-published book. 2011. No ISBN.

Farrell, Joseph P. *The Third Way: The Nazi International, European Union, and Corporate Fascism.* Kempton, Illinois. Adventures Unlimited Press. 2015. ISBN 978-1-939149-48-0.

Fleming, Peter. *Operation Sea Lion: The Projected Invasion of England in 1940—An account of the German Preparations and the British Countermeasures.* New York. Simon and Shuster. 1957. NO ISBN.

Friedrich, Christof. *Secret Nazi Polar Expeditions.* Toronto. Samizdat Publishers, Ltd. No date. No ISBN.

Gehlen, Reinhard. *The Service: The Memoirs of General Reinhard Gehlen.* Trans. from the German by David Irving. New York. Times Mirror. 1972. ISBN 0-529-04455-2.

Godwin, Jocelyn. *Arktos: the Polar MUth in Science, Symbolism, and Nazi Survival.* Kempton, Illinois. Adventures Unlimited Press. 1996. ISABN 0-932813-35-6.

Goodrick-Clarke, Nicholas. *Black Sun: Aryan Cults, Esoteric Nazism and the Politics of Identity.* New York. New York University Press. 2003. ISBN 978-0-8147-3155-0.

Goodrick-Clarke, Nicholas. *The Occult Roots of Nazism: Secret Aryan Cults and their Influence on Nazi Ideology.* New York. New York University Press. 1992. ISBN 978-0-8147-3060-4.

Harris, John, and Wilbourn, Richard. *Rudolf Hess: A New Technical Analysis of the Hess Flight, May 1941.* Stroud. Spellmount (The History Press). 2014. ISBN 978-0-7524-9708-2.

Hecht, Ben. *Perfidy.* New York. Julian Messner, Inc. 1961. No ISBN.

Hess, Wolf Rüdiger. *My Father Rudolf Hess.* Translated from the German by Frederick and Christine Crowley. Tiptree, Essex. W.H. Allen & Co., Plc. 1987. ISBN 978-0-352-32214-4.

Hess, Wolf Rüdiger. *Who Murdered my Father, Rudolf Hess? My Father's Mysterious Death in Spandau.* Trans. from the German by Sonja Ruthard. Decatur, Alabama. Reporter Press. 1989. (Argentine printing: Buenos Aires. Talleres Graficos Genesis. 1991. Argentine ISBN 99234-4-3.)

Irving, David. *Hess: The Missing Years 1941-1945.* Dorney, Windsor, United Kingdom. Focal Point Publications. 2010. ISBN 978-1-872197-21-3.

Ivinheim, Michael. *The Secret Alliance: The Unknown Alliance between the Third Reich and Argentina.* Hernando, Florida. Sharkhunters International. 2001. ISBN 9781460919767.

John, Robert. *Behind the Balfour Declaration: The Hidden Origins of Today's Mideast Crisis.* Costa Mesa, California. Institute for Historical review. 1988. ISBN 0-939484-29-3.

Kerr, Peter. "Body of Adm. Byrd's Son, 68, Found in Empty Warehouse," *New York Times*, October 9, 1988.

Kilzer, Louis. *Hitler's Traitor: Martin Bormann and the Defeat of the Reich*. Novato, California. Presidio Press, Inc. 2000. ISBN 0-89141-710-9.

Melaouhi, Abdallah. *Rudolf Hess: His Betrayal and Murder*. Washington, DC. The Barnes Review. 2013. ISBN 978-1-937787-18-9.

Mosley, Leonard. *The Reich Marshal: A Biography of Hermann Goering*. Garden City, New York. Doubleday and Company. 1974. No ISBN.

Nesbit, Roy Conyers, and van Acker, Georges. *The Flight of Rudolf Hess: Myths and Reality*. Stroud, Gloucestershire. The History Press. 2011. ISBN 978-0—7509-4757-2.

Padfield, Peter. *Night Flight to Dungavel: Rudolf Hess, Winston Churchill, and the Real Turning Point of WWII*. Lebanon, New Hampshire. University Press of New England. 2013. ISBN 978-1-61168-531-2.

Picknett, Lynn, Prince, Clive, and Prior, Stephen. *Double Standards: the Rudolf Hess Cover-Up*. London. Sphere (Little Brown and Company). 2014. ISBN 978-0-7515-322-3.

Quigley, Carroll. *The Anglo-American Establishment*. New York. Books in Focus, Inc. 1981. ISBN 0-916728-50-1.

Robert, James. "Britain's Secret War in Antarctica." *Nexus Magazine*. Volume 12, Number 5, August-September 2005. https://www.bibliotecapleyades.net/tierra_hueca/esp_tierra_hueca_13.htm

Robert, James. "Britain's Secret War in Antarctica." *Nexus Magazine*. Volume 12, Number 6, October-November 2005. https://www.bibliotecapleyades.net/tierra_hueca/esp_tierra_hueca_15.htm

Robert, James. "Britain's Secret War in Antarctica." *Nexus Magazine*. Volume 13, Number 1, December 2005-January 2006. https://www.bibliotecapleyades.net/tierra_hueca/esp_tierra_hueca_16.htm

Schön, Heinz. *Mythos Neu-Schwabenland: für Hitler am Südpol: die deutsche Antarktis-expedition 1938/39*. Selent, Germany. Bonus-Verlag. 2004. ISBN 3-935062-05-3.

Simpson, Christopher. *Blowback: The First Full Account of America's Recuitment of Nazis, and its disastrous Effect on our Domestic and Foreign Policy*. New York. Collier Books. 1988. ISBN 978-0-02-044995-X.

Stevenson, William. *The Bormann Brotherhood*. New York. Harcourt, Brace, Jovanovich, Inc. 1973. ISBN 0-15-113590-8.

Summerhayes, Colin, and Beeching, Peter. "Hitler's Antarctic base: the myth and the reality." *Polar Record 43(224):* 1-21. 2007.

Thomas, W. Hugh. *The Murder of Rudolf Hess*. New York. Harper and Row, Publishers. 1979. ISBN 0-06-014251-0.

Toland, John, *Adolf Hitler*. Volume II. Garden City, New York. Doubleday & Company, Inc. 1976. (No ISBN)

Toland, John. *Adolf Hitler*. Volume I. Garden City, New York. Doubleday & Company, Inc. 1976. (No ISBN)

Von Lang, Jochen. *The Secretary: Martin Bormann, the Man who Manipulated Hitler*. Translated from the German by Christa Armstrong and Peter White. New York. Random House. 1979. No ISBN.

COVERT WARS & BREAKAWAY CIVILIZATIONS
By Joseph P. Farrell

Farrell delves into the creation of breakaway civilizations by the Nazis in South America and other parts of the world. He discusses the advanced technology that they took with them at the end of the war and the psychological war that they waged for decades on America and NATO. He investigates the secret space programs currently sponsored by the breakaway civilizations and the current militaries in control of planet Earth. Plenty of astounding accounts, documents and speculation on the incredible alternative history of hidden conflicts and secret space programs that began when World War II officially "ended."

292 Pages. 6x9 Paperback. Illustrated. $19.95. Code: BCCW

HIDDEN FINANCE, ROGUE NETWORKS & SECRET SORCERY
The Fascist International, 9/11, & Penetrated Operations
By Joseph P. Farrell

Pursuing his investigations of high financial fraud, international banking, hidden systems of finance, black budgets and breakaway civilizations, Farrell investigates the theory that there were not *two* levels to the 9/11 event, but *three*. He says that the twin towers were downed by the force of an exotic energy weapon, one similar to the Tesla energy weapon suggested by Dr. Judy Wood, and ties together the tangled web of missing money, secret technology and involvement of portions of the Saudi royal family. Farrell unravels the many layers behind the 9-11 attack, layers that include the Deutschebank, the Bush family, the German industrialist Carl Duisberg, Saudi Arabian princes and the energy weapons developed by Tesla before WWII.

296 Pages. 6x9 Paperback. Illustrated. $19.95. Code: HFRN

THRICE GREAT HERMETICA AND THE JANUS AGE
By Joseph P. Farrell

What do the Fourth Crusade, the exploration of the New World, secret excavations of the Holy Land, and the pontificate of Innocent the Third all have in common? Answer: Venice and the Templars. What do they have in common with Jesus, Gottfried Leibniz, Sir Isaac Newton, Rene Descartes, and the Earl of Oxford? Answer: Egypt and a body of doctrine known as Hermeticism. The hidden role of Venice and Hermeticism reached far and wide, into the plays of Shakespeare (a.k.a. Edward DeVere, Earl of Oxford), into the quest of the three great mathematicians of the Early Enlightenment for a lost form of analysis, and back into the end of the classical era, to little known Egyptian influences at work during the time of Jesus.

354 Pages. 6x9 Paperback. Illustrated. $19.95. Code: TGHJ

THE THIRD WAY
The Nazi International, European Union, & Corporate Fascism
By Joseph P. Farrell

Pursuing his investigations of high financial fraud, international banking, hidden systems of finance, black budgets and breakaway civilizations, Farrell continues his examination of the post-war Nazi International, an "extra-territorial state" without borders or capitals, a network of terrorists, drug runners, and people in the very heights of financial power willing to commit financial fraud in amounts totaling trillions of dollars. Breakaway civilizations, black budgets, secret technology, occult rituals, international terrorism, giant corporate cartels, patent law and the hijacking of nature: Farrell explores 'the business model' of the post-war Axis elite.

364 Pages. 6x9 Paperback. Illustrated. $19.95. Code: TTW

COVERT WARS & THE CLASH OF CIVILIZATIONS
UFOs, Oligarchs and Space Secrecy
By Joseph P. Farrell

Farrell's customary meticulous research and sharp analysis blow the lid off of a worldwide web of nefarious financial and technological control that very few people even suspect exists. He elaborates on the advanced technology that they took with them at the "end" of World War II and shows how the breakaway civilizations have created a huge system of hidden finance with the involvement of various banks and financial institutions around the world. He investigates the current space secrecy that involves UFOs, suppressed technologies and the hidden oligarchs who control planet earth for their own gain and profit.

358 Pages. 6x9 Paperback. Illustrated. $19.95. Code: CWCC

ROSWELL AND THE REICH
The Nazi Connection
By Joseph P. Farrell

Farrell has meticulously reviewed the best-known Roswell research from UFO-ET advocates and skeptics alike, as well as some little-known source material, and comes to a radically different scenario of what happened in Roswell, New Mexico in July 1947, and why the US military has continued to cover it up to this day. Farrell presents a fascinating case sure to disturb both ET believers and disbelievers, namely, that what crashed may have been representative of an independent postwar Nazi power—an extraterritorial Reich monitoring its old enemy, America, and the continuing development of the very technologies confiscated from Germany at the end of the War.

540 pages. 6x9 Paperback. Illustrated. $19.95. Code: RWR

SECRETS OF THE UNIFIED FIELD
The Philadelphia Experiment, the Nazi Bell,
and the Discarded Theory
by Joseph P. Farrell

Farrell examines the now discarded Unified Field Theory. American and German wartime scientists and engineers determined that, while the theory was incomplete, it could nevertheless be engineered. Chapters include: The Meanings of "Torsion"; Wringing an Aluminum Can; The Mistake in Unified Field Theories and Their Discarding by Contemporary Physics; Three Routes to the Doomsday Weapon: Quantum Potential, Torsion, and Vortices; Tesla's Meeting with FDR; Electromagnetic Phase Conjugations, Phase Conjugate Mirrors, and Templates; The Unified Field Theory, the Torsion Tensor, and Igor Witkowski's Idea of the Plasma Focus; tons more.

340 pages. 6x9 Paperback. Illustrated. $18.95. Code: SOUF

NAZI INTERNATIONAL
The Nazi's Postwar Plan to Control Finance,
Conflict, Physics and Space
by Joseph P. Farrell

Beginning with prewar corporate partnerships in the USA, including some with the Bush family, he moves on to the surrender of Nazi Germany, and evacuation plans of the Germans. He then covers the vast, and still-little-known recreation of Nazi Germany in South America with help of Juan Peron, I.G. Farben and Martin Bormann. He then covers Nazi Germany's penetration of the Muslim world including Wilhelm Voss and Otto Skorzeny in Gamel Abdul Nasser's Egypt before moving on to the development and control of new energy technologies including the Bariloche Fusion Project, Dr. Philo Farnsworth's Plasmator, and the work of Dr. Nikolai Kozyrev. Finally, he discusses the Nazi desire to control space, and examines their connection with NASA, the esoteric meaning of NASA Mission Patches.

412 pages. 6x9 Paperback. Illustrated. $19.95. Code: NZIN

REICH OF THE BLACK SUN
Nazi Secret Weapons & the Cold War Allied Legend
by Joseph P. Farrell
Why were the Allies worried about an atom bomb attack by the Germans in 1944? Why did the Soviets threaten to use poison gas against the Germans? Why did Hitler in 1945 insist that holding Prague could win the war for the Third Reich? Why did US General George Patton's Third Army race for the Skoda works at Pilsen in Czechoslovakia instead of Berlin? Why did the US Army not test the uranium atom bomb it dropped on Hiroshima? Why did the Luftwaffe fly a non-stop round trip mission to within twenty miles of New York City in 1944? *Reich of the Black Sun* takes the reader on a scientific-historical journey in order to answer these questions. Arguing that Nazi Germany actually won the race for the atom bomb in late 1944,
352 PAGES. 6x9 PAPERBACK. ILLUSTRATED. $16.95. CODE: ROBS

THE SS BROTHERHOOD OF THE BELL
The Nazis' Incredible Secret Technology
by Joseph P. Farrell
In 1945, a mysterious Nazi secret weapons project code-named "The Bell" left its underground bunker in lower Silesia, along with all its project documentation, and a four-star SS general named Hans Kammler. Taken aboard a massive six engine Junkers 390 ultra-long range aircraft, "The Bell," Kammler, and all project records disappeared completely, along with the gigantic aircraft. It is thought to have flown to America or Argentina. What was "The Bell"? What new physics might the Nazis have discovered with it? How far did the Nazis go after the war to protect the advanced energy technology that it represented?
456 pages. 6x9 Paperback. Illustrated. $16.95. Code: SSBB

SAUCERS, SWASTIKAS AND PSYOPS
A History of a Breakaway Civilization
By Joseph P. Farrell
Farrell discusses SS Commando Otto Skorzeny; George Adamski; the alleged Hannebu and Vril craft of the Third Reich; The Strange Case of Dr. Hermann Oberth; Nazis in the US and their connections to "UFO contactees"; The Memes—an idea or behavior spread from person to person within a culture—are Implants. Chapters include: The Interplanetary Federation of Brotherhood; Adamski's Technological Descriptions and Another ET Message: The Danger of Weaponized Gravity; Adamski's Retro-Looking Saucers, and the Nazi Saucer Myth; Dr. Oberth's 1968 Statements on UFOs and Extraterrestrials; more.
272 Pages. 6x9 Paperback. Illustrated. $19.95. Code: SSPY

LBJ AND THE CONSPIRACY TO KILL KENNEDY
By Joseph P. Farrell
Farrell says that a coalescence of interests in the military industrial complex, the CIA, and Lyndon Baines Johnson's powerful and corrupt political machine in Texas led to the events culminating in the assassination of JFK. Chapters include: Oswald, the FBI, and the CIA: Hoover's Concern of a Second Oswald; Oswald and the Anti-Castro Cubans; The Mafia; Hoover, Johnson, and the Mob; The FBI, the Secret Service, Hoover, and Johnson; The CIA and "Murder Incorporated"; Ruby's Bizarre Behavior; The French Connection and Permindex; Big Oil; The Dead Witnesses: Guy Bannister, Jr., Mary Pinchot Meyer, Rose Cheramie, Dorothy Killgallen, Congressman Hale Boggs; LBJ and the Planning of the Texas Trip; LBJ: A Study in Character, Connections, and Cabals; LBJ and the Aftermath: Accessory After the Fact; The Requirements of Coups D'État; more.
342 Pages. 6x9 Paperback. $19.95 Code: LCKK

ORDER FORM

10% Discount When You Order 3 or More Items!

One Adventure Place
P.O. Box 74
Kempton, Illinois 60946
United States of America
Tel.: 815-253-6390 • Fax: 815-253-6300
Email: auphq@frontiernet.net
http://www.adventuresunlimitedpress.com

Please check: ☑

☐ This is my first order　　☐ I have ordered before

Name

Address

City

State/Province　　　　Postal Code

Country

Phone: Day　　　　Evening

Fax　　　　Email

Item Code	Item Description	Qty	Total

Please check: ☑

Subtotal ▶

Less Discount-10% for 3 or more items ▶

☐ Postal-Surface　　Balance ▶

☐ Postal-Air Mail　Illinois Residents 6.25% Sales Tax ▶
　(Priority in USA)　Previous Credit ▶

☐ UPS　　Shipping ▶
　(Mainland USA only) Total (check/MO in USD$ only) ▶

☐ Visa/MasterCard/Discover/American Express

Card Number:

Expiration Date:　　　　Security Code:

✓ SEND A CATALOG TO A FRIEND: